CAPTAIN JOHN H. ROGERS, TEXAS RANGER

Captain John H. Rogers. Courtesy Texas Ranger Hall of Fame and Museum, Waco

Captain John H. Rogers, Texas Ranger

Paul N. Spellman

Number one in the Frances B. Vick Series

The University of North Texas Press
Denton, Texas

The paper in this book meets the minimum requirements of the
American National Standard for Permanence of Paper for Printed Library
Materials, Z39.48.1984

Permissions
University of North Texas Press
PO Box 311336
Denton, TX 76203-1336
940-565-2142

Captain John H. Rogers, Texas Ranger is
Number one in the Frances B. Vick Series

Library of Congress Cataloging-in-Publication Data

Spellman, Paul N.
Captain John H. Rogers, Texas Ranger / by Paul N. Spellman.
p. cm. – (Frances B. Vick series ; no. 1)
Includes bibliographical references (p.) and index.
ISBN 1-57441-159-4 (cloth : alk. paper)
1. Rogers, John Harris, 1863–1930. 2. Texas Rangers—Biography.
I. Title. II. Series.

HV7911.R645 S67 2003
363.2'092–dc21

2002151871

Design by Angela Schmitt

Table of Contents

List of Illustrations

ACKNOWLEDGMENTS

Because the bulk of the materials for this biography of John Harris Rogers came from the official records and files of the Texas Rangers, most of my work was done at the Texas State Library Archives in Austin. My sincere thanks to Donaly Brice and his staff for the hours of work they put in to assist me. This also includes the staff in the Genealogical Room and in the Government Documents archives. I am also indebted to Christina Stopka, Judy Shofner, and the staff at the Texas Ranger Hall of Fame and Museum archives in Waco. A third source of Ranger materials came from the Center for American History (Barker Texas History Center) in Austin, and my appreciation to those who helped me there on several occasions.

For the research on Rogers' early years and the family's arrival in Texas, I so appreciate the diligence of Jacki Gross, assistant library director at the Seguin-Guadalupe County Public Library in Seguin. Jacki tracked down several key pieces of information from deep within the county property and deed records. Archivists and staff at the libraries in La Grange, El Paso, Columbus, Laredo, and Del Rio also assisted me. Ron McCandless is a great resource for genealogical information on the Internet, and he solved several puzzles for me.

The staff at the Texas Room of the Houston Public Library has helped me so many times and I appreciate their interest and support always. Both through e-mail and in person, the very helpful staff at the Austin History Center of the Austin Public Library system led me through many difficult paths to trace the family's history in Austin between 1907 and 1930. Newspaper articles, city directories, police records, and early city and cemetery maps were all made readily available to me during my research.

For the U. S. Marshal records, I was assisted by Cindy Smolovik and the staff at the National Archives and Records Administration, Southwest regional offices, in Ft. Worth. Anne Saba helped from the U. S. Customs archives office, and Keith Welch found resources for me at Central Presbyterian Church in Austin. The staff at the University of Houston main library helped on this subject as well.

The other wonderful resource for this biography was the family of Captain Rogers, especially the Reeves kin in the San Antonio area. John Leslie Reeves, Charlie and Mills, and Bub and Marian Reeves were so delighted to help me with this project. I am also grateful to have spoken with Rev. Curren Rogers "Tex" McLane of Fort Worth, Kid Rogers' grandson. They all told me great stories that had come down through three generations, and allowed me the privilege to sort through myriad letters, newspaper clippings, artifacts, and photographs—so much of what has personalized this book. I thank each of them and dedicate this book to the family.

I am grateful to Harold J. Weiss, Jr. and Mike Cox for their critical eye and sound knowledge on the subject of the Rangers; they helped make this biography more polished and of broader interest to readers with their suggestions.

And an understated word of appreciation to my family who still puts up with me as I go about my work of research and writing. Their encouragement is unflagging, their support unwavering. How invaluable that is to a writer.

INTRODUCTION

John Harris Rogers stood motionless at the window of his new office, his hands clasped behind his back, his head bowed. He opened his eyes when a twinge of pain in his right shoulder interrupted his silent prayer. He turned and walked around to the large chair that sat behind his desk. A blank piece of paper still lay on the desktop, a pen resting beside it. Rogers finally sat down, picked up the pen and began to write. "After giving due credit to all loyal friends who stood by me so nobly and endorsed me so unqualifiedly," he wrote in long sweeping strokes, "I nevertheless attribute my success to Almighty God, whose I am and whom I serve and to whom I solemnly pledged if He would favor me for said position, I would use the office for His glory, which pledge I now ratify, relying upon Him for His help and guidance."

It was a spring day in 1913, and the April colors outside Rogers' Waco office were resplendent like the rainbow that arched near the horizon. The forty-nine-year-old lawman pondered the beginnings of his new career as United States Marshal for the Western District of Texas. He had retired from the Texas Rangers after twenty-eight remarkable years, then put in these last two years as a deputy marshal out in El Paso. Now this new office. Some of his new responsibilities would be as familiar as the days when he rode the Ranger trail after desperadoes of every sort and kind. Some of the paperwork would be familiar as well, he sighed to himself. That came with it.

But transcending all of the vagaries of this or any job in law enforcement was the firm resolution of the Master who continued to call on John Rogers for his service. "The Captain," as everyone called him for thirty-seven years, believed without question that his career, his life, was in good hands. "It is my desire that what additional influence I might have by reason of my office," Rogers wrote in conclusion, "shall be used for Him."[1]

The life and times of Texas Ranger John H. Rogers represent some of the most exciting years in the history of Texas, ranging from the Civil War to the Great Depression. Rogers was born of strong Tennessee farming stock in Guadalupe County, Texas, even as the Civil War reached its climax. His father and uncles served with distinction in that war. Eager to be more than a planter, the young adult Rogers headed after the railroads as they moved west, where he encountered his own future with the Texas Rangers. After a decade as a private, Rogers' obvious leadership qualities moved him upward to a captaincy by 1893, a command where he served the state of Texas for the next eighteen years. After ten years in the marshal's office and a stint as a police chief, the venerable captain returned to the Rangers for the last three years of his life.

John Rogers was one of the first Ranger captains of his generation, along with compatriot Bill McDonald, to serve as a United States Marshal, and the only Ranger captain to serve eighteen years and then return to his company's command after a sixteen-year absence.

Along the trail as a lawman John Rogers witnessed some of the most legendary incidents in the history of the Rangers, from the Conner Fight along the Sabine to the El Paso Prizefight of 1896, and from the confrontations in a quarantined Laredo to his capture of Gregorio Cortez, one of the most elusive and famous fugitives ever hunted in the American Southwest. Along the way he brushed up against fabled characters such as John Wesley Hardin, Bat Masterson, Pancho Villa, and the notorious John Barber, and escorted two presidents—American and Mexican—to a vitally important conference along the border. Rogers was wounded three times during his illustrious career, twice seriously—both times his wife was incorrectly informed that he had been killed in action, and came closest to being killed when the infamous Hill Loftis got the drop on him. His escape from that moment he evermore credited to his strong faith.

And it was that faith, along with the strict adherence to the law and a self-discipline unsurpassed in Ranger history, that set Rogers apart from his peers. Convicted as a teenager to the tenets of the Christian faith, he let his beliefs guide him for the remainder of his life, encouraged by his wife and soul mate Hattie for more than three decades. His faith was open and unyielding, and he carried it on his sleeve as well as in his pocket Bible, and perhaps even to a fault. Ranger chronicler Walter Prescott Webb wrote of Captain Rogers: "There was just one quality that the Borderlands held against Rogers, and that was one which would have added to his reputation in another portion of the state. He was a bit too much the Presbyterian—the Sunday School man—to wholly please the Border."[2] The Captain would have taken that as a great compliment.

Even as he kept a Bible close to his heart, however, Captain Rogers never hesitated to use whatever force might be necessary to enforce the law or rein in a criminal. Like other "Christian Rangers" such as Thalis Cook, Augie Old, and Lone Wolf Gonzaullas, he was as famous to his Ranger compadres for his ability to disarm a crook as he was to read the Scriptures to that same man while sitting around a trail campfire. In the latter days of his career a biographical article said this in its introduction: "It is indeed a rare pleasure to know this splendid Christian gentleman. If any has the impression that a man cannot be a Christian and be actively engaged in the enforcement of the law they have only to meet this quiet, dignified and unassuming man face to face."[3]

John Rogers found himself involved in a number of shootouts during his lengthy career, and several fugitives found their final justice at the other end of his bent-stock Winchester rifle. Ever the conscientious family man, Rogers invariably responded to any of his children's queries about killing bad guys with, "There were bad men who were shot in my presence." Rogers was largely responsible for the creation of the office of chaplain for the Rangers, and for the appointment of fellow Presbyterian Pierre Bernard Hill to that office. John H. Rogers was a lawman and a man of God, the two parts inextricably connected.

The history and lore of the Texas Rangers covers nearly all of Texas' history since the arrival of Stephen F. Austin and his "Old Three Hundred" colonists. Austin assigned men to "range" the outer areas as a security force principally against Indian attacks. In 1835 the Texas Rangers were formally organized into three companies with several officers and fifty-six men. During the era of the Republic the Rangers served mostly as escorts and scouts, and the organization was expanded during the Lamar administration. Almost every able-bodied Texas frontiersman served at least a three-month hitch as a Ranger during that period, and charismatic leaders such as John Coffee "Jack" Hays, Ben and Henry McCulloch, and "Big Foot" Wallace put their indelible stamp on the Ranger legend.

The Rangers became known outside the Southwest during the War with Mexico. With their Walker Colt revolvers on each hip, and led by Hays and Samuel Walker, the Ranger forces charged ahead of the U. S. Army into battle after battle, their courage contagious, their flair for the dramatic and obstinate resistance to obeying orders a thorn in the side of every army commander.

In his book *Lone Star,* T. R Fehrenbach says of Jack Hays: "He was no talker but a born partisan who liked to ride the wild country by the North Star; not a great gunman, but a leader who rose by sheer ability from among his peers; and a superb psychologist who could bend both friend and foe to his will. Ben McCulloch, Sam Walker, L. H. McNelly, John H. Rogers, and even Big Foot Wallace were similar."[4]

The period of the Civil War and Reconstruction witnessed a breakdown in the Rangers organization and responsibilities as the Confederacy sent these men off to a conflict far away, and those who returned found their old duties now being taken care of by the army or the State Police. But in 1874 the State Legislature reorganized the Rangers into two units: the Special Force under Captain Leander H. McNelly and the Frontier Battalion commanded by Major John B. Jones. McNelly achieved fame as he led his Rangers against the lawless brigands who roamed the State; Major Jones created a prototypical character of Ranger leadership and bravery in the Indian Wars that carried over into the next generation. Fehrenbach writes: "The Ranger captains had to be not only field generals but superb psychologists, understanding the enemy and their own men. They found their greatest strength in a legend of superiority, which in the early years they genuinely won."[5]

Over the last two decades of the nineteenth century, the Rangers pushed the dangerous Indian frontier far out beyond the Llano Estacado, concentrated its efforts on the thieves and desperadoes that roamed the large state, and established itself as a law enforcement agency unlike any other in the United States. Toward the end of the century four men rose to the rank of captain in the elite four-company force: their inheritance of the high character and indefatigable perseverance of those who had gone before enhanced the Texas Ranger story and brought them the collective title of "The Four Captains." Wrote Woodford Mabry, their adjutant general, in a stirring endorsement: "A Texas Ranger is the synonym for courage and vigilance. A bold rider, a quick eye, and a steady hand, he is the terror of the criminal, and merely his presence has its moral effect and acts as a wholesome restraint."[6]

John Rogers served as one of the legendary "Four Captains" of the Texas Rangers during the 1890s and until 1911, and was the only one Texas-born. John A. Brooks with whom he worked and fought alongside in their early years, John Hughes, and Bill McDonald helped form the quartet of commanders that led the transition from the old Frontier Battalion days into the twentieth century. These were steadfast men of the law, unapproachable by fraud or graft, fearless beyond measure, and relentless in pursuit.

John Abijah Brooks was born in Kentucky in 1855 and came to Texas in 1876. He joined the Rangers the same year as Rogers and was the first of the four to rise to the captaincy, in 1889. Although most of his Ranger career was in central and east Texas, Brooks and his company were seen in the Rio Grande Valley and at the El Paso prizefight. Brooks stood with Rogers against fence-cutters and thieves, and in the Conner Fight lost three fingers in the dramatic skirmish.

Brooks retired in 1906 and began another full career as a legislator and county judge out of Falfurrias. He died in 1944.

John Reynolds Hughes was born the same year as Brooks, in Illinois, and came to Texas around 1880. He joined the Rangers in 1887 and worked his way up the ranks in Company D to become captain when the Ranger Force was organized in 1901. Known for his persistence on the trail of a felon, Hughes never gained the spotlight as others did, but his exploits are nevertheless manifold. He retired in 1915 and lived as a private citizen another thirty-two years.

The most flamboyant of the four was William Jesse McDonald, born in Mississippi in 1852. "Bill Jess" came to Texas as a teenager at the end of the Civil War, his family settling in Rusk County. After early business tries as a grocer and teacher, McDonald joined the Texas Rangers and was elevated to the captaincy in 1891. He was at the El Paso prizefight with the rest of the Rangers, at the center of the controversy of the 1906 Brownsville investigation, and served as bodyguard and escort to two American presidents. Two of the great Ranger sayings come from McDonald: his memorial "No man in the wrong can stop a man in the right who just keeps on coming"; and his response to the Dallas administrator who had called for help, that as there was only one controversial prizefight, they only needed one Ranger to stop it. "One riot, one Ranger" was born. Captain Bill left the Rangers in 1907 to become a revenue agent, and died of pneumonia in 1918 after serving six years as a U. S. Marshal.[7]

From the leadership and example of the "Four Captains" came the next generation of Ranger legends: Frank Hamer, Will Wright, Tom Hickman, and Lone Wolf Gonzaullas, among others. And because of their tutelage and collective wisdom the Rangers survived the especially difficult times that followed between 1910 and 1919. Rogers testified at the signal Canales investigation in 1919, adding clear and convincing testimony to the importance of the force for Texas despite the irregularities and tragic consequences of the dark days of the Borderlands' "special" Rangers.

When his Ranger days were done, John Rogers served another decade in law enforcement at the federal level, two years for the American Railway Express, then a year as chief of the Austin police force. He was a lifelong Democrat whose support was eagerly sought by politicians at every party level. And when the bootlegging days of the late Twenties seemed too much for standard law enforcement, a new Texas governor called on the aging but able Rogers for one more turn of service to his state. The fiercely prohibitionist captain was "in uniform" when he died in 1930 at the age of sixty-seven.

Historian A. J. Sowell listed Rogers in the same company as John Hays, L. H. McNelly, and John B. Jones—good company, and Webb adds Ben McCulloch to that same list of distinctive Rangers.[8] Known for his religious convictions, the principled Rogers was also soft spoken and humble in manner, several times being mistaken for an ordinary citizen or even a local minister until, that is, it was time to mete out Ranger justice. His descendants tell a favorite story of Rogers stepping off a train in a West Texas town at the same time as a rough-hewn cowboy, the official welcoming committee mistaking the much bigger man for a Ranger and ignoring the quiet captain in suit and vest.

From 1883 to 1930, Captain Rogers' duties spread from across the wild frontier days of fence cutters in a wide-open West Texas to car chases after bootleggers and gamblers in the Texas capital streets. He worked out of Laredo, Del Rio, El Paso, Cotulla, Alice, and Austin, and found himself in Ranger camps from Brownsville to Fort Hancock and Vernon to Hempstead. He traveled literally hundreds of thousands of miles over a long career, on horseback and by rail, and even made his way into Mexico, to Arizona and Kansas, and into Indian Territory (Oklahoma).

In fact, the story of John Harris Rogers is importantly a story of the settlement of much of the Lone Star state. When the railroads headed into West Texas in the 1880s, the populace followed close behind. Then came the troublemakers, which necessitated the arrival of the Texas Rangers to restore order. As a young Ranger private then, John Rogers experienced the evolution of a civilizing, if not civilized, Texas. He served in Colorado City, Rio Grande City, and Cotulla. He maintained order in Snyder and McCamey and Thurber, in Roby and Mullin and Rocksprings. As a Ranger captain he tracked criminals to Hemphill and Hempstead, and from San Antonio to San

Angelo. The path of Rogers' career is a trail of the birthing of half of a state.

The Captain was a family man as well, never knowing his father, dedicated to his mother, and faithful to a faithful woman, Hattie, his wife. He dearly loved his "kid" brother Curren who served under him in the Rangers, but suffered the tragedies of burying that brother at too young an age and his own nine-year-old son who drowned near an Austin dam. John's other two children, Pleas and Lucile, lived long, full lives and brought their children to visit "Grandaddy" at his Austin home on San Antonio Street. Pleas Rogers fulfilled a career in the military with distinction, carrying on his father's legacy, and recalled with affection years later that his father "was a total abstainer from liquor and I never heard him utter an oath of any kind. He was very fond of smoking cigars, but when [I] was born he gave up the habit in order not to set a bad example. When he caught [me] smoking at the age of sixteen," Pleas notes, "the reason for his abstinence was removed."[9] Lucile's grandchildren and descendants, who have helped so much in the making of this biography, still tell the Captain's story today.

When he died, John Rogers was revered and respected by men and women from across the Southwest. The letters of condolence to his widow included high-powered Democrats, small town pastors, bankers and judges and cowboys, and Rangers who only knew him by reputation. Newspapers of every sort and size eulogized him, and articles appeared in journals and chapters in books, ensuring the captain's legendary status. Said his pastor at the funeral, "Shall not we as we are gathered around his bier pledge our hearts' allegiance to those finest things of life to which, and for which, he so unstintedly gave his whole life?"

This, then, is the unique story of a lawman who tracked an unimaginably large countryside for most of four decades, committed to the preservation of law and order in order to make a world more peaceful and secure for everyone. This is the story of a God-fearing man who stood out among his colleagues, though not purposely so, and whose remarkably quiet voice then still rings its clarion call for peace.

A eulogy for Captain Rogers in the *Waco News-Tribune* may be the most succinct in its portrayal of this man. In part it says: "Those who admire the brave and the gentle in public servants, sworn to enforce the law and uphold its majesty, will regret the passing of this Ranger chief who in early manhood rode with fellow Rangers who protected the Rio Grande border against outlaws and desperadoes from both sides of the historic river.

"[But] Rogers never boasted of his own achievements. He never had a press agent. He never wrote a book of adventure with himself as the hero. He lived an unostentatious life and he died the death of a Christian gentleman who believed in the immortality of the soul and life everlasting." And it would be presumptuous to claim the following but neglectful not to include it: "His Ranger life would be read, if placed in book form, like a romance of a knight of old. Its adventures and its thrilling incidents would furnish rich material for a biographer who knew how to whip the material into shape and give the narrative a thousand thrills."[10]

This is one humble effort.

CHAPTER 1

The Guadalupe Homestead

ISAAC SAMUEL ROGERS STOOD STRAIGHT and tall at the center of the small Bolivar Courthouse assembly room. He pulled at his tight starched collar, the twenty-one-year-old Tennessee farmer uncomfortable in suit and tie on this cold March evening. But the occasion of his wedding kept him resolute, somber, uncomplaining. To his left stood his brother William, like Isaac a farmer in the Hatchie River Valley of Hardeman County, Tennessee. Seated just behind him in the straight-backed hickory chairs were several members of the Elkins family— the elder William, his wife and a cousin or two sat ramrod straight at the edge of their seats. On Isaac's right stood eighteen-year-old Mahala Elkins, soon to be his bride. Woodson Vader, justice of the peace for the Bolivar area and a neighbor and friend of the Rogers clan, intoned the civil ceremony then pronounced the couple husband and wife. Isaac was pleased to loosen his collar for the remaining festivities that Tuesday evening. It was March 18, 1834.[1]

Although both bride and groom were natives to the Hatchie Valley—born and raised long before Hardeman County's 1823 organization—they felt a pull to the west to start their married life together. And so they packed their few belongings, bade farewell to kith and kin, and headed for the newly opened Chickasaw Country.

Forty-five miles to the west and just south of Bolivar lay the Old Chickasaw Trail making its way from Mississippi into Tennessee, skirting the Tennessee River Valley. The Nonconnah River, a tributary that ran north-south nearly to the state line, displayed a welcoming valley of rolling hills and rich farm land. Families from both states were moving in even as the American Indian Nation was removed.

Isaac and Mahala Rogers settled there in the fall of 1834 on a small homestead that straddled the two states. Their first child Michael was born the following spring and quickly followed by James, Martin Van Buren (named for the current president in 1839), Richard, and John Harris. Their fifth son, Pleasant William Miles, was born in 1844 and the last child, and only daughter, Leonora, arrived in 1850 just weeks after the census taker had come by the farming community. Because of the proximity of the farm to the two states, five of the children claimed Shelby County, Tennessee, as their birthplace, while Richard and Leonora claimed De Soto Township, Marshall County, Mississippi as theirs. The census taker in June of 1850 placed the homestead in Mississippi.[2]

In 1836 the first school was begun in that area and named Rock Springs. Four years later, amid the clutter of mercantile trading posts, the first of several churches was organized not too far from Pigeon Roost Road. The makings of a real community were in place by the mid-1840s.

But even as the farming community grew, the American West opened again after the War with Mexico and the stunning discovery of gold way off in California, and Isaac Rogers contemplated another move for his large family. The gold fields were no place to raise a family, although there were riches to be had there, and the Great Plains remained something of a mystery to all but the bravest who crossed it in search of wealth. But reports continued to laud Texas, now the twenty-eighth state of the Union, as a Paradise itself.

In the fall of 1856, after a decade on the fringe of the Chickasaw Trail, Isaac decided to move the homestead southwest across the Red River. His adult sons Michael and James made different decisions—Michael would accompany his family while twenty-year-old James stayed behind on the family's farm.

And so it was that Isaac Rogers purchased a humble 162 acre homestead in Guadalupe County, Texas, in the fall of 1856 and moved his family there. Guadalupe County and its county seat of Seguin already had a long history in the Southwest stretching back to the Spanish and Mexican days, a center for unrest during the Texas Revolution in 1835-1836, and now a prospering community of farms and ranches. The Guadalupe River, though unpredictable and even vicious in the spring and fall rainy seasons, nonetheless had provided fertile soil for thousands of years, dug out beautiful valleys among the softly rolling hills, and left natural springs and unusually dependable—for Texas—creeks every few miles.

In 1838 Mathew "Old Paint" Caldwell and thirty-three other Texas Rangers, fresh from their exploits during the Revolution, surveyed several leagues of land in Guadalupe County as payment for their military service. They organized the first community of Walnut Springs, which was soon renamed Seguin after the legendary Tejano war hero, and began clearing land. As Robert Hall wrote of the experience later, "We clubbed together and bought land from old Joe Martin and laid out the town. Although I lived a ways from there, twelve miles from Gonzales, I helped clear about a half league of land some nine miles east of Seguin. I was what they called a chain carrier, clearing the scrub trees and brush. Got into it with an old doe," he recalled, "and took a shot at her but just grazed her on one leg. She didn't clear out, just limped around and watched us while we worked. They called her 'Hall's old doe' for as long as she and I was around."[3]

In the early 1850s the Robert Hall league was subdivided and sold off in small parcels. Thomas and Margaret Halsel bought a homestead at the headwaters of Jacob Darst's creek several miles north of the Guadalupe, adjacent to the W. W. Arrington Tract. On November 7, 1856, they signed a contract selling their land to Isaac Samuel Rogers for $810. The first semblance of a market road between Seguin to the west and Luling to the east tracked along less than a mile north of the Rogers property, with Darst Creek and a deep ravine outlining the eastern boundary.[4]

The Rogers family soon expanded and divided, as the boys married and some bought property of their own. Richard married

Josephine "Birdie" Adams in 1861, and Pleasant married neighbor Mary Amanda Harris on January 5, 1863, under the serious eye of Deacon Frederick Butler, an itinerant Methodist Episcopal pastor. Martin married Peneca Davidson one year later. Richard and Martin bought land along the banks of the Guadalupe and moved their families there in the early 1860s.

The first grandchild of Isaac and Mahala was a girl, Valverde, born in June of 1862, daughter of Richard and Birdie and named after a just-waged Civil War victory by the Confederates in New Mexico. The next grandchild was John Harris Rogers, the subject of this story, born October 19, 1863, just nine-and-a-half months after Pleasant and Mary's wedding day, and named after Pleasant's older brother.[5]

Isaac lived to enjoy the delights of several of his grandchildren, but he died on November 1, 1867, fifty-four years of age and having lost three sons to the vagaries of war; his wife Mahala died that same year. Twenty-three-year-old Pleasant Rogers became the administrator of his parents' estate along with neighbor C. M. Garity, filing in the county court on November 25—noting there was no will—and declaring the assets and debts of the estate on December 12 and again on January 28, 1868. The court records state that the "sole heirs" of the Rogers probate would be Martin, Pleasant, Leonora, and Valverde (still a minor at age five and currently under the guardianship of her mother and Frank M. Pearce, whom Birdie wed after Richard's death.)

The court declared an auction to be held in order to pay off the debts that amounted to some $850. The first auction date of February 15, 1868, was moved to March 20. On that day, at the home of Martin Rogers on Nash Creek, friends and neighbors arrived throughout the afternoon to bid on the few cattle, horses, furniture, and farming tools from Isaac's estate. The auction was successful enough to pay off the debts while preserving the land itself for the family, and the estate sales record was filed on March 30.[6]

John Harris Rogers was barely four when his grandfather died. His mother's clan had long since become more than just neighbors of Isaac Rogers; they had become family as well.

Also from Tennessee, John Wesley Harris was born November 27, 1809, in Wilson County just east of Nashville and on the south banks of the mighty Cumberland River. One of their neighbors was the Adamses from Virginia. On December 8, 1832, eighteen-year-old Laura Adams married John W. Harris. Their family grew quickly, with Frank Wesley born in the early autumn of 1833, John Wesley on May 11, 1834, and Jane Elizabeth on June 12, 1836. Three more children rounded out the Harris family—William (1839), Laura Adams (1841) and Mary Amanda on February 6, 1845.

Shortly after Mary Amanda's sixth birthday, the family made their move to Texas along with so many others who formed caravans and left "G.T.T." signs swinging on gates and doors and storefronts. On December 12, 1851, John Harris signed a deed for land on the old Joseph Kent claim in Guadalupe County. This acreage lay along Mill Creek about seven miles east of Seguin. Neighbors included the expansive family of Asa Sowell, his brothers and sons and their kin.

In 1855 Jane Elizabeth Harris married Nathaniel Benton, already a storied Texan whose adventures from Mexico to California had gained him a reputation as one of the foremost frontiersmen of his era. Jane bore "Cap'n Nat" Benton three children over the next five years. J. Wesley Harris married Emarita Swift on January 20, 1860, and eleven months later his sister Laura married Guadalupe County resident John Eckols on November 26. With Frank and Mary Amanda following suit, John—a "grand old Tennessee gentleman" - and Laura Harris proudly watched over in-laws and a brood of grandchildren for the next two decades. The Harris and Rogers kids grew up together and went off to local country schools together. They worked the fields every spring, summer, and fall, rode and swam, and got into mischief together. They befriended other children in that farming community, including the many Sowells, the Noltes, Dunns, and Colemans.[7]

But most of that third generation had not been born when the Civil War broke the country wide open in 1861. Instead, it was their fathers who packed off to fight for the Confederacy, and their mothers who prayed and fretted and anxiously awaited their return or the tragic news that might come to their doorsteps.

The year 1860 brought with it an acceleration toward secession by most of the slave-holding states across the American South, and

Texas was no exception. The election of "the Black Republican" Abraham Lincoln to the presidency signaled a final political challenge met on December 20 by the official vote of secession by South Carolina, the first of eleven who would form the Confederate State of America. Texas called its secession convention in February, 1861, and overwhelmingly the delegates—biased already to the inevitable outcome—voted to leave the Union. By March, the election of Jefferson Davis to the Confederacy's presidency and Lincoln's installation in Washington, D.C. left only the when and where, not if, of civil war. That came early in the morning of April 12, 1861, when the Charleston guns began their bombardment of Fort Sumter.

In Guadalupe County, Texas, the fever for secession was prevalent across the eastern part of the county and into the city of Seguin itself. The local castle of the mystery-cloaked Knights of the Golden Circle, led by John Wright, spoke clearly for war and would be the first to "join up." To the west, however, the large and growing contingent of German immigrants—748 were counted in the 1860 census—fought the idea of secession. Some had been in Texas for two decades and were not interested in leaving a Union they had worked so hard to get to from Europe. J. F. McKee, a leading Unionist voice in the county, gathered sympathizers to his side in a futile attempt to sway the vote. It was never to be—the local county tally for secession was a persuasive if far from surprising 314 to twenty-two, the German voters obviously discouraged from showing up at the polls. The Rogers and Harris, Nolte and Sowell clans cast their lots with the Confederacy.

Enlistment officers began to make their way through Seguin even before the first shots of the war were fired. Tom Green was there, and Peter Cavanaugh Woods from San Marcos. William P. Hardeman recruited men from the area, and locals such as Nat Benton, Ben and Henry McCulloch, and J. Wesley Harris quickly accepted officer assignments and began to recruit from the farmlands of the Guadalupe. Philip Noland Luckett rode up from Corpus Christi calling for men to come to designated camps in Austin and San Antonio, and as early as May the would-be soldiers began to arrive. The fever for war was pitched.

Nat Benton organized a company of men in June, 1861, and they assembled on the Guadalupe courthouse lawn on the morning of June 28, a huge crowd of family and well-wishers cheering in a large circle around them. Several young women modestly presented a company battle flag and a Confederate flag to Benton, who accepted it graciously and with a brief speech. John Wesley Harris stood there in the company that had named itself "The Knights of Guadalupe," and so also Richard Rogers, John Eckols, and Peneca's brother, William Davidson. Pleasant Rogers, only sixteen and too young to enlist, cheered at the edge of the crowd with the rest of his family.[8]

But Benton's company was soon discharged without ever leaving the county. Nat's wife Jane became seriously ill that same month forcing her husband to stay by her bedside. Despite medical and loving attention, Jane Benton passed away on August 5, and the bereaved widower lost interest in a distant war.

Meanwhile other recruiting continued in and around Seguin. Company A of the Fourth Texas Cavalry recruited in the area, and Asa and James Sowell and Martin Rogers were three who enlisted under William Hardeman on August 8, 1861. They marched off to war in the fall of 1861, and over the winter found themselves part of Henry Hopkins Sibley's Brigade and on the front lines of the Confederacy's New Mexico Campaign. In February, 1862, the Fourth Texas crossed the Rio Grande near Union-held Fort Craig, skirted the bastion across a rough desert trail, and met the Yankees at the Val Verde river crossing. The battle was intense and the Confederates managed to drive the Union forces back to the fort. It was an important victory for the South, although perhaps no more than a broad skirmish, and brought much-needed good news back home. Martin's letter to his family may have been what prompted his brother Richard to name his first daughter, born that June, Valverde. Creeks, a town, and a county in Texas still bear that Civil War name.

The victory quickly vanished under the uneven leadership of General Sibley and a devastating defeat at Glorieta Pass in April, and the Confederate forces limped home. Months later the 4th Texas was back in action, this time in Southern Louisiana attempting to hold against an aggressive Union naval blockade and invasion of the Delta. On

April 14, 1863, along the coastal St. Mary's Parish, the Confederates fought two battles outside of the town of Franklin, Louisiana. The Texas soldiers pushed hard against the Union forces at Irish Bend and hours later set up along a rail fence near Nerson's Woods. As the Union attacked the Confederates blistered the field and won the day. During the battle, however, a rifle ball glanced off one of the rails and struck Martin Rogers with such force that he was thrown to the ground badly wounded. It was the end of the war for Martin and he was discharged and sent home by June.[9]

On November 25, 1861, seventeen-year-old Pleasant Rogers signed up with Company E of the newly formed Third Texas Infantry under Colonel Philip Luckett. Augustus Buchel was lieutenant colonel and Charles A. Schreiner of Kerrville was the ordnance sergeant. It may be that Pleasant lied about his age to get in, but get in he did and marched off to war. Luckett's Regiment of 648 soldiers landed at Fort Brown in the Rio Grande Valley over the winter. For whatever reasons—climate or drilling or army rations—young Pleasant became ill and spent most of March and April in a sick bed at Fort Brown. Still without seeing any action, he was then discharged on July 12 presumably when his correct age was discovered.

Pleasant came home to the Darst Creek farm, turned eighteen on October 19, courted and proposed to Mary Amanda Harris, and married her on January 5, 1863. As news of the war continued to reach back to Texas, the young married man could not stand to be left out, even with a wife who announced she was pregnant that spring. On July 15 he enlisted with Captain Bill Martin's Company D of the Thirty-sixth Texas Cavalry, a unit that included his brother-in-law Will Harris and good friend Montraville Harrell. He would now be off to war alongside his oldest brother Richard and the others of Company B.[10]

The Thirty-sixth Texas Cavalry was commanded by Colonel Peter Cavanaugh Woods, a Tennessee native who had lived for ten years in nearby Hays County. Nat Benton served as lieutenant colonel. Although the regiment had spent a year patrolling the German-populated Texas hill country where Unionist sympathizers created more suspicion than unrest, real action now seemed imminent with the threat of a Union invasion by General Nathaniel P. Banks. Pleasant accompanied the troops to Indianola where they remained from July to the following March, 1864, with only one notable incident to report during that interlude.

On September 9, 1863, this cavalry unit was ordered dismounted, its now-foot soldiers to be sent by rail to Beaumont and its horses requisitioned for the Confederacy. The men were furious, especially since nearly all of the horses were owned by the soldiers. Colonel Woods protested but to no avail. The infantry unit marched and countermarched through the fall and winter, grumbling constantly. On February 1, 1864, 157 of the men decided enough was enough and they deserted en masse, headed for home. Woods scurried after them and after some fast talking got them to return without penalty. However, district orders on February 20 reinforced the dismounting orders and many of the men prepared to walk away again. The war came to them just in time.

Union General Banks was marching deep into Louisiana and General Richard Taylor's army needed support to stop him. The remounted Thirty-sixth headed for the front lines March 12, arriving at Pleasant Hill on April 9 just hours after the significant battles at Mansfield and Pleasant Hill. But three days later the Texans encountered a battle-worn enemy at Blair's Landing on the Red River. In this heated exchange the immensely popular Texan General Tom "Daddy" Green was killed instantly by a point-blank cannon shot as he charged a Union gunboat from the riverbank. The Confederates managed to chase the Union flotilla northward, no little thanks to the courage of the just-arrived Texas forces who were later commended in an official report: "conspicuous in their valor, their desperate courage baffled descriptions."[11]

A skirmish ten days later at Cloutierville was followed by a ranging battle near Monette's Ferry on April 23. Regiments from both sides pushed at one another across an area pocked with deep gulches and muddy bayous. Back and forth they fought until the Yankees, mistakenly believing the rebels were retreating, made a hasty charge across a field. Texas companies B and D found themselves in the open with a Union cavalry bearing down on them. Pleasant Rogers made a dash across flat ground pursued by a platoon of mounted Yanks. Attempting to leap a ditch, his horse lost momentum and rolled into the gully, turning upside down with Rogers underneath. Trapped and sure to be killed or captured, the nineteen-year-old managed to pull his pistol and prepared to go down fighting. Suddenly a familiar face appeared on horseback in the ditch beside him—Second Lieutenant J. Wesley Harris dismounted in the fray, pulled his in-law free, and the two mounted Harris' horse and escaped the onslaught.[12]

The Thirty-sixth remained in Louisiana for another month, repulsing every offensive by Banks' army from Bayou Rapides Bridge to Alexandria to Yellow Bayou on May 18. A later report again commended the Texans for "greatly distinguishing themselves" during the campaign, the excitement tempered with the dozens of casualties along the way and the serious injury to Colonel Woods, who lost the use of his arm from a rifle ball at Yellow Bayou.

As the Union line finally withdrew from western Louisiana, the Thirty-sixth Texas was ordered back to their home state where they patrolled east Texas and the lower Sabine for the next nine months. In February, 1865, they rode to Galveston Island where they stood in defense until the war finally came to a close on April 9. Official discharges from the now-defunct Confederate army came in the fall; Pleasant received his on October 4, two weeks before his son John's second birthday. All of the Guadalupe boys of Companies B and D had survived the war, not without scratches and wounds, and had arrived home by the end of May to the delight of wives and children and neighbors alike. But not all the Rogers boys would come home.[13]

Michael and John Rogers joined up with Company D of the Fourth Texas Infantry in late 1861, and Will Harris transferred to their company in 1862. These soldiers provided the core of what became Hood's Brigade, one of the most decorated and active troops of the Civil War fighting under the general command of Robert E. Lee and his Army of Northern Virginia from Manassas to Appomattox. Mike and John fought against McClellan in the Peninsular Campaign and at Second Manassas, against Meade at Antietam, and marched to Fredericksburg in December, 1862, to face Ambrose Burnside's Army of the Potomac. Hood's Brigade found themselves on Lansdowne

Valley Road two miles south of the city in a holding position against the Union's left flank. A small skirmish just after Noon on December 13 near Deep Run resulted in the Yankees' maneuver stopped in its tracks, even as the larger battle was playing out along Marye's Heights to the north.

John found his brother lying mortally wounded not far from the road where the skirmish had taken place. Bandaged and piled into a wagon, Michael was rushed to a Richmond hospital during the rainy, freezing cold night. He died the next morning.

John Rogers and Will Harris went on to fight at Chancellorsville and Gettysburg, and carried on against the ever-increasing odds as Sherman marched across Georgia in 1864. Will was wounded at Cold Harbor, Virginia, in June, 1864, and both survived the horrible siege at Petersburg which took Lee's army to the end of the war. After a week long dash across southern Virginia, Lee agreed to meet Ulysses S. Grant at the Appomattox Courthouse at Noon on Sunday, April 9. There he surrendered his proud but haggard and badly depleted army. The war, for all intents and purposes, had come to an end.[14]

Whether from the wounds of war or the vagaries of disease, the records show only that Mike Rogers died in the war; there are no extant records that also indicate how and when his brothers Richard and John died as well, although the yellow fever that cut a deadly swath through Texas after the war may have been a possible cause. But in the fall of 1867, Isaac Rogers was dead and so were three of his sons.

John Harris Rogers was only one-and-a-half years old when his father Pleasant returned from the war. He would not have remembered the excitement and relief that mixed with the family's tragedies in those months. As life made feeble attempts to return to normal during the early years of Reconstruction, John was soon joined by his two siblings. Laura Henrietta was born March 25, 1866, and his kid brother Curren Lee arrived April 2, 1869. Laura's name came from the family heritage, Curren's was a combination. A distant Tennessee cousin named Curran Michael Rogers, chaplain for Morgan's Raiders during the war and a Methodist minister afterwards, preached in Texas and visited his Guadalupe County kin in the late 1860s, impressing his gathered congregations with the Gospel word as well as his personal war stories. John's brother's middle name no doubt paid homage to the Confederate general himself. For all that, Curren Lee was called Kid most of his life.[15]

The 1870 census has Pleasant W. M. Rodgers [*sic*] and his wife Mary Amanda Harris Rodgers residing on the old homestead with their children and Pleasant's sister Leonora, age twenty. The Harrises and Sowells still made good neighbors, and Wesley and Emma Harris' only son Tupper, who turned four that year, would become a life-long friend of John's. Another neighbor, fourteen-year-old Ed Nolte would also have an impact on John's life along the way. Many of those families took that time to remember those who were no longer there, those lost in the war and the terrible yellow fever plague that rampaged across Texas in 1867, leaving graves in its path.

In November of that same year, although seven-year-old John might not have had any more than a faint memory of it, excitement came to his doorstep once more as a call for Rangers went out to hunt down the marauding Kiowas and Comanches of west Texas. Fifty-two men from Guadalupe County volunteered and rode out in mid-November.[16]

From Old Paint Caldwell to Robert Hall to the McCullochs and to Nat Benton and the Sowell brothers, ghosts and voices and adventures of the Texas Rangers were never far from John Harris Rogers' life even from childhood. Maybe it was something in the water; it surely was in his blood.

A second, much less destructive outbreak of yellow fever scorched the lower Guadalupe and Colorado valleys in 1873, with particularly tragic losses in nearby Washington County, but life carried on. Pleasant worked the small farm, his brother Martin moved his family to the Luling area, and the community's children attended, on occasion, the small country schools in their neighborhood and up and down Mill Creek.

On John's twelfth birthday in 1875, his father was sick, an illness that did not diminish. On December 18, at age thirty-one, Pleasant William Miles Rogers died and was buried on the homestead property.[17] Devastated and left to operate a farm with three children in tow, Mary Rogers found relief from an unlikely source and in a re-markably short period of time.

There were two things that arrived in Guadalupe County around 1870 that thrust the small farming community into the progressive post-war economy. One was the arrival of the cattle drives. The other was the railroad. Both came from Fayette County. So did Will Crier.

When the war finally dragged to its conclusion, a serious deple-tion of beef back along the Eastern seaboard caused from feeding the burgeoning Union army for four years presented a minor crisis for some and a golden opportunity for others. One of those who saw that glass half full was Joseph McCoy, an enterprising railroad man who already had his sights set on Kansas and a little rail junction named Abilene. McCoy scouted the Great Plains, including Texas, in search of meat on the hoof that could be transported—through his town and on his railroad—back to the hungry and wealthy city folks in the East. Reports from Texas ranchers of literally millions of wild Long-horn cattle in south Texas and along the Rio Bravo brought the first cattle drives by 1868, up trails that became known as the Sedalia and Chisholm and the Western.

The Chisholm Trail started in the San Antonio area and moved almost directly north along a line of longitude that took the herds to the awaiting stockyards in downtown Abilene, Kansas. Several paths swept northward through Fayette, Caldwell, Hays, and Kendall coun-ties, and in 1869 the first trail came through the western half of Guadalupe. Ranchers made investments in the lucrative market. "Cap-tain" Eugene Millett put together the first cattle drive out of the Seguin area in 1869. Thomas Perryman of Seguin became one of the wealthi-est men in Texas by 1870. Teenage boys hired on for the adventures on the cattle drives and the pay at the end of the trail, not the least of which included the saloons and bawdy houses in Abilene. Some of the Guadalupe cowboys that made a name for themselves on the Chisholm Trail included J. K. Alley, Dan Denman, and L. B. "Cow-boy" Anderson.[18]

At the same period the railroads were coming to Texas. Ironically they would soon make the cattle drives unnecessary as the stockyards and transportation came into the Southwest and there was no need

13

to lug the longhorns a thousand miles to Kansas. The Southern Pacific arrived in Fayette County by 1870 through its subsidiary Galveston-Houston & San Antonio (G.H. & S.A.) Railway Company, and three years later it inched its way west toward San Antonio. Word of the railroad's arrival became the exciting news of 1872 in Seguin. A road-bed was cut just north and parallel to the Old Seguin to Luling Road between 1873 and 1875, and the first rails put down by the end of that year. In 1876 the first train made its entrance on the Guadalupe County stage to the delight of the entire community. The town of Kingsbury—named after a Texas dentist turned railroad man—established itself that year eight miles northeast of Seguin and on the rail line.

The Rogers homestead now stood only two-and-a-half miles south of the railroad and Kingsbury, increasing the value of that land and assuring a decent future for all of the families in that area.

William C. Crier came from old Texas stock. His grandfather was one of the original settlers, part of Stephen F. Austin's "Old Three Hundred." Their land grant became a part of Fayette County when it was organized. Will was born in 1856 and by the time he was only fourteen he had participated in his first cattle drive. When the railroads needed workers to head west into Guadalupe County, and as the cattle drives began to dissipate by 1874, Will hired on with the G.H. & S.A. He worked for the Rogers family during that time as well as a ranch hand. When Pleasant Rogers died in December, 1875, Will, though turning only twenty a few weeks later and eleven years younger than Mary, offered to become a permanent part of the family.

And so as J. M. Baker, an ordained minister, made his way through the countryside in the spring of 1876, he found Will Crier and Mary Rogers waiting for him to perform their wedding, which he did on March 1. John's half-sister Maggie Amanda Crier was born September 27, 1877, and Haywood on September 21, 1883.[19]

The 1880 census shows the expanding family—except of course for Haywood, residing still on the old Isaac Rogers farm but with a Kingsbury address. Will claimed his occupation as a stock driver, and sixteen-year-old John Harris Rogers told the census taker to write down "farmer" beside his name. Laura was fourteen and Curren eleven.

Next door still lived the elderly John Wesley Harris, seventy, and his wife Laura, age sixty-seven. Their grandson Nat Benton, nineteen, who had come to live with them in 1861 when his mother died, still resided with them. Another stop away was the Elder Harris's son J. Wesley, forty-six, and fourteen-year-old Tupper. With several Sowell farms surrounding the Rogers and Harrises, John's Uncle Martin Rogers and Aunt Peneca lived closer to the Guadalupe River, with cousin James Harris boarding there.[20]

Everyone was settled and happy. Everyone except John Harris Rogers, "farmer."

CHAPTER 2

Colorado City Ranger

JOHN ROGERS STARED DOWN INTO the dark Guadalupe County soil, holding his hand where the rattler had just sunk its fangs. Working the field clearing rocks, he never saw the coiled snake until it struck. Now as it slunk away the teenager kicked a chunk of dirt in its general direction, turned and strode calmly but briskly back to the barn. As he walked he pulled the sweaty kerchief from around his neck and wrapped it around his wrist just above the two red marks, pulling it tight with the ends of the cloth in his good hand and clinched between his teeth.

When he reached the vicinity of the corral he made his way deliberately into the throng of chickens that pecked away at their morning feed scattered on the hard ground. His arm throbbed and a slight discoloration had already appeared on the back of his hand. The young man reached down and grabbed the nearest hen and deftly twisted its neck, killing it in one swift motion. John pulled the knife from his pocket and slit the dead chicken at its gullet. Blood spilled out onto the feathers as he untied the tourniquet and tossed it aside. He cut a similar slit across the back of his hand, wiped the knife on his pants and put it back in his pocket. Then he thrust his wounded hand deep inside the warm carcass.

As John leaned casually against the corral's rail fence, the old remedy for snakebite worked its magic. The chicken carcass turned a deep blue, then charcoal black as the rattler's poison spent itself from John's hand. Several more minutes passed. John felt lightheaded but not enough to fear fainting. When the slight dizziness had passed, he tossed the blackened chicken into a gulch behind the barn, wrapped a clean cloth around his hand, gulped some water down from the pump, and went back to work in the field.

John intended to be the best farmer in Guadalupe County. To do that meant going to agricultural school to study the latest technology—tools, crop rotation, irrigation, and so on. Thirty-five miles southeast of his home, in DeWitt County and just a few miles from Cuero, the ten-acre campus of Concrete College sat along Coon Hollow. The small school had been established nearly twenty-five years earlier and had a local reputation for its agrarian classes as well as its religious disciplines. Presbyterian Reverend John Van Epps Covey currently served as the school's president.

John was accepted to the school in the fall of 1880, and attended only after the crops had come in. No more than a long day's ride on horseback from home, he would stay in the tiny dormitory for awhile and often commute back home to help with the farming responsibilities. Professors Hueber, Woolsey, and Bonney taught most of the courses there, including business and commerce. President Covey taught a required Bible course. Adjacent to the college campus lay a broad field expressly for the purpose of experimenting with the latest farming techniques. Here John and the other students learned what they would need for their future careers.

John also found himself fascinated with, and perhaps convicted by, Reverend Covey's Bible studies. This may have been a beginning for the strong Presbyterian discipline that would rule and guard the rest of his life. In later years Rogers never spoke of a single "conversion experience," but rather that "Christianity came to me quietly and gradually after much study of the question. Years of religious reading," he continued in a 1928 interview with Harry Van Denmark, "gave me the conviction that Christianity should dominate a man's life, no matter in what occupation he might be engaged." Here, then, was its start.[1]

During the winter break that extended into January, 1881, however, the financial situation of an already struggling Concrete College finally came to a head—the school would have to be shut down. Whether John Rogers had planned to return for a spring session now became moot. School was over. What with the new activities and excitement brewing in Guadalupe County that spring, it may be that Rogers never intended to return to DeWitt County anyway. Ahead there lay a whole new world—and his own future—and it was in west Texas.

Three ingredients led to the opening of west Texas in the late 1870s. The first was the end of the Red River Indian Wars with the "settlement" of the Kiowa and Comanche on reservations and the gradual end to the buffalo hunting. The second factor surrounded the spread of ranching as far as the Panhandle and Llano Estacado. And the third was the arrival of the transcontinental railroads.

In 1875 U. S. Army Colonel Randall Mackenzie and his "Raiders" rounded up the last of the recalcitrant Comanches after the attack at Palo Duro Canyon and accompanied most into Indian Territory. A military road was constructed during that period along the Upper Colorado River and in the general vicinity where many believed Francisco Coronado had marked a trail in 1543. The old Bexar District, which at the time covered most of the otherwise uninhabited western portion of Texas, was subdivided by the state legislature, and Mitchell County was formed on the Colorado under the administration of nearby Shackelford County leaders. Towns and county seats and farming communities would not be far behind.

At the same time as the Indian Wars drew to a close, so too did the reason for the years of violence—the slaughter of the American bison in western Texas. Hired by the railroads after the Civil War, buffalo hunters roamed the Southwest killing literally millions of buffalo between 1868 and 1878. On the Upper Colorado men such as John Wesley Mooar and his brother Wright, Joe McCombs, George Waddell, and I. F. Byler piled tons of buffalo bones and hides and carted them to Fort Griffin or Fort Worth. Out of camps on Champion Creek and Morgan Creek, McCombs and his party killed over five thousand bison in 1876 alone. By the end of the 1870s most of the buffalo were gone.

Massive west Texas ranches began to organize just behind the cattle drives and just ahead of the railroads. Charlie Goodnight and Oliver Loving operated the JA Ranch. In what would soon be Mitchell County, John Wright and William P. Patterson organized some of the first ranches, and John W. Mooar came in from the last of the buffalo hunts to start his own ranch in 1879. So did George Waddell. Colonel Isaac Ellwood and his son arrived, and Joseph Glidden of Illinois sent his new invention—barbed wire—into the Texas market. The Snyder brothers organized what became the Renderbrook Ranch, and smaller ranches by the dozens began to pop up on Lone Wolf Creeek and Silver Creek. Brice Hughes even tried his hand at cultivating a peach orchard there.

In 1876 the state legislature rewrote several land and rail bills that eased some of the requisites for the expansion of the railroads across Texas. At the same time Collis P. Huntington was marching his railway eastward from Southern California, and the notorious Jay Gould had his eyes on the Southern Pacific making its way to meet Huntington in El Paso. In 1877 Gould and his partner Russell Sage put up three-and-a-half million dollars for the Texas and Pacific (T&P) Railway Company that had already reached Fort Worth. By 1880 they had connected a line out of Sherman, Texas, and were ready to make their way across west Texas. Gould hired Grenville Dodge to supervise the operation.

By June, 1880, the T&P reached Weatherford, thirty-one miles west of Fort Worth. Another 120 miles was completed by the end of the year. Speculators, investors, and merchants scrambled to look at survey maps and guess where the rails would go next—a correct guess meant a new town and nearly instant prosperity. William Dunn and his son-in-law predicted a route that would cross the Colorado River near Lone Wolf Creek and in August, 1880, they opened the Dunn, Coleman, and Company store there. They guessed right.

As the route became clearer by the beginning of 1881, Mitchell County was formally organized on January 10 and elections held. J. R. Dobbins became the county's first judge. The tiny clump of stores on Lone Wolf Creek, known as the town of Colorado, was selected as the county seat—its population had just passed the 150 mark. The

T&P roadbed came through Colorado [City] in the early spring, and on April 16 the first train chugged into the depot that sat on George Waddell's property. "Civilization" had arrived. Elm and Oak Streets were laid out on May 1, perpendicular to First Street. Storefronts and other businesses poured in to line the streets. In June the inaugural—and a crowded—passenger train emptied wide-eyed new residents into the Colorado City streets.

Among the first founders of Colorado City were the mercantilist Snyder brothers, "Uncle Mack" McClintock, and A. W. Dunn. Will Dobbyns hurried to town to start its first newspaper, the *Colorado Courant*. He got there so fast he arrived without any paper and used brown wrapping paper from Dunn and Coleman's store to print the first editions. The Burns, Walker Store, which soon became the Smith & Walker Company, opened that spring and the JA Ranch bought its supplies from that establishment. T. H. Lee had a drugstore, and the Grand Central Hotel went up, boasting a billiard parlor on its ground floor.

John Birdwell, an ex-Ranger and former frontier marshal, opened the first saloon in Colorado City, its first weeks situated under a large canopy tent. Right on schedule Reverend Oscar Fitzallan Rogers showed up there to preach against the evils of drink. In March, 1881, Rev. Rogers organized the first Sunday School class in town.

The cattle ranching industry erupted in Mitchell County. Fifteen brands were registered in the first months of 1881 alone and more the next year. Clay Mann bought land south of town and had over 26,000 head of cattle there two years later. D. W. "80 John" Wallace, one of the first African-American cattle ranchers, hired on with Mann during these formative years. In 1883 forty-one-thousand head were shipped through Colorado City and one-hundred-thousand the next year. An interested observer wrote: "Cattle cars were the first things we saw, hundreds of them lining sidetracks for more than a mile, marking the edge of the city."

Word spread of the wealth and opportunity in Mitchell County. John Garland James resigned as president of Texas A & M College to partner up with his brother and open a bank in Colorado City. Lots on Oak Street sold for six thousand dollars each, a "boom town" price tag. By the end of 1882 the population had soared to over six-thousand. Colorado City boasted seventy-five business establishments, four banks, a dozen lawyers, seventeen doctors, a dentist, and a barber. There were four theatres and seven billiard parlors. By early 1883 a water line was under construction, seventy telephones were operating, and an opera house opened in 1884.

On the seamier side of any boom town, Colorado City also claimed twenty-eight saloons, a liquor store, and three dance halls that stood side by side. The Nip and Tuck Saloon was the town's largest. Prostitution presented its own set of problems, although the regional newspapers admitted that such an institution was a "necessary evil." One observer noted: "Everywhere we looked were gambling dens and dance halls, cowboys staggering about the streets, some arm in arm with painted women."[2]

Law enforcement was in the hands of the county judge, an itinerant marshal, and the Texas Rangers whose camp had been in place in that area on Hackberry Creek since 1877. Captain Bryan Marsh, one-armed and absolutely fearless though not often sober, led Company B, and his former sergeant Richard C. "Dick" Ware, who most Rangers believed had fired the shot that killed Sam Bass, served now as sheriff.[3]

Two of the ranchers who arrived in Mitchell County during this early period were A. M. K. Sowell and James Wesley Benton, both from Guadalupe County and former neighbors of John Harris Rogers. And John came with them. At seventeen, he was not old enough to stake his own claim, but certainly mature enough to start out on his own and begin as a ranch hand working for someone he knew. It is likely that part of John's decision to head west, apart from the prospect of excitement and adventure and prosperity appealing to any young man, was the realization that the Rogers farm would probably never be his to own and operate. His stepfather Will Crier was only seven years older than John and likely to live long enough to be in charge well after John was ready to inherit the responsibilities. Heading out to west Texas may have been as pragmatic a decision as it was alluring. He bade his family farewell and made his way to Mitchell County where he worked on a Lone Wolf Creek ranch for about a year.

How fascinating it must have been for the farm boy from Guadalupe County to find himself on the boom town city streets. On his own, but often just plain alone, John worked hard on the ranch and limited his trips to town to obtaining supplies. When he did ride into Colorado City the sights and sounds must have been a world entirely different from Seguin, the only large community he had ever known. Brothels and saloons dotted every street, noisy cowboys whooped it up on Saturday nights, or maybe any night, and the flurry of bustling crowds arrived at the rail depot and spilled down First Street.

John may very well have spent some time with Reverend Rogers, the Presbyterian minister who traveled in that area and may have been a distant relative. A lifetime of Sunday church-going may have begun there, at least as soon as the first organized church came to town. When Reverend Rogers organized the Sunday School, John might have been seen in that group on as regular a basis as he could manage.

Prior to John's arrival in Mitchell County, although the stories would still have been fresh, a mud-slinging campaign had been waged between Richard Ware and William P. Patterson for the office of sheriff. Patterson, already an established rancher in the area, was a popular candidate backed by arrogant gambling man John Good and many of the local ranchers. His opponent Ware was a Texas Ranger when he entered the race in the spring of 1881, known to be tough-skinned and fair. The two sides displayed little respect for each other during the campaign and Ware won by a single vote. He retired from the Ranger force and set up shop in a small office near 1st and Oak. There was no jail yet in Colorado City and a chain around a large mesquite tree at the edge of town served that need.

It was to that very tree that W. P. Patterson found himself chained one May morning after a loud night of drunken carousing in which shots had been fired inside and outside of a local saloon. Patterson was released later that same day—laws against carousing were minimal in a boom town, but by that night he was back at his antics again, sore about his election loss and unimpressed with the local constabulary. When his outbursts persisted through the week, Ware, perhaps uneasy about how personal a confrontation would look, finally called on the Rangers for assistance.

On the night of May 16 Corporal J. M. Sedberry and privates Jeff Milton and L. B. Wells walked in from their riverside post when they heard shots being fired in town. Outside the Nip and Tuck Saloon the Rangers confronted Patterson and his friend Ab Adair in the street, both citizens drunk and pistols pulled. Sedberry calmly asked Patterson for his revolver. Patterson refused: "Damn you, you'll have to go examine somebody else's pistol." Most witnesses claimed later that Patterson fired a shot in the corporal's direction, missing him. Private Milton drew his gun and shot Patterson, who fell to the ground. New to the force and probably unnerved by the close quarters shootout going on, Wells pulled his revolver and shot Patterson who now lay on the saloon floor. Patterson died where he had fallen.

News spread through town like a west Texas prairie fire. In a matter of minutes a crowd—a hanging mob—had gathered inside the large saloon, John Good spurring them on. Ware arrived hastily, and at his suggestion the three Rangers surrendered their arms to him and went before Justice Smith two days later. In most cases such as this the Rangers were given the benefit of the doubt and released. But the judge, in a room crowded with angry townspeople, indicted the three for murder, then released them on fifteen-hundred dollars bond each when Captain Marsh let it be known his boys would be going to camp with him, not to jail.

Soon a lengthy trial was underway. Rumors and gossip surrounded the trial, that the Rangers had murdered Patterson in cold blood on behalf of their fellow peace officer Dick Ware. Other testimony hinted that Patterson and Ware had come to blows months earlier and that a vendetta of sorts existed at the time of Patterson's death. The trial was moved to Big Spring and finally Abilene in October, 1883. Although the charges were finally dropped after an agonizing three years of trials and testimonies, bitter feelings remained on both sides of the incident.

Captain Neal Coldwell, quartermaster of the Rangers' Frontier Battalion, and veteran Ranger D. W. Roberts soon arrived in Colorado City to investigate the matter. They decided the Ranger camp needed to be moved farther from the city to eliminate any trouble that might occur from this unfortunate incident. Company B relocated another twelve miles southwest of town and soon thereafter moved on to Big Spring to look after the railroad camps. Coldwell also reported that Company B was in disarray, Captain Marsh hardly sober enough to command, and the relationship with the townsfolk quickly deteriorating. On the other hand, Roberts reported, "Patterson was a drinking man and very troublesome while under the influence of liquor. Considered a dangerous man under those circumstances." He noted that there was "a good deal of sensational talk, and some threats," but neither he nor Coldwell "saw anything ominous of any further trouble here."

The new adjutant general, Wilburn Hill King, who had just assumed that office upon the death of the legendary John B. Jones, inherited the Mitchell County situation as his first challenge. Believing that Captain Marsh needed to be disciplined but wanting of the rubric or precedent that would justify a court martial, King did the next best thing—he disbanded Company B. Marsh was relieved of his duties and his officers as well. Sedberry, Milton, and Wells were transferred to Company E "for their own safety." Upon Coldwell's subsequent recommendations the adjutant general then reorganized Company B, keeping a handful of the Rangers who had served previously (including Sedberry and Wells), brought Lieutenant S. A. McMurry over from Company F and promoted him to captain.[4]

Captain McMurry needed recruits for his reorganized company of Texas Rangers. One of those would be John Harris Rogers, who enlisted on September 5, 1882, just shy of his nineteenth birthday, signing up along with J. F. Green and W. H. Meador that same day. Despite the accusations that flew at the Rangers from some of the citizens, John's background had long since established a huge respect for this unique Texas law enforcement organization. Whatever "call" he might have had during his year as a ranch hand in Colorado City, this was an opportunity that presented itself clearly and he answered without hesitation. His days as a farmer and rancher were now behind him; his whole life, as a peace officer, now lay before him.[5]

Texas Ranger Private John Harris Rogers' first activity with Company B included a fourteen-hour train ride to El Paso on October 30 to watch over the state and local elections that were being held later that week. The company stayed until November 8; there were no incidents of trouble to report and they returned to their Mitchell County camp.

Over the winter and during the spring and summer of 1883, Private Rogers worked in the Mitchell County area as well as up and down the T&P line. Trouble in and around the railroad camps from Midland (first known as Midline) to Big Spring and back to Abilene kept the Rangers on the move. With almost no law enforcement to speak of in the rail towns, a call to Company B was a regular occurrence. Rogers himself does not appear in any of the monthly reports as having made specific arrests of his own, but he earned his monthly thirty dollar paycheck working crowd control, keeping the peace in the livelier districts of the towns, and so on. He spent camp time on Hackberry Creek, but also in Big Spring, and got to know men like Sedberry and Jeff Milton, the huge Buffalo Bill Jenkins, and others of the company.

Even as the last stage of the Ranger trials was about to commence in Abilene in the fall of 1883, and where Private Rogers would be assigned to help keep order, the state legislature had left the Texas Rangers organization in its budget-cutting wake. The companies were to be consolidated and limited—the last to be recruited would be the first to go.

On September 4, 1883, Rogers signed on for another year as a Ranger in Company B; other names on the list included Charles Trentham, John McNelly, J. W. Woods and John's in-law cousin Nat Benton. But John Rogers drew his last thirty dollar paycheck on October 31, 1883, and instead of jumping the rail to Abilene found himself a victim of budget cuts and on the way back home to Guadalupe County. Just turned twenty, John stayed four months with his mother and Will Crier on the farm, contemplating his now uncertain fate.

But the future turned bright for him quickly as a new call for Ranger recruits went out after the first of the year. The Eighteenth Texas Legislature added ten thousand dollars back to the Rangers allocation as of February 28, 1884, thus allowing for the addition of dozens of new privates. John Rogers wrote Adjutant General King of his desire to reenlist and received an invitation to join Captain Joe Shely's Company F in Cotulla, where he arrived around March 1. He would draw pay as a Texas Ranger for the next twenty-seven years.[6]

Joseph Cotulla got right to work when he learned that the International & Great Northern Railway Company was headed out into south Texas. By the summer of 1881 he had purchased and prepared 120 acres of land for the rail line and by the next year the first small depot in La Salle County awaited the arrival of the trains. As if on cue settlers and speculators arrived quickly, with a general store, a post office and a jail on the site. By 1883 the town of Cotulla had been designated the county seat and a raft of mercantile establishments dotted the landscape along the upper Nueces River.[7]

With the arrival of the railroads came the trouble that nearly always followed. Company F was transferred to Cotulla in the fall of 1883 after moving through outposts in Pearsall and Yorktown. John Rogers joined them there the next March.

The Texas Rangers force in 1884 numbered an unusually strong 136 officers and men in the field. Still, there were some across the state who thought the usefulness of the old Frontier Battalion had come to an end. When a state congressman questioned the budgetary funds, however, Adjutant General King responded quickly: "I could exhibit hundreds of private and official letters speaking in terms of honest praise for the Rangers," he said. "I could show the proceedings of citizens' meetings and large stock conventions all over the border in which formal and open recognition was given in favor of the frontier force and its valuable service to the people. I could cite you the constant and earnest efforts, and the moving appeals made for years past, by legislators from all over Texas to have this force kept in the field, as the only sure defense of the orderly, honest and law-abiding citizens of the frontier against the criminal classes."[8]

Company F reported over sixty arrests in April 1884 alone, and forty-nine more in May, many of them within a day's ride of troublesome Cotulla (later called "the rustler capital of the world" by another Ranger). King was quick to note these facts to that same congressman "as evidence of the positive good from this force," specifically naming Captain Joe Shely and Company F. Disturbing the peace led the list of crimes as railroad workers and cowboys drank and fought and generally kept the little town lively. There was at least one assault charge and a burglary, and two horse thieves were tracked down and arrested.

In August Shely was sent to Anahuac in Chambers County on orders from Governor John Ireland. Six of the company including Privates John Rogers and John Brooks accompanied him—they may have been the first Rangers ever to set foot in that county on business. Cattle thieves fearlessly roamed the coastal plains and a local cattlemen's association finally asked for outside help. Company F made short work of the criminal element there, garnering a letter of high praise from the locals. There is no record of additional complaints by that particular congressman.[9]

Ironically for the still-wild West there were local ordnances in many Texas towns, enforced by the Rangers, that made carrying a concealed weapon illegal. Apparently carrying a .45 pistol in plain view on your hip was all right, although the Rangers themselves were encumbered by General Order No. 13 (January 7, 1884) requiring that they be unarmed unless on duty. Several arrests were made in Cotulla that year for breaking the concealed weapon law and who knows how many close calls along the way for unarmed Rangers in tough scrapes.

That same order from the top now required every Ranger to carry a written identification listing his height, eye and hair color, and any distinguishing characteristics, so as to prevent any confusion should a man claim himself to be one of the elite force. John Rogers' list hardly wavered throughout his career—five feet, ten inches tall, blue eyes, mustache, fair complexion, and hair that went from brown ultimately to "iron gray." Those eyes and the stare that emanated from them caused more than one criminal to quake in his boots, as well as a saying oft repeated, that "a man wouldn't want to get in the way of those gimlet eyes."[10]

The first written record of action by Private J. H. Rogers appears in the September, 1884 monthly report of Captain Shely. Richard Jones, a Cotulla resident, had been involved in an ongoing affray with

John and Curren Rogers, about 1885. Courtesy Texas Ranger Hall of Fame and Museum, Waco

another man which finally escalated into attempted murder on September 1. The next day Rogers hauled Jones into Cotulla and deposited him at the sheriff's office.

One month later Rogers was sent on a wider hunt, this time to Karnes County where Dan Butler had gone to escape a warrant for his arrest in La Salle County. Butler was wanted for murder. Reports of his whereabouts near Karnes City reached Company F and Shely sent Rogers to get him. John took the train up to Alice and Three Rivers, then northeast into Karnes County. He found the wanted man on October 12 after a day's search and returned him to Cotulla on October 14.

Having successfully fulfilled that tracking job, Rogers was sent out again in December to DeWitt County in search of a forgerer named Joseph Megler. The Ranger private returned with his subject on December 13. That close to his family, it is still unlikely Rogers took the time for even a quick visit with them—there was business to be taken care of, after all.

In February, 1885, Rogers and Company F survived a cut in personnel so serious that the company itself was actually in line to be disbanded altogether. With a relatively quiet lower Rio Grande Valley at the time, it seemed to King a reasonable place for the necessary cut to be made. What saved the company, ironic as it seems, was a renewal of violence with raids on both sides of the river by Mexican banditos. Cattle were being rustled with impunity and the local citizenry had killed several of the bandits, arousing even more trouble in the valley. At the behest of a concerned Governor John Ireland, Adjutant General King caught the International & Great Northern train to Encinal that same month to meet personally with Company F officers Shely and Scott and survey the threatening situation himself. Company B was put on alert and in March both companies arrived near William Votaws' ranch to quell any more outbursts from either bandit or citizen. A truce was called and it held. But Company F was now needed; unfortunately for others, as George Baylor's Company A was disbanded instead. The surviving companies were then reduced in force to seventeen men and their officers.[11]

And so Rogers'—and Company F's—work continued into the spring of 1885. When there wasn't a pressing need for the whole company to be active in the Cotulla area, there was plenty of Texas still to be covered by the peace officers. In fact, as the spring wore on the little town of Cotulla began to settle down, enough that the adjutant general considered a shift for his companies. In addition, the Nineteenth Legislature had once more cut funds to the Rangers necessitating a reorganization by Adjutant General King. One company of Rangers would now be required to watch over all of the Lower Rio Grande Valley as well as a number of counties in south Texas. In May Company F was moved to Uvalde County eighty miles west of San Antonio to carry out that far-reaching responsibility.[12]

Uvalde County had been named after the old Spanish governor Juan de Ugalde by the citizens who organized the county in the mid1850s. The little hamlet of Encina organized by Reading Black in 1853 was renamed Uvalde at the same time. Although Fort Inge stood nearby, the region was known mostly for its lawlessness for the next three decades, much of which was related to border violence. When the Galveston, Harrisburg & San Antonio Railway made its way there in 1881, trouble increased and the Rangers were finally called in. The town of Uvalde was not officially incorporated until 1888, but by then its population rapidly approached 2,000, including over sixty businesses and a newspaper.[13]

During this period one of John Rogers' Ranger comrade-in-arms was John A. Brooks, a good friend and sergeant of Company F, a Ranger whose own career and reputation would ascend to legendary heights over the next three decades.

John Abijah Brooks was born November 20, 1855, in Bourbon County, Kentucky. He came to Collin County, Texas, as a twenty-year-old, working as a cowboy and a miner. He joined the Rangers in 1883 and rose to sergeant quickly. He stood straight on a lean frame, wore a mustache nearly his whole life, and spoke quietly though always firmly. By contrast, John Rogers was taller than Brooks, but like his friend sported a mustache and made his point in a calm, soft voice regardless of the situation. He and Brooks would stand together on many occasions, the most deadly of which awaited them only months away.

But in the summer of 1885 the Rangers' work was typical. On July 11 Private Rogers brought in Reinhart and Peter Wingus, brothers who had stolen several head of cattle in Edwards County fifty miles northwest of the Ranger camp. Nine days later John Brooks brought in the third brother accused of the same crime. Rogers kept busy in late August bringing in horse thief Jesse Parker to the Edwards County sheriff on the 22nd and two days later hauling in John and "Windy" Hart for stealing hogs near Rocksprings.

On October 5 an order came down requiring the downsizing of all the Ranger companies from seventeen to twelve men plus officers. John Rogers survived that reduction in force but one-third of Company F was sent home. The extra-large geographical region under the supervision of Company F, and now reduced in size, meant only more work and longer trips. Two weeks later Privates Rogers, Moore, and Collier traveled over 200 miles north to San Angelo to arrest three cattle thieves, then returned them to Uvalde and deposited them in the jail.

In what must have been a surprise transfer, Company F loaded up in November, 1885 and moved due north from Uvalde to Wilbarger County on the Red River and Oklahoma border. They set up camp outside the town of Vernon, a particularly troublesome town for the past two years, replacing Company B which also been moved. During this period Captain Joe Shely was replaced by William Scott who had served as lieutenant of Company F since its reorganization in 1884.[14]

John Rogers had served as a Texas Ranger for most of three years. He turned twenty-two just before his company transferred to north Texas. He was as far from his family as he had ever been. John had survived three reorganizations of the force already and was quickly developing a reputation for his steadfastness, his dedication as a peace officer, and his perseverance on the trail of a criminal. He had yet to draw his gun in a deadly encounter. But that time was coming, soon, and it would nearly be the death of him.

CHAPTER 3

The Fence Cutter Wars

ON A COLD DECEMBER MORNING in 1885, Private John Harris Rogers stood in the middle of Doan's Store; not a building, but a town, of sorts, situated only several thousand yards west of where the Red River turned suddenly south on its wayward journey down from the high plains. Doan's Springs were just to the north, as was Doan's Crossing, a wide flat bank of the river that led Texans into Indian Territory. Not only Texans, but hundreds of thousands of cattle had been driven across the river there over the past seventeen years. For here the Chisholm Trail and a wide northeastern swing of the Western Trail converged. So too converged cowboys and soldiers, reservation Chickasaw and Apache, merchants and whiskey salesmen, rustlers and thieves, and prostitutes and the like. What a place, thought the young Ranger.[1]

Ranger companies B and C and now F had taken turns trying to tame this northern section of Wilbarger County, to no avail. Beyond the rowdy saloons—there were two - and the drunken brawls that spilled into the dusty streets, the proximity to the Texas border and Indian Territory made Doan's Store a likely spot for crooks to escape the law. In August of 1883 alone there were arrests made of eight cattle thieves in five separate incidents, two whiskey merchants selling liquor to the Indians, a burglar, and two wanted men on the run—all as they headed to cross the border and disappear into the reservations.

This common occurrence at Doan's Crossing brought Private Rogers and five others from Company F up from their Vernon camp. Warrants for several Texas fugitives spurred the Rangers to track them across the river. The Apaches and Chickasaws lived along this portion of the Red River and the small Anadarko Reservation lay a hundred miles into Indian Territory north of Fort Sill.

Company F rode out of Doan's Store on December 1 and would not return for nineteen days. The made their way to Fort Sill where they checked in with officers of the U. S. Army stationed there. Receiving the papers that allowed them legal jurisdiction should they find any Texas fugitive, the Rangers pressed on, skirting the sharp rise of the Quartz Mountains and enduring the rough terrain of gulleys and ravines along their way. The weather deteriorated into a series of wintry squalls—the normally high winds in that region spiked prickly cold—making the journey more than uncomfortable. But on December 17 they arrested felons Sam Davis and Jim Blankenship in Anadarko country; the two gave up without a fight. With winter settling in, the Rangers decided to quit while they were ahead—they were back in Vernon late on December 20, the two fugitives deposited in the small log cabin that served as the town jail.[2]

In north Texas 1886 came in cold and snowy, a far different clime from where John had grown up and likewise a contrast to the dry, dusty cold of Cotulla's winters. On January 30 Rogers and Private J. B. Harry rode east to the Wichita County line and arrested Tom Comfort and Tom Moelhull. The two had been spotted after a break-in of the Smith ranch house near there. No rest for the weary, however—two days later Private Rogers and Jim Moore were on the train to Colorado City to disperse a mob that had gathered around a criminal in the city jail. They stayed on several days to guard the prisoner until he could be transported to safer surroundings.

When violent railroad strikes hit Fort Worth that spring, Company F joined Companies B and C for nearly three weeks in April restoring order. An attack on a train April 2 outside of Fort Worth resulted in one death and several injuries. When it became known that a Missouri labor leader had ordered the ambush, local authorities called for outside help. U. S. marshals and Rangers responded, and Governor Ireland sent three hundred state militia to back them up. The depots and railway camps were shut down and the Rangers kept twenty-four hour vigil until an agreement was reached between the organized workers and the T&P management. Company C returned to its Rio Grande post after several days, while the other companies remained. Adjutant General King reported calm in the Fort Worth area: "Quiet and orderly and without uniform of any kind, the sturdy and determined manner and appearance of the Rangers, and their well established character for the fearless observance of order made a powerful impression on the minds of the strikers, and had due weight in bringing about a condition of peace."[3]

Not all of Company F went to Fort Worth. The company's sergeant, John A. Brooks, and two others were called instead to the Choctaw lands in Indian Territory. Fugitives hiding along the Red River raft region had eluded federal authorities and the U. S. Army asked for help. Tracking the criminals to their hideout, Brooks found himself engaged in a deadly shoot-out. The felon, one Albert St. John, was killed. What seemed a fairly ordinary circumstance, however, would return to haunt Brooks.[4]

On May 16 Barry Thompson and J. A. Carroll shot and killed a man in southern Wilbarger County. There was certainly some history of an ongoing dispute, for the murder was premeditated. A warrant was immediately issued for their arrest. Rogers and Harry went on the trail and found the two after three days. They were returned to Vernon.

One month later Rogers and four others of Company F—now commanded by the just-promoted Captain William Scott—were sent to the town of Harrold where they reported to Ranger Captain McMurry and his company already patrolling the streets. Harrold sits about sixteen miles east of Vernon, and until 1884 had been the sleepy little hamlet of Cottonwood. But Bar-X Ranch owner Ephraim Harrold had promoted the area and succeeded in bringing in the railroads. Almost overnight the newly named town claimed a rowdy population of fifteen hundred, plus sixteen saloons. When the crowds got crazy on those summer nights, the Rangers had their hands full.

Barely back to the Vernon camp after restoring order in the Harrold streets, Company F received orders to move to Hemphill, Sabine County. For nine weeks the force would find itself deep in the east Texas Piney Woods and only a stone's throw from Louisiana. During their brief stay the Rangers dealt with border troubles of a different sort and the foreshadowing of an event that would lead to tragedy a year later and a dramatic escape from death by the young Ranger from Guadalupe County.[5]

"I had rather be a pack mule out west than be a million heir [*sic*] in this brush." So wrote Captain William Scott from the Ranger camp near Hemphill. "We have been going out every day and each man brings back Ticks. Enough to keep him scratching and Kussing all night. Yes it is sure rough country on man and beast, but I can stand it if I can only get back to the prairie alive."[6] The Rangers, accustomed to wide open country and landscapes that trailed to far horizons, did not care for the Piney Woods. That distaste included some of the citizens as well.

One of the most notorious of the Sabine Valley clans was the Conner family, headed up in those days by "Uncle Willis" Conner. Ranger William W. Sterling describes them as "the most audacious band of desperados in deep east Texas (who) lived like savages in the dense thickets, trapped, stole livestock, and defied the local authorities." Another account describes them "living like Indians in the wilderness."[7] They had not always been so, however, for before the feud began they were law-abiding farmers who raised hogs on land along Bull Creek east of Hemphill. A personal dispute between Uncle Willis's son Charles and neighbor Kit Smith escalated in 1883. On December 5 Smith and his friend Eli Lowe rode down a rough trail in the piney woods. Their bullet-riddled bodies were found that evening.

Charley and his older brother Frederick, known as Fed, were arrested, tried, and convicted of the two murders. Charles went to prison, while Fed's conviction was overturned. Awaiting these decisions in December, 1886, the Conner boys broke Fed out of the Hemphill jail and disappeared into the dense woods with their father, defying the authorities, always on the move to makeshift camps, living like wild animals throughout the spring, and sending messages to family members protesting their innocence.[8]

That summer their primitive campsite lay hidden in the thicket several miles south of Hemphill and butted up against the swampy edge of the Sabine River. It was country a stranger could get lost in and perhaps never be seen again. The thick woods near Walnut Creek and Lick Branch would eventually become part of the aptly named "Scrappin' Valley." In early July of 1886 the local authorities asked for the Rangers' help to bring in the Conners and Company F was sent.[9]

On July 10 Captain Scott and his men made camp just on the outskirts of Hemphill. They quickly set to work interrogating members of the several families involved in the latest bloodshed, although they were unable to locate the Conner men. In fact the search for the Conners and any others involved in the summer's violence proved as irritating as the ticks the men pulled off their legs every night. Early in August, Captain Scott got on the trail of Alfred (also known as Alfie) Conner, one of Uncle Willis's boys and wanted for questioning. The trail took Scott across the Sabine and to Calcasieu Parish, Louisiana, where another day's search was successful—Scott arrested Alfie Conner after a brief scuffle, handcuffed and returned him to the jail in Hemphill.[10]

With Conner's arrest the violence in that area temporarily quieted down. It would not stay that way for long, as the blood boiled through the Conner clan for vengeance, and a new target—the Texas Rangers—now grabbed their full attention. One of the bloodiest confrontations in Rangers history was less than six months away.

In an unrelated incident while Company F remained in Sabine County, Privates Rogers and Caldwell were sent into the western part of the county, near Pineland, to arrest one Dave Edding for rape. They returned the wanted man to the jailhouse on September 8. Only eight days later, Adjutant General King recalled Company F to west Texas, this time to Brownwood, where they would remain for five months before accepting the unpleasant task of returning to Sabine County.[11]

Notably absent during much of this first action on the Sabine River was Sergeant John A. Brooks. In a surprising turn of events,

A dapper Private John H. Rogers, 1886. Courtesy Charlie, Lauren, and Carley Reeves, San Antonio

Brooks was called to Little Rock, Arkansas, in August to appear before a federal judge and face a murder charge. As the case would unfold, it appears that the death of Albert St. John back in April had come under the scrutiny of the federal authorities—perhaps the very ones who had asked for the Ranger's help in the first place. Brooks had been indicted and charged. The case would stumble along into 1887, requiring occasional trips by Brooks back to the Arkansas court. He was found guilty of murder, discharged from the Rangers, pardoned by the governor of Texas and returned to active duty all in the span of several weeks in the summer of 1887. Brooks was exonerated even during the same period he was being promoted to lieutenant and then captain of the Texas Rangers.[12]

Company F took two weeks to establish their new camp near Brownwood. On their way in two separate groups, they traveled the rails by way of Rusk and the penitentiary there, delivering five prisoners as ordered. One of the prisoners was Alfred Conner, who was released soon thereafter—to the disgust of the Rangers—and allowed to return to his family now plotting their revenge.

Brownwood was established in 1857 along Pecan Bayou forty miles north of where the stream spills into the Colorado River and seventy-five miles southeast of Abilene. In the mid-1880s the growing town boasted two banks and two hotels, a street full of saloons, a newspaper, and two mills down the river. The Gulf, Colorado, and Santa Fe Railroad came through in 1885 and in two years the city had a waterworks and an opera house.[13] Although a certain amount of railroad town rowdiness certainly occurred and the kept some of Ranger Company F busy, it was another crisis that had called them to the wide country—the fence cutters.

Western author Walter Prescott Webb introduces the fence-cutting wars: "The invention of barbed wire in 1873 made it possible for the first time to fence the western portion of Texas. Though the day of free grass was about over, many men—long accustomed to believe that the Great Plains could not be used by farmers—were loath to believe or accept the fact. When they saw all the lands going under fence, they seized their wire-cutters and used them in the determination to keep the free range. . .The horse thief was caught with the horse and the cow thief with the cow, but the fence-cutter rode away from the curling steel tendrils with no evidence upon him. He had to be caught on the job through detective work."[14] The Texas Rangers became those detectives.

Texas counties from the Pease River valley south nearly to the Rio Grande suffered from these fence-cutting wars during the 1880s. Brown County, situated more or less in the center of this activity as well as in the heart of cattle country, had its share of troubles. The sparsely populated county—only 544 people counted there in the 1870 census—grew rapidly to over 8,400 a decade later. Many of these new families were small time farmers, and the larger landholders in many cases simply, literally, fenced them in. A natural dispute arose between the haves and have-nots, along with the obvious problem of there being no gates for the small farmers to transport their produce. In addition, another group of Brown County citizens—the free range ranchers—watched with frustration as the open grasslands disappeared.

In the spring of 1883 fences belonging to the Coggin brothers and also to Brooks W. Lee, Sr. were cut. Four more miles of fence became tangled strands by August of that year. The next month L. P. Baugh defiantly strung two miles of new fence along his property line. Three days later he found a note nailed to a post. It read, "Mr. Baugh, take down this fence; if you don't, we will cut it and if we cut it and a drop of the cutter's blood is spilled, your life will pay the forfeit." Baugh scrawled his response on the bottom of the piece of paper and left it hanging there: "You cowardly cur," he wrote, "this is my fence, and you let it alone." A mile of the fence was cut the next night.[15]

In December of that same year a so-called "fence cutter's convention," J. B. Scruggins in the lead, rode into Brownwood for what everyone knew would be a bloody confrontation. Brownwood Sheriff W. N. Adams negotiated a truce and averted violence on that day, but the threats and fiery speeches acknowledged the dispute was far from over.[16]

Similar incidents across the plains counties finally led Governor Ireland to call a special session of the state legislature in the spring of 1884. The *Galveston News* reported one million dollars in damages in Brown County alone. War stories had spread across the whole country by now, and a Chicago newspaper blared bold headlines: "Hell

Breaks Loose in Texas!" After heated debate, the Texas Legislature passed a law making fence-cutting a felony. Far from settling the crisis, the new law only spurred the defiant cutters to more action. Local law enforcement was sure to be inadequate—the Rangers would have to be called in.[17]

In Brown County L. P Baugh and his brother continued to be harassed by fence-cutters and several face-offs had occurred in 1885. The Baughs would not back down and instead supplied a long list of the names of the felons to Sheriff Adams. A grand jury sat in March, 1885, to hear the evidence and returned indictments against ten men. Among the indicted were Amos Roberts and Jim Lovell, Ace and John Matthews, three Johnson brothers, and Bob Parrock. Overwhelming eyewitness testimony resulted in a second indictment against Lovell. But the courts did not take action and the case sat on the bench for a year. A continuance postponed it again to September, 1886. By then tempers had boiled over, fences were still being cut, and Adjutant General King received a message from the governor to take care of the volatile situation.[18]

King sent Ranger Ira Aten to Brownwood to consult with Sheriff Adams and survey the situation. Upon his arrival Aten determined that he would gain more information by working undercover. He took the train to Coleman, bought a pony and rode back into Brown County posing as a cowpoke looking for work. A sympathetic farmer took him in and trusted him to such an extent that he sent Aten to Belton with horses the farmer had stolen and was trying to sell off. Aten corraled the horses some miles away until he could take care of that situation later, and went back to work.[19]

Meanwhile, the Baugh brothers had persuaded neighbor Joe Copeland to do the same as Aten, gaining the confidence of the cutters and setting up more evidence against the perpetrators. By the end of October, working together, Copeland and Aten wormed their way into the fence-cutters' operations and learned of a plan to destroy miles of fence on the night of November 9. Aten wired King, and King sent Company F.

The targeted fence stood along a property line about fourteen miles due north of Brownwood. On November 8 Captain Scott rode to the Baugh ranch accompanied by Sergeant John A. Brooks and Privates Jim Carmichael, Bill Treadwell and John H. Rogers. There they met with Copeland and Aten and several of Baugh's hired hands. After darkness had set in on the evening of November 9, ten riders made their way to the targeted fence and hid in bushes nearby.

Near midnight the fence-cutters rode up to the fence line. There were several whose gray silhouettes could barely be made out in the night. Two of the riders dismounted only a few yards from the concealed Rangers and began their destructive work. Captain Scott stepped from his hiding place, hollered "Texas Rangers," and shouted through the pitch-black darkness for the culprits to stop what they were doing. The men still on horseback vanished into the night, but the two cutters on the ground, caught completely off guard, reacted swiftly. Jim Lovell grabbed for his Winchester rifle leaning against a post. Amos Roberts ran for his horse and pulled his rifle from its scabbard. The Rangers stepped out from the bushes, spread ten yards wide on either side of their captain, and opened fire in two rapid volleys. Rogers and Carmichael fired through the darkness first, bright orange flame spitting from the barrels of their guns. Lovell dropped his rifle, grabbed at his chest and fell backwards, mortally wounded. Scott and Aten opened fire. Roberts had taken a step toward the Rangers, but was driven back head over heels when bullets slammed into his torso just under his left shoulder blade.

In an instant it was over. The Rangers holstered their guns and looked after the two fallen men. Neither had been able to get off a shot. Lovell died within the hour, having never risen from where he fell. Roberts hung on, and was taken into Brownwood to the local doctor. One of the bullets was removed from his chest, but by dawn he too was dead. Their bodies were delivered to the undertaker who buried them in the only cemetery available, on the property of L. P. Baugh.

On the morning of November 10 the Rangers walked through the town streets. Word spread rapidly of the shoot-out from the night before and Brownwood citizens poured out into the streets to get the latest reports of what had transpired. Will Butler, a deputy sheriff (and some said one of the fence-cutters) confronted Joe Copeland out in the street, demanding that he turn over his pistol while in town. Ranger Jim Carmichael, standing at Copeland's side, pulled his revolver and pointed it at Butler. Sheriff Adams stepped into the staring contest and leveled his pistol at the Ranger. Everyone in the street held their breath. Just then, Captain Scott appeared. He calmly suggested that everyone holster their weapons, which they did. Copeland had been deputized as a Ranger, explained Scott, and had a right to carry his pistol in town. But Scott also ordered the Brown County farmer to head for home. On his way home, seven miles out of Brownwood crossing Salt Creek, Copeland was ambushed by revenge-seeking fence-cutters. He managed to escape when the mule he was riding bolted even as the first shots were fired.

The consequences of this deadly action were interesting. A third fence-cutter from that night's action, Wood Runnels, was arrested on November 24 by Sergeant Brooks, and two weeks later Brooks also hauled in Frank Johnson for the same crime. A grand jury indicted Ace Matthews, Frank Johnson and one of his brothers, and Bob Parrock following the November incident, but in early 1887 all of the charges were dismissed. In August of that same year new indictments were brought by a grand jury for the attempted murder of Joe Copeland, and Private Rogers and seven others from Company F brought in Bob Parrock, Ace Matthews, Wood Runnels, and Bill Green. In June of 1888 those charges were dropped as well.[20]

Meanwhile, Captain George Schmitt of Ranger Company C officially criticized Captain Scott for his hasty actions that resulted in the death of two fence-cutters and the dismissal of the other charges. Although Schmitt had not been present, he wrote into the official records his opinion that Scott could have spared those two lives and put the others in prison if he had acted more responsibly. Irascible and from the "old school" of discipline, George Heinrich Schmitt expended a great deal of vitriolic energy over several years on Scott and what Schmitt considered questionable leadership abilities.

When Ned Perry succeeded Will Adams as Brownwood's sheriff shortly after these incidents, one of the indicted fence-cutters, still at large and with wanted posters circulating the county, tried to escape arrest by hiding in a neighbor's hay wagon headed out of Brownwood. Suspicious, Perry stopped the wagon and asked if the fugitive might be hiding there. The farmer said, "Oh no, not a soul," whereupon Perry replied in a loud voice that he thought he might set the hay wagon afire just in case. The fugitive hollered from the bales, "Wait a minute, Ned," and crawled out in surrender.[21]

For John Rogers, the fence-cutting wars in Brown County proved a sobering experience in his life. For the first time in service as a law enforcement officer—for the first time in his life—he had killed a man. It would be an experience he would never forget, and would forge in his own mind and soul a determination to never pull a gun unless he was absolutely sure it was necessary. And he knew at that moment, and would tell other Rangers under his command in the years to follow, that once they had pulled their guns, to use them with absolute resolve.

Never would that resolve be more significant in Rogers' life than in the confrontation that would follow only nineteen weeks later. The combination of these two events less than five months apart led the twenty-three-year old to a faith-journey that would lift and carry him for the next four decades. His taking of a life, and his own subsequent brush with death, reinforced the meaningfulness of a life led in faith.

Throughout December the Ranger company roved the wide Texas country tracking down reports of fence cutting in McCulloch, Concho, and Lampasas counties. In January, 1887, Scott reported no fence-cutting incidents in that region— the Rangers had accomplished their mission.[22] A new, and much more deadly one, awaited them now.

In March, 1887, Company F was recalled to Hemphill and Sabine County where new violence had broken out involving the Conner clan. Local law enforcement, either unable to quell the violence or too afraid to try, needed help. But was this a calculated trap by Uncle Willis Conner? Did he know he could entice the Rangers back into his own backyard and take revenge against the very company that had disrupted his family months earlier? Whether premeditated or not, the gun battle that took place on the night of March 31 was one of the bloodiest of the Texas Rangers in that era. And John Rogers found himself in the thick of it.

John Rogers *(standing)* and brother Curren, 1887. Courtesy Curren Rogers McLane, Ft. Worth

CHAPTER 4

The Conner Fight

CAPTAIN SCOTT AND COMPANY F arrived at the camp near Hemphill where they had been the previous autumn. It was the last week of March and a meeting with the local authorities convinced the Rangers that the Conners were on a rampage, intimidating the locals then recoiling back into the safety of the dense forest and bayou country like a deadly snake. Scott retained the "deputized" services of a small-time Sabine County crook who could communicate with the Conners and track them into their lair. Scott also deputized Judge James Polly from Hemphill, and Judge William Wallace Weatherred, a district judge from nearby Milam (and later a deputy marshal), came along as well. Henry Harris and John Toole, local merchants, and Milton Anthony rounded out the posse of deputized citizens.[1] These men knew the country, knew the Conners, and were good with a gun.

With Scott on this manhunt was his sergeant John Brooks, and Privates Jim Carmichael, Jim Moore (just transferred from Company C), William "Billy" Treadwell, Bob Crowder, Ed Caldwell, Len Harvey, Bob Fenton, and John Rogers.[2] On the morning of March 25 the posse rode south out of Hemphill four miles until they crossed the deep gulch of Housen Bayou. They continued south about ten miles, first along Walnut Creek and then to the county border along Brushy

Creek and Big Sandy. Working their way back northward with the help of their guide (who may have been Redden Alford), the Ranger posse searched high and low for the elusive Conners. Five days went by, the men silently complaining about the elements but pressing on in their search of the rugged wilderness that enveloped them. On March 30 they picked up what they thought might be a trail which took them back to Walnut Creek and then east about one mile. They were less than ten miles south of Hemphill.

As the sun set to their backs, the Rangers stared with uncertainty into the black forest. An abandoned house stood at the edge of a meadow; the spy said he believed one of the Conners used to live there. Two hundred paces east lay two small graves with roughly carved stones indicating the deaths of two small children ten years earlier.[3] Somewhere just a few hundred yards farther east and down a steep hillside was a shallow but running stream named Lick Creek (or Lick Branch) meandering its way slowly toward the Sabine. The infiltrator told Scott that the Conners had been moving their camp up and down the creek bed, but that they kept a bell on their packhorse when moving in the thick underbrush. The Rangers could position themselves to hear the bell and capture the Conners while they slept. The spy disappeared, presumably to locate the Conner camp, and was gone for several hours.

Midnight passed. The Rangers kept silent in the darkness. The informer returned about two o'clock and pointed into the blackness where he had spotted the campsite in a deep dry gulch. At a hand signal the men dismounted at the abandoned structure, the Ranger horses obediently silent in this tense situation. Scott motioned to his men and they quietly divided into two prearranged groups. Crowder, Caldwell, Weatherred, Polly and the other three locals moved off to the left; Scott took the rest of his company and moved right. Their plan was to find the Conner camp somewhere between them and descend upon the criminals from both sides.

In the black night, both parties walked right past the camp without ever spotting it. Later reports indicated that the Conners had stumbled onto the Ranger trail at some point earlier, took the bell off the packhorse, doused their torches and a kerosene lamp, and waited to launch their own attack. With them were four vicious hunting dogs, also laying in wait. The group sneaking to the left did not participate in the action, hearing too late the gunfire that signaled the blood-bath in the deep piney woods.

Brooks walked down into the gully and motioned to Scott that they should make their way back up this gulch in case it was the one where the campsite was located. The six Rangers, guns drawn and senses sharpened, spread abreast and began stalking the gully. They had walked less than a hundred yards when they became vaguely aware that it was first light, only a half-hour until daybreak, March 31. But in the solid forest the darkness prevailed.

The Conners—Uncle Willis's sons Fed, John, and Bill—were hiding in the camp while the old man took up a sniper's position. Uncle Willis spotted the Rangers at nearly the same instant that one of the Conners was seen moving behind some brush. Brooks and Rogers saw the shadowy figure, realizing that the two sides in the coming fight weren't fifty feet apart. Rogers whispered in the figure's direction, thinking it was one of the men from the other party. The figure stood, a shotgun coming to his shoulder, as Brooks hollered a warning.

Then all hell broke loose.

The first sounds after Brooks' shout were terrifying growls from the throats of the hunting dogs as they sprung from their hiding places and made for the Rangers, teeth bared and trained to kill. The next was the first volley of gunfire coming from the Rangers. Scott, Brooks, and Rogers raised their guns and fired simultaneously at the figure they had first spotted. Thirty-two-year-old Bill Conner dropped where he stood, one bullet in his brain and two more in his chest. He was dead before he hit the ground, although one story had him firing even as he went down. Jim Carmichael and Billy Treadwell took aim at the lunging dogs.

Uncle Willis Conner fired next from behind the trees where he hid. Jim Moore had taken one stride toward the enemy when a bullet pierced his heart. He toppled over backward, his gun thrown aside. Jim Carmichael, only a few feet away, knelt beside his comrade. Moore managed a brave smile but a second later he was dead.

In the same concentrated volley John Rogers was also hit, a bullet pounding into his chest at the left ribcage, spinning him around, then slowing as it struck the small daybook in his vest pocket. The notebook he kept as did many Rangers certainly saved his life. Later stories claimed it was his Bible that had shielded him—untrue, as good a story as it would have made. Rogers kept on his feet and raised his Winchester for a second shot. Hardly had he pulled the trigger before another bullet struck him in his left arm, slicing into muscle just above his wrist, careening off bone and nerve near his elbow and exiting downward toward his hip. Temporarily paralyzed by the two gunshot wounds, Rogers dropped to his knees, his pistol still raised in his one good hand. At some moment during the firefight he pulled himself over to a tree and sat up against it, cradling his left arm and pressing it against his chest wound. Years later he admitted that he couldn't remember anything that took place after being shot, but one of the others there claimed that Rogers propped his rifle on his knees, working the lever of the rifle with his right hand, and pulled the trigger repeatedly until he ran out of ammunition.

Captain Scott took a shot through a lung during the same volley that had dropped Rogers and he too fell to the ground. That left Brooks, Carmichael, and Treadwell to continue the fight, but Treadwell's gun jammed on him and he was forced to seek cover and watch the remainder of the battle. The volleys came hot and heavy from both sides, the Conners stepping out from behind the trees and firing single shots, the last two Rangers advancing steadfastly along the gulch, rifles and pistols blazing.

The four dogs were dead before they had reached their targets; the packhorse had taken several ricocheting bullets as well and lay dead.

A bullet found John Brooks as he stepped over Bill Conner's body—it left a groove as it glanced along his rifle barrel and smashed through both of his hands as he gripped his gun while firing. The three middle fingers of his left hand hung mangled and bloody; the bullet lodged in the palm of his right hand. Brooks tried but failed to continue the fight and was forced to crawl back to Rogers on his knees and elbows, blood streaming down his left arm. A handkerchief became a temporary tourniquet.

Fed Conner took a bullet in the last volley, and then with a shout the remaining fugitives retreated up the gulch into the dense brush and vanished in the gray dawn. The surviving Rangers agreed that over one hundred shots had been fired in a matter of minutes, none at targets of more than forty or fifty feet distance. Two dead men, three wounded, five dead animals, and a dozen pockmarked trees along Lick Branch substantiated that claim.[4]

Jim Carmichael went immediately to work on the injured men who lay all about the bloodied gully. He confirmed to Brooks that Jim Moore was dead, and he believed the captain's wound also to be life-threatening, although Scott would in fact survive. Treadwell chased the Conners with a borrowed rifle until he lost their trail, but raised the alarm that brought the other party that had advanced to the left to the scene a few minutes later. Captain Scott wrote in his official report of the fight that "the citizens being more accustomed to hunting deer than desperadoes held their stand, not being more than eighty yards distant from the fight and [did] not even come to our assistance for minutes after the fight was over. Had the squad come," Scott added, "we would have captured the entire Conner gang."[5]

Carmichael, whose rapid fire and deadly shooting, all agreed later, had likely saved the lives of the others, propped Captain Scott up with his head elevated on his coat so as to keep him from strangling on the blood that seeped into his lungs. In difficult drawn breaths and coughing up blood, Scott issued several orders to his company. Judge Weatherred and Private Crowder were to head immediately for Hemphill, the former to find the first doctor he could and the latter to ride on to San Augustine and locate a surgeon if possible. They were then to accompany the physicians back to this spot immediately; no one else was going anywhere for the time being. The others were to retrieve the horses and stand guard in case the Conners counter-attacked. "I then had [the Conners'] camp equipage & effects destroyed," Scott wrote later.[6]

James Polly took a piece of notebook paper and a pencil and scribbled a note: "Capt Scott and two of his men was [sic] shot this morning by the Conners and wishes that you come at once to this place as they need & wish your service and attention on them. Be sure & come right away as they are badly wounded." He tore off the piece of paper and handed it to Weatherred with instructions to get it in the hands of Dr. Frank Tucker up at San Augustine.

Surprisingly, the first person Bill Weatherred encountered in the still-quiet streets of Hemphill an hour later was Miss Vernon Scott, the Ranger captain's sister who had accompanied them to Hemphill and happened to be awake and outside when the messengers rode in. She immediately located a wagon and team while Weatherred raced to wake Dr. J. W. Smith, the local physician.

Bob Crowder rode on another twenty miles to San Augustine with Polly's note in hand and sought out Dr. Frank H. Tucker. Tucker folded Polly's note into a vest pocket and headed for Lick Creek. Arriving later that evening, he was the first to send word of the fight to Adjutant General King in a telegram on April 2. Reporting one dead and three badly wounded Rangers, Tucker added: "A Winchester ball entered apex of Captain's left lung & come out at lower border scapular. Hope to save his life," the telegram concluded. On May 11 Tucker wrote up a more formal report of the incident, indicating Scott's wounds "had not been dressed for he was expected to die," and noting that "the Winchester ball had carved away Brooks' fingers, nothing left to do but clip off ends of bones and wrap hand." [7]

Doc Smith and Miss Scott raced to the bloody scene with the marshal as guide, where the captain's fretful sister assisted as a deputized nurse while Smith went to work. Smith relates the events in a letter to Ranger Captain Lam Sieker in Austin on May 19: "I lost no time in getting to the men and found Capt. Scott in a faint and dying condition, but by the use of restoratives he began to react [later that] night. I extracted the ball about Noon which relieved the difficulty of breathing to some extent. I was very doubtful as to his reacting. . .I amputated three fingers for Brooks on one hand and removed a ball from the other hand.

"Rogers' wounds in the arm and side were dressed by me using great care to remove all extraneous matter in the track of the balls.

"I remained in the woods with the wounded men until the next evening and carried them to Hemphill. Capt. Scott was carried on a litter, the other two men in a wagon. I remained with them or nearby

Note from James Polly at Conner battle site, March 31, 1887. Courtesy Texas State Library and Archives Commission, Austin for 10 days, abandoning all other practice and gave my time exclusively to them, believing their safety depended upon our close attention."[8]

With Miss Scott also in attendance for most of that time along with Drs. Tucker and Smith, and a constant flow of sympathetic ladies from the town bringing flowers and nourishment, the Rangers slowly recovered from their wounds. Brooks and Rogers both stated years later they thought for certain they were going to die—not from their wounds but the wagon ride through the piney woods.

James F. Perkins wired Adjutant General King on April 2 to report the fight, that he had sent word to the penitentiary for some bloodhounds to track the Conners, and that "Judge Bower in Sabine says Conners can be easily captured if you will come now." He also noted that Private Rogers "had a ghastly wound in the side, also shot through his left arm."

Jim Moore's body was carried into Hemphill and buried there, although he was from Center Point in Kerr County. Nearly all of the citizens turned out for his funeral. His uncle, Sheriff Frank Moore, arrived two days later and returned his nephew's horse and possessions to his family.

William Scott recovered fully from his near-fatal wounds but resigned from Ranger service the next year, moved to Mexico, and went to work there as a successful railroad contractor. Jim Carmichael resigned from the Ranger force later that year, left Texas in 1888, and only returned as an old man in the 1930s. Billy Treadwell—"a lovable vagabond, loyal, trustworthy and a fightin' fool," said a friend, eventually went to work on the Pettus Ranch near Goliad. John A. Brooks never made much fuss about his amputated fingers and learned to operate the weapons and tools of his trade with only seven digits for the remainder of his long life. The loss certainly did not diminish his accomplishments nor his courage in future deadly encounters. Nor did the permanent injury ever impair his promotions through an outstanding Ranger career.[9]

Ranger George H. Schmitt was less than sympathetic with the entire incident, blaming Scott for the failed assault in a letter to Captain Sieker: "It looks like Capt Scott and his men got the worse of it, and three of the criminals got away. It seems to me that Capt Scott had not men enough with him or else he could have captured the whole gang. This is a very unfortunate affair and I feel sorry for them." Only days earlier Schmitt had complained to Sieker that Scott had allowed his men (especially Treadwell) to "get drunk and insult and abuse local citizens," and that Scott's company had been "drawing full rations & supplies—having picnic times—even though only half of the men were in camp." John Rogers had, in fact, been in Hot Springs for an extended period of time earlier that year.

The disabled John Rogers remained in San Augustine for two more weeks recuperating under the watchful eye of the two physicians. Well enough to travel by the last week in April, he was escorted home to the Kingsbury ranch for an extended stay with his family. When he rejoined his company in late May, now camped out west of Fort Worth near Weatherford, he was accompanied by his little brother Curren "Kid" Rogers. Caught up in the excitement of his brother's adventures, and perhaps concerned to keep an eye on him at the same time, Curren enlisted in Company F on June 1. He would ride with his brother and the Rangers for much of the next decade.[10]

There were no lasting problems from the wounds Rogers received and he recovered fully the use of his left arm. Ironically, a more damaging injury, to his other arm, was still twelve years away.

Bill Conner was buried in the tiny cemetery a few feet from the children's graves near where he had fallen. They were in fact two Conner children. Those in Company F who could still ride tracked the Conners for two months. Using bloodhounds, they searched in the deep piney woods and as far as the Atoyac River bottoms. They rounded up eight men who were arrested as accomplices in the Conners' getaway, but the principals had escaped.

Six months later a company of Rangers tracked the remaining Conners into that same Sabine County territory. In a firefight much like the first but with far different results, forty-one-year-old Fed Conner was killed on October 25 and buried near his brother Bill. Leander Conner was tracked into Louisiana and captured; John Conner made his escape as the last survivor of the Conner gang, riding into the piney woods never to be seen nor heard from again. Shortly thereafter a private detective tracked Uncle Willis to his hideout and on November 15 killed the sixty-five-year-old and his ten-year-old grandson at his side. They too were buried in what is now marked as the Conner Cemetery.[11]

Thus ended one of the most desperate and deadly confrontations in the history of the Texas Rangers.

John Barber and his gang waited restlessly in the thicket as the train huffed and blew to a stop at the Mulberry Creek Bridge a mile east of Flatonia. It was a hot June afternoon and no breeze stirred. Barber wiped the sweat from his face with a kerchief. Time to go—he signaled to Brack Cornett, Charley Ross, and Ike Cloud with a nod, pulled the grimy old Stetson down on his forehead, and dug his spurs into his horse's flanks. As the last metallic noises echoed away from the locomotive, the four men rode up to the tracks at an even pace. Bud Powell turned and headed for the engineer while Barber led the others to the lone passenger car. The gang's leader noticed with a smile that a freight car sat coupled just behind the Pullman.

They made quick work in the sweltering midday heat. With the engineer covered by a Winchester, Barber and his cohorts boarded the passenger car, stepping from saddle to stair onto the steel landing, and pushing through the heavy door. Pistols drawn at their hearts, the dozen or so startled people inside were quickly parted from their valuables, rings, necklaces, and money. One man surrendered over one thousand dollars in cash and received a pistol whipping for his troubles. John Barber fired a shot into the mail car while his men finished their work. He got the drop on the lone security man who had nodded off anyway, and slung the small payroll box out the sliding side door to Ed Reeves who was waiting there.

With a wave to the front of the train as he leapt to the ground, Barber signaled for the man at the locomotive to send the train on its way. The thieves rode briskly for the hills to the north of the G.H. & S.A. line, paying no attention to the chugging bursts of the train as it pushed on eastward.[12]

Two weeks later, Deputy U. S. Marshal William Van Ryper waited patiently outside the small wooden church in Cisco, his hat in his hand. It was Sunday, July 10, just after noon, and the service was letting out. Although the marshal had never met John Rogers before, he spotted him in the tiny crowd without difficulty. The young Ranger sported the beginnings of a moustache, walking ramrod straight as he stepped out of the double front doors of the church, not all that tall but seemingly so because of his posture and just the way he carried himself. As he raised the white ten-gallon hat to his head, Rogers was clearly still favoring his left side even three months after the Conner fight.

The deputy marshal introduced himself and the two law officers rode out of the little railroad town together. They headed north in the general direction of the Brazos, into Stephen County. John Barber, recent train-robber, had been spotted two days earlier making his way north on a trail that would likely lead him to the Doans' Store crossing and into the safety of Indian Territory. Barber had lived in the Cherokee Nation before and his usual operation was to seek safety there. Van Ryper and Rogers tracked the desperado for four days, knowing they were close but frustrated by the dusty trail that left so few markings. In the end they admitted defeat and parted company.[13]

John Barber [Barbour] would live to break the law again and John Rogers would be on his trail another day. For now, though, the Ranger private headed back for the Cisco camp. The company had been there less than two weeks, having hopped from Hemphill to Weatherford in June, then another 100 miles west along the rail line towns to Cisco. Captain Scott continued to convalesce from his serious wound. Sergeant Brooks had been discharged out of Weatherford when the courts in Fort Smith, Arkansas, had found him guilty at the trial that had haunted him for two years. Although he would be pardoned by the Texas governor shortly and return to his company in September, Brooks' absence left no officer on site. Private Rogers had taken up that responsibility for the time being.[14]

On the first of August, 1887, Callahan County rancher John Wilson reported eight head of cattle missing and presumed stolen, and Company F responded. Rogers led three men on a four-day search for the thieves but came back empty-handed. No sooner had they returned to the Cisco camp than they were again called to Brown County to deal with the next, and one of the last, incidents related to the fence-cutting shootout from a year before. The eight-man company arrested four men for the attempted murder of Joe Copeland, the rancher who had assisted the Rangers in what had led to the deaths of two fence cutters.

While in Brownwood, Company F received orders to remove their Cisco camp another one hundred miles west out the rail line to Ballinger in Runnels County. The tiny rail town was barely a year old, another oasis sprung up as the Gulf, Colorado, and Santa Fe Railway moved west, and in fact named after one of the railroad company's trustees. Already Ballinger claimed a hotel, a couple of saloons, and a newspaper. Now it had the Texas Rangers. The official records note that Private Rogers was in charge of this move. The camp was established at the edge of town by the end of August. Captain Scott and Sergeant Brooks returned in September and resumed their duties.[15]

This brief charge was Rogers' first taste of command, one that he carried out as well as everything else he did, with determination and quiet control. He was well organized and had the respect of the rest of the company even though no higher in rank than the others. The experience would serve him well as promotions awaited just around the corner.

On October 4 word came to the Ranger camp that a stagecoach had been robbed outside San Angelo less than thirty miles away. This particular crime had become almost commonplace in Tom Green County due to increased commerce since 1884. A sensational series of robberies that year and the next resulted in the arrest, trial, and conviction of two robbers (one of whom was shot after his escape from jail), and the addition of Army escorts for some of the payroll stages. An observer out of Fort Concho noted in 1886 that "the tough element is pretty well cleaned out. The citizens have done much to encourage the officers of the law and by that means discourage the rowdy elements."[16]

But as the railroads grew closer to San Angelo and the west Texas town picked up its pace as well as its population, robbers were at it again the next year. Rogers and Brooks and two others from Company F arrived in San Angelo on October 5, the day after the robbery. Brooks took one of the Rangers and headed north on the trail, while Rogers and the other private looked for signs to the south.

Hardly had the two parties divided when a report came to Rogers that a horse thief named George Bright had been spotted outside of town. Diverting from their route the two Rangers tracked Bright and cornered him in a motte of trees near the Concho River. Bright pulled his pistol but Rogers drew faster and fired, felling the thief with the first shot. Wounded but not mortally, Bright was taken to the Tom Green County jail and deposited there. The Rangers continued their pursuit of the stage robbers, but with no success.[17]

As his twenty-fourth birthday drew near that month, John Rogers must have taken some of his personal time to meditate on the violence of the career he had chosen. In less than two years he had covered thousands of miles of Texas and Indian Territory, been drawn on three times, killed three men, and been seriously wounded himself. He believed that God had called him into this career, and he believed that God was protecting him as well. His brushes with death had grown him up in a hurry.

John returned briefly to his home near Kingsbury where his sister Laura married Robert Johnson on October 19, John's birthday. Robert and Laura would raise three sons, nephews to proud "Uncle John." It was a fine family reunion, but duty beckoned once more and the Texas Ranger headed for San Angelo.

Company F moved into Tom Green County on November 11, 1887, and set up their camp on the Concho two miles east of San Angelo. But the work of law enforcement never dawdled. Five days later Rogers and Bob Crowder tracked down and arrested three cattle thieves; two weeks later they brought three more into the county jail. Finally, 1887 drew to a close. It had been more than an eventful year for Private Rogers and Company F. The next year would not be any less so, as company records indicate these men would travel a total of 47,781 miles in 1888, arresting 249 men without the loss of one Ranger.[18]

On January 7, 1888, a message from Fort Concho indicated that an Army recruit by the name of J. K. Hogan had deserted. Private Rogers went after him, found him, and escorted him back his post. Hogan had at least had the benefit of one evening around a trail campfire with Rogers, whose Christian witness had offered consolation to the distraught young man.

Stealing horses seemed to be the crime of the month in Tom Green County, at least as the Ranger records show. Rogers arrested Jim Philips and Tom Price for that crime on January 19, and then tracked Tom's brother Sam Price for five days in February for the same incident. This brother eluded the Ranger.

A surprise awaited Rogers when on March 1 his cousin Tupper Harris rode into the Ranger camp with the intention of enlisting in Company F. The two had grown up together along the Guadalupe and now would ride with Kid Rogers for most of the next decade. Tupper would be a faithful comrade and fellow officer when promotions finally came to Company F.[19]

Another surprise, a deadly one, awaited Rogers.

CHAPTER 5

Captain of the Rangers

ON MARCH 3, 1888, WORD CAME to the Ranger camp near San Angelo that horses had been stolen up the river and the thieves identified as Bill Neil and Bill Davis. Private Rogers took half the company and headed northwest, picking up the thieves' trail between the Concho and Colorado valleys until they crossed into Mitchell County on March 6. Rogers met up with Mitchell County deputy sheriff Y. D. McMurry, and the two men went north while the other Rangers headed out along another trail.

The next day as Rogers and McMurry ambled along a dusty trail, two men on horseback crossed from the nearby woods onto the road—it was the horse thieves. Neil grabbed for his pistol and had it out of the holster when Rogers' first shot rang true, striking the man in the arm and forcing the gun to the ground. McMurry nearly made a fatal blunder as he turned to watch the first man fall from his horse, leaving Bill Davis an instant to draw his own weapon. However, a steely look from Rogers, gun pointed at Davis's heart, encouraged the thief to rethink his position and he raised his hands skyward. The two men ended up in the Tom Green County jail.

Two weeks later Rogers and two other Rangers rode the train east one hundred and twenty-five miles to the rowdy rail town of Mullin in

Miles County. Created by the rail company that had pushed through there that winter, Mullin was already overflowing with raucous rail workers and the accompanying riffraff that always managed to come out of the woodwork when a new town rose up in west Texas. The three Rangers remained there a week, curbing the growing violence in the one street town, "restoring peace and order" as the records describe it.

Upon their return by train to the Concho River camp, the Rangers were informed that new orders had come from Austin—Company F was bound for Ballinger again. Here they would spend two more months before yet another move. In April Private Rogers was recalled to Mullin to quell renewed violence, arresting a John Williams for aggravated assault and remaining in the town several days.

With word that the elusive train robber John Barber and his gang had been spotted making their way south, Company F went on the trail. But on April 29 they returned to the Ballinger camp without success. In September the Cornett-Whitley Gang robbed a train out of Harwood. Barber escaped but several others were tracked down, arrested or killed. Barber himself died in 1889.[1]

Rogers and the others rode into camp filled with frustration, and this would be the last foray by the young private. Not bad news, however, for orders came on May 1 that John H. Rogers had been promoted to Ranger sergeant. His friend and comrade in arms John Brooks rose to the rank of lieutenant and, with the untimely resignation of William Scott ten days earlier, Brooks became the commander of Company F.[2]

This was a coming of age for Rogers, his first step up in command but not his last, and the result of obvious leadership skills he had exhibited over the previous year. It was a logical decision out in the field as well as in Austin, and Company F applauded the news.

No rest for the diligent and dedicated, however, rings ever true for the Texas Rangers. On the same day Captain Scott had announced his resignation from the force, another stage had been robbed. This one, near the town of Miles in Runnels County, had been westbound for San Angelo. The unusually polite crook, almost apologetic as he emptied the pockets of the passengers, announced that they would wait until the eastbound stage came by, which he planned to rob as well. Growing impatient when the other stage was delayed, the thief (who had identified himself as Rube Burrows while they waited) thanked the passengers for their cooperation and rode away.

Two weeks later a reported sighting in Mills County of the polite robber brought Sergeant Rogers back to Mullin. But the trail evaporated and the robber, who it was later determined was not the infamous Alabama crook Burrows, managed his escape into the Texas wilderness. A stage robbery on June 23, 1888, near the Willow Watering Hole on the San Angelo-Abilene Road, was thought to be the last such crime in that part of Texas as law enforcement cracked down along the stage lines and as those same stage lines finally gave way to the more expeditious railroad travel.[3]

John Rogers made one more extended trip out of Ballinger before Company F picked up and moved. On May 15 he rode southeast to San Saba after reports of street violence had reached the Ranger camp. The company's sergeant returned several days later to report that everything was now quiet in the San Saba streets.

Company F spent its summer in Kerrville dealing with a reprisal of fence cutting in that ranch country and generally keeping the peace in the region. Kid Rogers was discharged after one year of service, went home for a few weeks, then returned and reenlisted in July, a practice he would repeat for most of his thirteen year Ranger career.

Kid's big brother arrested a fence cutter named Tom Secrist in June, and chased down cattle thieves in Uvalde and Bandera later that same month. Working the Kerrville streets in July, Sergeant Rogers arrested one Bill Stapleton for breaking the concealed weapons law, and brought in a mule thief to the Kerr County jail ten days later. Walt Greenwell was caught with false cattle inspection certificates after a routine search by Rogers in August, and a horse thief named Claude Bramlet was tracked south past San Antonio all the way to Atascosa and captured by the Ranger sergeant. Soon thereafter the sergeant caught up with and captured a horse thief named A. G. Peters in Gillespie County near Fredericksburg.[4] John Rogers was quickly earning his reputation as a tireless and perseverant tracker.

In October Company F was temporarily divided into two camps and sent south to the Rio Grande Valley. Lieutenant John Brooks commanded the force out of Rio Grande City, the main camp, while Sergeant Rogers took the others and established a smaller camp outside of Laredo. With the exception of occasional forays into other parts of the state, Rogers would enforce the law in south Texas for the next sixteen years, from Corpus Christi to Alice and Cotulla to Santa Maria, but never far from the Texas-Mexico Borderlands.

The first order of business was in Rio Grande City itself where desperate street rioting had left many injured and bad blood between Anglos and Tejanos. A Mexican-American named Abraham Recendez had been arrested for robbery by Starr County sheriff Warren W. "Wash" Shely, Ranger Captain Joe Shely's brother. Recendez was then gunned down while trying to escape from Shely's companion Victor Sebree, who was the U. S. Customs Inspector there. Shely was considered a racist by many in that area and a newspaper campaign was waged against the local Anglo authorities, a campaign led by a journalist named Catarino Garza who claimed that Recendez had been killed in cold blood. When Garza accidentally encountered Sebree on a Rio Grande City street that September, an argument turned into bloodshed, Garza's. Sebree then retreated to the safety of nearby Fort Ringgold. A two-hundred-man mob of mostly Hispanics was dispersed by the Army post commander, but trouble continued to brew and word spread that race riots were imminent in the Valley. Even a Montana newspaper proclaimed hyperbolic headlines that warned of war between the United States and Mexico.[5]

By mid-October two-hundred-and-fifty law officers had descended on Rio Grande City, including Ranger companies D and F, the Third U. S. Cavalry, and with state troops awaiting word as reinforcements if necessary. The Rangers helped keep peace and order in the area, arresting twenty-six Mexican-Americans in the meantime. Nothing more came of the anticipated riots, but bad blood simmered there and the name Catarino Garza would soon be heard from again.

Sergeant Rogers and Company F finished the year 1888 in routine fashion, at least compared to the tension in the Rio Grande City streets that October. Half of Company F watched over the voting booths in small Valley towns the first week of November; Benjamin Harrison and the Republicans wrested the White House back from the Democrats in a stunningly close national election. Rogers and four others spent four days in the tiny village of Saliñeno twelve miles up the Rio Grande from Roma. The quaint Hispanic hamlet dated back to the early 1700s, but had hardly grown since that time. On December 3 Rogers tracked down and captured Antonio Espinosa, wanted for smuggling along the border. And on December 22 he brought in Phil Morley, wanted for murder in Goliad.[6]

The year 1889 unfolded across the Valley as relatively peaceful, perhaps because the troubles of the previous fall had increased the presence of the U. S. Army and other law enforcement officials, including the Texas Rangers. Sergeant Rogers worked out of Rio Grande City for the first nine months, and the official records were written up by John Brooks who was promoted to captain on May 1 after nearly a year as ex-officio company commander. Rogers began the year with the capture of alleged murderer Margarito Castanedo on January 2, and in February and March he also tracked down and captured two other Mexican-Americans wanted for murder, one in Saliñeno and the other near Rio Grande City.

In May Rogers and three of his privates tracked Juan Garza from Edinburg to Brownsville, where Rogers remained for a month as a security force of one at the District Court there. He spent a week in June at the Edinburg courthouse before returning to the trail where he arrested nine criminals in a period of fifteen days.

August was as bad a month as June had been successful; the monthly record indicates that Rogers and others of Company F tracked wanted murderers across Hidalgo and Duval counties without making a capture, and lost a band of robbers who had ransacked a store on the border and crossed safely into Mexico. The Rangers made up for this bad run with Rogers' arrest of three thieves in late September. Captain Brooks took a six-week leave of absence during this period, and Rogers assumed command of Company F, a responsibility that would be repeated several times in the future and ultimately lead to his next promotion.[7]

In October with Brooks' return Company F was again divided, with most of the Rangers at Rio Grande City while Rogers took the rest and made camp near Santa Maria. The town of only three hundred had a long history back to Spanish days, and lay twelve miles southwest of Harlingen in Cameron County, eighty miles from the other Ranger camp. This allowed the force to work over a larger area of the lower valley, and it put Rogers in command for the next eight months at one site or the other before the company was rejoined at Cotulla. This was a challenging time for a Texas Rangers force depleted by cuts in the state budget and thinned across an ever-growing Texas population. Through the end of 1889 Company F worked quite actively, registering twenty-one arrests in the two counties, many recorded by Private Tupper Harris.[8]

On January 5, 1890, Sergeant Rogers moved his command to Rio Grande City while Captain Brooks prepared to establish a camp near Edinburg. From that post Rogers made three arrests on his own in February and five more in March and April.

Between May 10 and 20 Company F moved their two camps to Cotulla in La Salle County. Over the next two-and-a-half years Rogers would find himself tracking dozens of fugitives over thousands of miles, meet one of his lifelong best friends, meet and marry his lifetime partner of the next thirty-eight years, and culminate this stage of his career in law enforcement with a promotion to Texas Ranger captain. It would also be the first of two long stays at the south Texas town, the other coming at the turn into a new century.

In 1890 Adjutant General W. H. King, faced with a thin budget and a thinning Ranger force, moved Company D out to west Texas and Presidio County even as the railroads and the Texas populace made their way to El Paso. This left a huge area to be watched over by Company F; thus the compromise move out of the Valley but still having responsibility to the lower Gulf Coast. The advent of so-called "special" Rangers had done little to mitigate the problem, and so the "regular" Rangers would now be expected to maintain law and order over an ever-increasing chunk of south Texas, essentially from Del Rio to Alice to Brownsville.

The sharp-witted Polish immigrant Joseph Cotulla foresaw the arrival of the railroads into that part of Texas and welcomed the International-Great Northern Railway Company in 1881 with tracts of land and other incentives. By 1890 Cotulla's population had risen to 1,000. Troublesome as most railroad towns tended to be at the start, legend has it the railroad conductors would announce the arrival at this depot with, "Cotulla! Everybody get your guns ready!" At least three sheriffs and more than a dozen residents were shot down in blazing street battles before law and order was restored with the arrival of Company F of the Texas Rangers.[9]

That wasn't the only problem there, as Adjutant General King reported in 1890: "Large bodies of organized, well-armed and desperate characters were raiding the ranches and driving away stock in droves, and bidding defiance to the citizens and peace officers, or so arranging their wholesale thefts as to defeat all attempts at arrest and punishment. A special Ranger force had been organized but this was not sufficient, and it required the presence of regular Rangers to afford any substantial relief." By the end of 1890 King was able to report that "wholesale stealing has been stopped, but the thieves are still there, and the permanent or even temporary withdrawal of the Rangers will be the signal for renewed activity in lawless stock driving and stealing." The Rangers were there to stay.[10]

Two days after his arrival at the Cotulla camp as head of the supply caravan, Sergeant Rogers was on the trail arresting Miles Elkins, one of the most wanted horse thieves in the area (wanted in three counties). Elkins resisted arrest but was convincingly subdued and taken to the Cotulla jail for prosecution.[11]

The summer of 1890 was spent in fairly routine fashion—for Rangers, that is, with arrests of horse and cattle thieves, murderers, and several in the town streets for carrying concealed weapons. The Rogers family remembered years later that the rough and tumble town sneered at the sight of the clean cut, religious minded, soft spoken Rogers when he first arrived with his company. However, by the end of that summer, when an impressive assembly of those same brigands found themselves behind bars, a whole new respect for the quiet efficiency of the Ranger sergeant emerged. On August 25 Rogers tracked Jim Knight, wanted for murder in Frio County, north and east all the way to Wilson County, capturing the fugitive near Floresville. From mid September to mid October Captain Brooks was again on leave and Rogers commanded Company F.[12]

It was during this time that Rogers met two of the most important people of his life— Harriet Burwell, the woman whom Rogers would marry and who would become his most faithful life partner; and "Colonel" Thomas Atlee Coleman, a rancher who would stand alongside Rogers as a friend for the next thirty years. Coleman owned a grand spread outside of town where he traded for and bred prize horses. His fame was widespread and his nickname, *Don Tomas,* indicated the respect and integrity he earned across cultural lines in southwest Texas.[13] Throughout his life he was a friend to the Rangers.

Administrative changes at the top of the Texas Rangers also took place during this period with the retirement of Wilburn King as adjutant general on January 23, 1891, and the appointment of Woodford Haywood Mabry as his successor. Also, William J. McDonald was promoted to captain of Company B in February, 1891, and John Hughes to sergeant the following year and then on to a captaincy as well. The famous "Four Captains," including John H. Rogers and John Brooks, were emerging from the Ranger force and rising to the top.[14]

Sergeant Rogers spent the first ten days of 1891 in Batesville, fifty miles northwest of Cotulla, guarding the inmates of the Zavala County jail as an unruly citizenry threatened to turn into a lynch mob. The threat dissipated with the presence of the Ranger. On January 13 a particularly heinous crime, the murder of Charles Adami's two sons by two brothers following an argument that quickly got out of control, resulted in Rogers' tracking Pablo and Pancho Saenz for two weeks across La Salle County, through Encinal County and into Webb County. Rogers reported on January 27 that the two fugitives had "mounted good horses and fled to Mexico." Reports that the two had crossed back into Texas brought another chase in mid February, but the Saenz brothers were never brought to justice.

On March 30 Sergeant Rogers and Private Tom O'Donnell arrested four men wanted as cattle thieves in Webb County, including brothers Sam and Bill Anderson and a man named John Conner. There is no record that this was one of the Sabine County clan who had vanished five years before.

A cattle rustling gone bad in May resulted in the death of one cowboy in Zavala County and Rogers went on the trail, arresting George Rumfield on May 19, and on May 22, his brother Jack along with three others.[15] Throughout the summer and fall the Rangers kept their vigilant eye on the massive square mileage of southwest Texas. Rogers traveled by train and horseback across La Salle and Webb counties, coursing southward through Duval and into Starr counties, and even to the northwest into the Uvalde region.

While in Cotulla, Sergeant Rogers attended the Presbyterian Church services every Sunday that he could. It was here on the church grounds that John met Harriet Randolph Burwell, ten years his junior and eighteen years old in 1891. Harriet's brother Will would become a good friend and fellow Ranger in the years ahead, as would nephew Charlie Burwell years later.

The Burwells claimed their roots four generations back to Dinwiddie County, Virginia, and moved to Jackson County, Texas, around 1870, where Harriet was born on July 29, 1873. Like so many others, the Burwells moved west with the railroads in the 1880s and were now a successful ranching family outside of Cotulla. Late in 1891 John Rogers asked Harriet's father for her hand in marriage. Burwell, and Hattie, said yes.

On May 2, 1892, Rogers wrote Adjutant General Mabry this peculiar wedding invitation: "Doubtless you will be surprised to hear that a Ranger Sgt even entertained such a thought as marrying. However strange it may appear I am to be married on tenth of this month at Cotulla. I fully recognize the fact that it is rather out of order for a man of my rank in the service. But Capt Brooks has kindly informed me I may still remain in my present position, even though it may be hard for me to fill when married. I shall not let it interfere in the least with my work," Rogers continued, "though I may be constantly in the saddle scouting. I do not flatter myself that you could attend but it would be a happy surprise to meet you there for that occasion."

Blair Burwell stood proudly with his daughter on May 10, 1892, as she and John were married. Their partnership would last over thirty-eight years and would be blessed with three children, two of whom would become prominent Texas citizens themselves, while one would be at the center of one of the greatest tragedies of John and Harriet's life. John also joined the Presbyterian Church there in Cotulla and made a lifetime commitment to that Christian denomination that would never waiver. He may even have taught his first Sunday School class there.[16]

But the business of law enforcement never strayed far from John Rogers' life, and marriage or no, as he had promised in his letter to Mabry, there was work that needed to be done. Even as the Ranger sergeant was courting his future bride over the winter of 1891-1892, the so-called "Garza Trouble" spilled out again along the Lower Rio Grande Valley. It had been three years since the near-riots at Fort Ringgold that had first called law enforcement's attention to Catarino Garza; now a brewing insurrection arose once more.

Catarino Erasmo Garza Rodriguez was born in 1859 in Matamoros and raised there, educated at San Juan College and served in the National Guard. His first marriage into a prominent Brownsville family had ended in divorce; in 1890 he had married again. After years of working in the United States, and serving briefly as a Mexican consul in St. Louis, Garza had enjoined a small but tempestuous revolutionary cell that stood—twenty years ahead of their time—in open opposition to the dictatorial Porfirio Diaz regime in Mexico. Garza and Gabriel Botello published the fiery *El Libre Pensador* out of Eagle Pass and became targets of the Mexican authorities after 1888.[17]

Garza spent a month in jail when his newspaper equipment was confiscated, but soon moved to Corpus Christi and started up again. It was at this time that he had his run-in with Wash Shely and Victor Sebree, his wounding on the streets of Rio Grande City sparking the unrest that brought Ranger Company F into action the first time. Now in the fall of 1891 Garza was gathering fellow revolutionaries for what seemed to be preparation for an invasion into Mexico. Although none of his activities were aimed at the United States or its government, still the uneasiness that already pervaded the valley towns was only exacerbated by the presence of a growing army of Garcistas.

In his annual report Adjutant General Mabry thought little of this purported revolutionary force: "These smugglers are citizens of Mexico who are outlawed by the Mexican government and [thus] are always ready to join issues under the banner of any revolutionary leader who promises to create trouble on the border. They are material for ready draft to any movement of the Garza character."[18] Authorities on the U. S. side of the Rio Grande wanted nothing to do with such ruffians— their presence only guaranteed trouble.

Catarino Garza issued a manifesto in September, 1891, and his motley "army" crossed into Mexico with the apparent objective of leading a people's insurrection against the Diaz government. It failed miserably and Garza and some of his men returned in haste to Texas. A second, then third, failed invasion now had everyone on both sides of the Rio Bravo up in arms and Diaz' army on the prowl. Some of the mercenaries, having lost interest in Garza's higher philosophy of revolution, now resorted to bandit raids along the valley. Company E gave chase first, but soon Company F had come into the affray.

In December a warrant was issued for Garza's arrest in connection with the bandit activities of those associated with him. The U. S. Army came onto the scene in January after an ambush against Company C, Third U. S. Cavalry, on December 30 and again when a Corporal Charles Edstrom was killed—the cavalry swung out of Fort Ringgold to join the hunt. With the arrival of Company F from Cotulla, Brooks and Rogers conferred with Sheriff Wash Shely at Rio Grande City, then took up the hunt near the little border town of Roma. Word was that Garza was in hiding and still had 165 men at his side. The only real "battle" that took place during the entire affair occurred northeast of Carrizo when Rangers and U. S. troops surprised an encampment of bandits who promptly fled leaving twenty horses and some supplies behind.

During the second week of January, 1892, Rogers and five men from Company F followed a trail that led them to a camp just recently abandoned by Garza's forces. A list of over forty names was found left behind, names of Garza's lieutenants. Concerned that the numbers might exceed even the rumors, Rogers was sent, twice, to Laredo to ask for reinforcements. Finally a squad of army soldiers responded.[19]

Even Adjutant General Mabry appeared on the scene, evidence of the growing concern of a situation seemingly headed out of control on this side of the border. Mabry stayed in the area the last ten days of January and filed this perspective: "The situation is a peculiar one, and the obstacles to a successful raid at one dash are nearly insurmountable. The resident population of the interior is composed entirely of Mexicans who claim citizenship in Texas, but are with singular unanimity in sympathy with the Garza movement. They harbor them secretly, act as spies, and notify the revolutionists of any approach of Rangers or U. S. troops."[20]

As a result of both the conspiratorial aid of the citizens of that region, such as it may have been, and also the elusive nature of these border bandits cum revolutionaries, the authorities spent two more fruitless months on the hunt. In early March Rogers and seven of his company tracked through the rough country to yet another abandoned camp. This one, however, had left indications that the Garza movement was deteriorating into small bandit gangs. J. S. McNeel's Company E found seven more abandoned camps that month and made the same evaluation. On March 20 several bandits were caught by Company E and one was killed. Two days later Ranger E. E. Doaty was ambushed and killed by bandits.

On March 27 Sergeant Rogers and a volunteer named Lee Hall took up a trail of two fugitives, and three days later they caught up with brothers José and Pancho Ramirez. By coincidence, these two had been charged with the murder of the army corporal four months earlier. Rogers rode into their camp and called for them to drop their guns. Both bandits dove into the underbrush, pulling their pistols. Gunfire echoed all around the camp for the next several minutes, with the Ramirezes firing as they zigzagged their escape, and Rogers astride his horse firing his Winchester with deadly effect. When the shooting stopped, José Ramirez lay dead; his brother vanished.

The violence had come to an end. Several arrests were made over the following weeks but no bandit gangs were found. In late April Rogers and several Rangers from Companies E and F brought four of the bandits to the Nueces County jail and delivered them to U. S. Marshal P. S. Levy at the district court. The four were indicted and later convicted of violating the U. S.—Mexico neutrality laws.[21]

As for Garza, his revolutionary plans in disarray he slipped out of the country to be heard from again in Jamaica, Cuba, and Costa Rica.

In 1895 he was killed while participating in a revolution of Panamanians against the Colombian army, although legend continued to swirl around his name and purported sightings of the Mexican hero made the news for years to come. What glory he may have ever found from his Texas manifesto was published by distinguished American journalists and war correspondents Frederic Remington and Richard Harding Davis, the latter of whom wrote profusely of both Garza and the "gallant" Texas Rangers in his book, *The West From a Car-Window*.

In fact, Davis' description of the Rangers he met aptly describes many of the men, in character if not necessarily in attire, including John Rogers: "Boots above the knee and leather leggings, a belt three inches wide with two rows of brass-bound cartridges, and a slanting sombrero make a man appear larger than he really is; but the Rangers were the largest men I saw in Texas. . .remarkably handsome in a sun-burned, broad-shouldered, easy, manly way. They were also somewhat shy with the strangers, listening very intently, but speaking little, and then in a slow, gentle voice. And as they spoke so seldom, they seemed to think what they had to say was too valuable to spoil by profanity."[22] Davis' talks with John Brooks and John Rogers are certainly reflected in these last words.

The end of "the Garza Trouble" only directed the Rangers' attention to the more routine matters of law enforcement that had not abated in the meanwhile. In fact, Rogers recorded the arrest of a man named Luciano Longoria for stealing horses near Zapata on March 22, the same week he was finishing up operations against the bandit revolutionaries.[23]

In June, 1892, Company F moved its camp from Cotulla south to Realitos, a small *villita* on the Texas-Mexican Railway lines in south central Duval County, and of course closer to the lower valley towns. Harriet "Hattie" Rogers stayed in Cotulla with her family. Company F assumed their duties in this wide-open, some would say godforsaken, country and diligently rode the trails out of their post for the remainder of the year.

A list of Company F personnel appeared in a June, 1892, news magazine article on several notable Ranger officers, a list that included Sergeant Rogers. Under his command: Pink Barnhill, George Bigford,

W. M. Bonwell, Will Evett, Walter Ellis, Tupper Harris, John Hess, Dan Johnson, R. C. Lewis, D. L. Musgrave, John and Joe Naties, Tom and Mike O'Donnell, George and Pool Piland, Ed Rowe, Kid Rogers, W. M. Spindle, Covet Thomas, and Neel Wilborn. Bigford was the oldest at 35; Ellis and Johnson were barely eighteen. "Sergeant Rogers says they are all good men," states the article, "who pride themselves on their conduct and appearance and strive to be looked upon as *men* rather than as toughs."[24]

Sergeant Rogers arrested a sheep thief in July, a cow thief in September, and a horse thief in October among his regular duties with the company. Kid Rogers and fellow Ranger George Bigford were involved in a deadly shootout in December resulting in the deaths of Juan and Gabriel Longoria, both wanted felons in the Valley. The October notation is the last for Rogers as a Texas Ranger sergeant, for on January 1, 1893, he was promoted to the rank of captain and given command of Company E, succeeding J. S. McNeel who had served so well for many years.

There was apparently some controversy surrounding McNeel's discharge, that it had not been voluntary and that a series of conversations with Adjutant General Mabry may have led to the dismissal. One report has it that Mabry did not appreciate McNeel's tendency to talk with nosy reporters about Ranger operations. On December 22 McNeel wrote to Mabry: "Your letter of the 16th inst informing me that my resignation to take effect Dec 31st^t 1892, would be accepted by you, has been received and contents duly noted. And in answer to same I beg to say that I do not wish to resign my position as Captain of Co E Frontier Battalion. If however you have any charges against me I insist upon an investigation. All I ask is justice."

Whatever the case, the men of Company E were upset enough with their captain's summary dismissal that they requested their own discharge *en masse*, the only known incident of its kind in Ranger lore. John Rogers made his first official report as captain on January 1 and broached that subject. "All the men went out with Capt McNeel. I am confident he persuaded them to do so by some unjust and selfish motive. I am surprised he having such influence on them for some who quit I had reason to believe disliked Capt McNeel in fact had been badly treated by him. I feel like it is all for the best, however, for I can soon get me a set of good men who have never been spoilt. Capt Brooks has quite a number of applicants for admission in his camp. He will have them report to me at once. How many men will I be allowed to enlist? Will I be allowed a corporal?"

In a postscript Rogers added, "Just had talk with one of Capt McNeel's men who went out on December 31. He [McNeel] told his men if they stayed I would discharge them and likely give them a dishonorable discharge. May enlist two or three of them who I know to be good men." [25]

Thus on January 1, 1893, Captain John H. Rogers of Company E had no company. Unfazed the new commander went right to work. He recruited his cousin Tupper Harris as sergeant of the company, and Kid Rogers joined up, too. J. W. Woods came on and was promoted to corporal in March. Mabry had apparently wanted to nominate a couple of his own favorites for officers in the reorganized company, but Rogers had acted quickly and later apologized for not "leaving [a] position vacant as you requested." Otto Roberts, Ralph Tucker, Dan Coleman, H. J. Wells, C. F. Huss, and W. M. Burnett signed on in January, as did W. V. Odin although he resigned in May. Tom Ross, J. H. Davis, and W. T. Hancock are also listed in Company E on the February roster.

The monthly records for January, 1893, indicate only one action, an arrest of one Pedro Sanchez for stealing horses in Starr County, a hunt that Rogers reported as being accomplished "by Companies E and F." This was in all likelihood the new commander's subtle way of explaining how a nonexistent company got their man that day.[26]

Company E would be assigned to a post in Alice, and Hattie would join her husband there with great relief to be by his side. Soon came the very special news that she was pregnant with their first child.

John Rogers now embarked on the next great phase of his career in law enforcement—eighteen exciting, event-filled years as captain of the Texas Rangers.

CHAPTER 6

The El Paso Prizefight

CAPTAIN ROGERS SURVEYED THE RANGER camp with a jaundiced eye at the pitiful supplies that lay in front of him. He made several notes that he would later record in his first monthly file as a Ranger commander. "Thirteen men," he wrote in the upper right hand corner of the oversized page, "twelve horses, four mules, and seven worthless tents." He wrote the same equipment notation every month for seven months until he at least had the small satisfaction of recording in August that "two of the tents were blown to pieces and gone." In October he noted that grass was scarce and that he had been forced to procure hay and grain from local Alice merchants. By November he had been amply re-supplied, the adjutant general's office finally acknowledging his appeal.[1]

Compared to the previous years, 1893 through 1895 were remarkably peaceful for Company E and its new captain. With Cotulla more or less "cleaned up," the work out of Alice seemed as routine as that could be understood in the life of frontier law enforcement. With his work now increasingly administrative in nature, Rogers seldom found himself in the field. In 1893 he only recorded three arrests made by him personally: a horse thief in the county in May, another in July, and yet a third in November. The last of the trio, Mariano Benavides, had been wanted out of Bexar County and Rogers returned him there on November 9.[2]

Tragically out of character for these Alice days, the mysterious disappearance of Private J. W. Woods caused great concern for the entire company. Cattle thieves in Menard County had created such a disturbance that the sheriff finally asked for help. Private Woods arrived there in June to work undercover. He went to work at a local ranch hoping to unveil the operations of the rustlers. Instead, he may have been found out himself, for in July he simply vanished. His body was never found and no arrests were ever made relative to his presumed murder.[3]

The men of Company E noted arrests in Kimble, Starr, and La Salle counties as well as several closer to home. Rogers' brother-in-law Will Burwell joined up on June 1, adding more of a family flavor to the company with Tupper Harris and Kid Rogers along as well.

Adding family was quite clearly the highlight of Rogers' days in Alice. Lucile was born in the Alice Ranger camp on August 31, 1893, and John and Hattie's second child and first son, Pleasant Blair, was born twenty-seven months later. Pleas was named after his two grandfathers. Captain Rogers became a dutiful father, leaving the child raising to Hattie but spending as much time as possible with the children as they grew up.[4]

The year 1894 picked up the pace a bit for Company E. Captain Rogers traveled south into Starr County on a number of occasions, making arrests in February, March, and April of men wanted for murder, including brothers Ben and Bill Bennett. In July Rogers recorded personal arrests in Bexar County and even up in Travis County. In the fall he was back in the Alice area.

Tom Goff joined up in December of 1893 as the company fluctuated in size between twelve and fifteen over the following months, and for the first time the annotation of "special rangers" appears in the official files. Men appointed out of the governor's office to supplement the Rangers force often brought more trouble than help, since some were appointees satisfying a political favor, while others seemed to be no more than hired guns who brought little character with them. The last arrest noted for the year 1894 is dated December 30, the captain noting that "C. L. [Kid] Rogers arrested a sheep thief and put him in the Alice calaboose."[5]

Family occasions made their way into John and Hattie's life as well. On May 1, 1894, the families joined to celebrate Kid's marriage to Bettie DeHand Chessher of Guadalupe County. Curren and Bettie celebrated the birth of three children over the next seven years: Margie Lee in 1895; Curren Randolph, a second daughter, in 1896; and Emrett Benton born in 1901. John and Hattie returned to the old home grounds in late March, 1895, to attend the funeral of John's great uncle John Harris, one of the original family members to come to Texas whose life had spanned eighty-six years.

In 1895 a rash of gambling men arrived in the booming little town of Alice and kept the Rangers busy, the situation provoked by the state legislature's cutback of monies that forced the adjutant general to reduce the companies to only eight men each. Everyone needed to step up the pace. Rogers arrested five men as part of a gambling ring on May 4, 1895, and Frank Reynolds was hauled in for disturbing the peace that same night. Another gambler, Cristobal Riojas, was tossed in the Alice jail in October. Sergeant Tupper Harris and his cousin Kid Rogers kept especially busy on the trail of outlaws as attested by the monthly records, but overall the year was quiet.[6]

In October, 1895, Company E consisted of its sergeant Tupper Harris and privates Kid Rogers, Will Burwell, C. F. Hiers, Tom M. Ross, Tom Goff, and J. W. Moore.

Hundreds of miles off to the west in El Paso, events were unfolding whose ripple effect would soon wash across Nueces County and call on every skill and strength that Company E possessed—and for that matter nearly every Ranger in the force. The trouble wasn't the fence cutters, nor cattle thieves or border bandits. It was a prize-fight.

"Nothing short of lightning or the destruction of the earth by fire or flood can stop the contests we have arranged to pull off," declared one Dan Stuart, sports promoter. "El Paso is the biggest little town in all this country and can handle anything from a cowman to a prize-fight," seconded the city's editor in the *Daily Herald*. "I intend to stop this fight if it takes the entire police force of the State to stop it," responded Governor Charles Culberson.[7] The challenge was on, inside the ring and out.

Boxing matches had caused various levels of consternation across the sports world and the politically and religiously righteous for a decade or more. The violence of the pugilistic contests enervated some, disgusted others. Sports promoters saw money to be made, while church leaders remained horrified at this example set for the nation's youth. The New York superintendent of police expressed the legal stance for most in 1891: "These knocking-out contests shall not be revived. There will be no prize fighting in this city. If these men get together and violate the law, it is my duty to arrest them and I will do so." With this caveat he concluded, "I cannot and do not desire to prohibit sparring exhibitions, but the law does not permit prizefighting." The gambling that accompanied the violent confrontations was too much for the morally upright, for even the *New York World* acknowledged "the prize fighter for what are regarded as manly if not heroic qualities."[8]

The principal fighters of that day were Gentleman Jim Corbett, John L. Sullivan, Robert Fitzsimmons, and Peter Maher. Sullivan had been the preeminent bare knuckles fighter of the 1880s but had retired from the ring to pursue an acting career. Still he lingered at the edge of the profession. In 1892 he gave way to Corbett who beat him in one of the all-time classic ring encounters. Two years later the red-haired, freckle faced Englishman Robert Fitzsimmons challenged Corbett for the world championship and was declared champ by the Olympic Club when Corbett snubbed him.

That's when Dan Stuart got involved. A professional gambler and sports promoter whose Dallas headquarters was the Coney Island Jockey Saloon and Restaurant downtown on Main Street, the Vermont native now prepared to bring the two great champions to Texas to fight in a spectacular fifty-two thousand seat coliseum he was designing. For all of Stuart's bravado and vision, however, the Dallas Pastors' Association would have none of it and by the summer of 1895 they had managed to block all of his attempts to construct the coliseum and bring the fight to Texas.[9]

The state also became involved in the controversial sport. As late as 1889 the law allowed for prizefighting in Texas as long as the organizers put up a five-hundred-dollar "occupation tax," but under re-form Governor James S. Hogg that law had been replaced by another. In part the 1891 statute declared that any person "voluntarily engag-ing in a pugilistic encounter between man and man, or fight between man and bull or between man and other animal, for money or any-thing of value, or money bet or waged, or to see which any admission fee is charged, shall be guilty of a felony and upon conviction shall be punished by a fine of not less than $1,000 [twice the 1889 statute fine], and by punishment in the county jail not less than sixty days nor more than one year [none in the previous law]."

"Prizefighting is manifestly unlawful," explained the state comp-troller in 1891, "and carries a maximum sentence for violations of a $1,000 fine and a year in the pokey." An Austin ministers' coalition chimed in. "Prizefighting is an enormous and useless waste of time, attracts a vast throng of disorderly and dissolute persons to these sav-age scenes, applies a seductive but poisonous temptation to the natu-ral feelings of inexperienced youth, and is brutal, cruel and danger-ous to the participants."[10]

But Dan Stuart was nothing if not determined, and he took the law into court, winning in front of a sympathetic judge who consid-ered the upcoming fisticuffs display to be legal after all. The Austin paper headlined, "Dan Stuart Triumphant." The *Dallas Morning News* published a poem that declared, in part, "'Great Scott!' shrieked the guv bird, 'what'll I do? My main vote play's gone up the flue; Now how, Mr. Crane, can I keep up with you? I'll call out the Rangers and the whole to do.'"[11]

The *Texas Christian Advocate* weighed in with a call for a special legislative session to end the controversy, and newly elected Gover-nor Culberson responded. On October 3 Culberson signed a bill making prizefighting in Texas a felony, the legislators spending only three hours in the one-sided debate. Stuart immediately revised his plans, junked the coliseum construction in Dallas, and went to In-dian Territory to arrange the fight. Stopped there, the perseverant promoter traveled next to Arkansas. The Rangers were already on the job—Rogers sent Private Tom M. Ross undercover to trail Stuart and Fitzsimmons in Hot Springs.

At this point the whole issue took a body blow when a frustrated and perhaps slightly nervous Jim Corbett backed out of the fight. Nonplussed, Stuart turned to Peter Maher, a heavy drinking Irish fighter who was already in the Southwest and who had lost a controversial slugfest to Fitzsimmons in 1892. A re-match would be the next best thing to what he had originally planned. By the end of November, 1895, the only question still to be addressed, at least as far as Stuart and his supporters were concerned, was where the fight would take place.[12]

A group of eager El Paso businessmen provided one possibility for Stuart: Juarez, Mexico. Even back in August railroad man B. F. Darbyshire and El Paso's ex-mayor Doc Albers had started a conversation about the economic benefits of bringing a world championship prizefight to west Texas. Action by the governor and legislature only called for creativity, not resignation. Saloonkeeper J. J. Taylor headed for Dallas to speak to Stuart; businessmen in Mexico were brought into the discussions.[13]

But so were Mexican President Porfirio Diaz and his government, pressed by the Texas governor and others to keep the fight out of the borderlands. Declared a Mexico City newspaper: "Mr. Stuart and his short-haired friends must not suppose for a moment that the fight may take place in any Mexican state." Merchants in El Paso waivered between the law and the potential economic boost. "We don't care for the scientific display of the manly art itself," wrote one, "but we want the samolians that the boys will bring with them."[14]

With many significant details still to be worked out, the fight moved toward El Paso. Fitzsimmons and his entourage arrived in the city on Christmas morning and, as an act of good will and self-promotion, the fighter played right tackle on an El Paso football team in a New Years Day game. Dan Stuart detrained on January 9, 1896, and Pete Maher showed up two days later before heading to Las Cruces, New Mexico to set up his training camp there. George Siler, sports editor of a Chicago newspaper, was selected as the referee, February 14 was set as the date for the fight, and famed frontier gunfighter Bat Masterson headed for El Paso as a promoter of the fight and chief of security for Stuart's operations. Some said he was bringing 150 men to make sure the fight went off without a hitch; others said Masterson could handle it alone. By January 25 every hotel room in El Paso was occupied.

Still, a "legal" location for the fight, not to mention the increasing resistance by the religious community, kept the prizefight far from being a certainty. The El Paso Ministers' Union, led by Methodist ministers C. J. Oxley and Adolf Hoffman, published "An Appeal to the Citizens of El Paso" explaining the detrimental effect of the fight bringing "many who by gambling will intend to take away money" and that "likely will come prostitutes. Shall the keepers of saloons, gambling dens and houses of prostitution dictate our city's business policy," the manifesto asked pointedly. Church women's groups circulated a second to that: "We hereby protest against having the fair name of our city and our character so besmirched. We wish it understood that we consider the carnival a disgrace to the city and an insult to every true woman of El Paso and womanhood everywhere."[15]

Pressure from the "morally outraged" segments of the community had an interesting effect. On February 5 New Mexico's United States Congressman Thomas Benton Catron introduced an "anti-fight bill" to Congress that was duly signed into law by President Grover Cleveland just two days later. When Mexican President Diaz concurred by stating, "I have a force of cavalry out scouting the frontier and I have ordered them to arrest anyone entering Mexico to take part in the prizefight," it appeared that Dan Stuart had finally lost the fight, figuratively and literally.[16]

But Stuart was undeterred, despite such resignation as the *Chicago Tribune's* comment that "with Congress arrayed against the fight on the one hand and Mexican troops with loaded guns ready to interrupt, it has dwindled down [for Stuart] to a case of pure luck." Friends and associates said the promoter slept well at night and was all smiles through each February day: Stuart had an ace up his sleeve, but no one could figure out what it might be. "The fights will take place," Stuart assured some merchants, "and those who contemplate a journey here to witness them can come on without the most remote misgivings or fear."[17]

Governor Culberson intended to keep the prizefight from ever coming off in his state. On January 31 he sent word to Adjutant General Mabry that the Texas Rangers would be needed. Mabry wired Captain

John Hughes in Ysleta to proceed into El Paso and work out a plan in cooperation with the city's law enforcement officers. Hughes replied that the men of Company D would be easily recognized by the promoters and merchants and that any undercover surveillance would thus be impossible. On February 3 Captain Rogers received a telegram from Mabry. "By order of Genl. Mabry," Rogers wrote into the official reports, "I sent [today] Sergt. [Tupper] Harris and Prvt. [Tom] Ross to El Paso for the purpose of ascertaining if possible the location of the proposed Prize fight, they to remain unknown to any one except Capt. Hughes to whom they were instructed to report." Captains Bill McDonald and John Brooks were also alerted to the situation, sent men undercover, and made preparations to head for El Paso themselves. Mabry then boarded a train out of Austin to reach the west Texas town and take over the Ranger operation in person.

John Rogers wrote on February 7, one week before the fight was scheduled to take place: "By order of Genl. Mabry I enlisted three men and left with my entire command for El Paso arriving there on February 9. While in El Paso we kept up such guard and watch each day and night as was deemed necessary to prevent the fight being pulled off on Texas soil."[18] Fourteen Rangers stepped from the Texas & Pacific train on February 9 onto the platform of the El Paso depot. They ate breakfast at the Pierson Hotel as word quickly spread of their presence. Harris and Ross had arrived earlier and were already working undercover.

The *El Paso Herald* reported the arrival of these "resolute looking strangers. The tightening of the lines around prize fighting are being drawn so close that the death rattle can be heard," the paper opined. "The calling out of Rangers and United States marshals sounds no uncertain tones the death knell to the prize ring in the United States." On February 12 the paper carried a poem entitled "The Carnival" which included this verse:

> The government vows it shall not be in Texas or in New Mexico,
> And Diaz vows within his bounds the boxers dare not go.
> But preachers may preach and rave and Rangers may scour the plains,

The hero of the carnival treats threats with cold disdain,
Dan Stuart says, "it shall be!"[19]

Dan Stuart had another problem by this time, however, which did
worry him. Peter Maher had come down with a terrible eye problem,
either from the gritty Texas dust or perhaps from stress for the coming battle. One El Paso merchant suggested that the local ministers
had "prayed the blindness of Peter" on the pugilist. Either way, he
was in no shape to take on Fitzsimmons and Stuart reluctantly postponed—but did not even dream of canceling—the fight for a week.
On February 10 Rogers reported to Mabry: "We are masters of the
situation—no fight will occur in Texas or any neutral ground between
Texas and any other country."

In the meanwhile Stuart and his cohorts tried to keep one step
ahead of the ever-vigilant Rangers and other authorities who dogged
the principals' every step. On the night of February 11 a train slipped
out of the depot carrying what some rumored was equipment and
supplies for the fight. Captain Hughes caught up with the train at
two-thirty the next morning and put four men on board—the search
turned up nothing. Stuart played on the tension by sending "work
crews" both east and west out of town with building supplies over the
next few days with no other purpose than to string out law enforcement—it worked. The feints and false alarms were maddening, but
Ranger confidence was high. Rogers reported to Mabry that same
day, "The papers claim that Stuart is serene—but I know he is badly
scared—his only hope is Old Mexico."

Mabry's patience finally ran out. He told Fitzsimmons and his
handlers "to keep out of the power of the U. S. Government." If they
insisted on going on with this fight, Mabry warned, "he would shoot
to kill first and do the arresting afterwards." He then accosted Stuart
with this: "I'm going to board that train of yours with my men at all
hazards," he promised. Undaunted, Stuart replied, "All right," and
then offered to pay for the Rangers' train tickets.[20]

Rogers and Company E patrolled the streets of El Paso along with
other authorities, maintaining a very tenuous peace as gamblers and
brigands from all over the Southwest poured into the town. Legisla-

tor Albert Fall arrived from New Mexico with deputy marshals and staff to watch over the proceedings. On the evening of February 18 the captain received word that a gang of robbers had just emptied the pockets of several folks at a nearby saloon. Rogers, Private C. F. Hiers, and a deputy sheriff tracked the villains down later that night, arresting Joseph Adams, Thomas Halligan, Frank Waldo and Charles Tallan for robbery and placing them in the El Paso jail.[21]

By Wednesday it appeared that the fight had been rescheduled for Friday, but its whereabouts remained a mystery to all but a chosen few at Stuart's side. Peter Maher's eyes were clearing up, ruse or otherwise. Fitzsimmons was still being escorted, literally, with two Rangers at his side nearly twenty-fours a day. In fact several Rangers, including Captain Rogers, accompanied Fitz over to his camp in Juarez and watched a lazy afternoon sparring exhibition. They noticed the Mexican troops in the vicinity as well, nearly one-hundred-and-fifty cavalry and assorted other personnel.

On Thursday, "Fight Day Minus One," the Rangers kept vigilant eye on all of the principals except for a brief time when they agreed to have their photograph taken on the courthouse steps. It is still one of the most remarkable snapshots of the Texas Rangers force taken in the nineteenth century, with Mabry and all four Ranger captains lined up along the front row and thirty others behind. Captain Rogers appears on the right end of the front row wearing a light brown suit in contrast to the black attire of the others. Kid Rogers stands on the back row in the center alongside the men of his brother's company.

Peter Maher arrived by train from Las Cruces at noon, took a carriage to the Astor House, bathed, and ate a large late breakfast. A Texas Ranger shadowed his every move. Another train had departed in the pre-dawn hours with freight cars loaded with lumber. And Rangers. It headed southeast and the rumor that quickly made the betting pools was that the fight would be at Fort Hancock forty-five miles away. But Mabry received a telegram from his scouts that finally gave up the real destination: Langtry, Texas, nearly four hundred miles down the Rio Grande. The telegram may never have gotten off if the Rangers had not occupied the telegraph office after Stuart's thugs threatened to shut it down to keep the location secret.

Texas Rangers in El Paso to stop the 1896 prizefight. Rogers is in the front row right.
Courtesy Charlie, Lauren, and Carley Reeves, San Antonio

Langtry meant Judge Roy Bean, and that was ever cause for con-sternation by law enforcement agents along the Valley. A self-ap-pointed prosecutor and sometime executioner to boot, Bean carried on in his tiny west Texas hamlet as king over kingdom. "The Law West of The Pecos," read the hand painted sign across the top of Bean's Jersey Lilly Saloon and "courtroom." And in that town, he was the law. It is no stretch of the imagination to believe that Judge Roy Bean had contacted Dan Stuart somewhere along the way and offered his humble fiefdom as host to the prizefight; the attention and whiskey sales alone would be reason enough for Bean. Langtry gave "in the middle of nowhere" whole new meaning, and a nearby stretch of sand-bar down the middle of the Rio Grande, with high bluffs for specta-tors on the Texas side, would be perfect accommodations. The spit of dry land was technically neither U.S. or Mexico, but for Bean it was, well, his.[22]

The real train bound for the fight site left out of El Paso at 9:45 P.M. Thursday night. A reporter from the *New York World* described the chaos: "Men were flying around packing up hampers of provisions and getting bottled goods ready and making general preparations for a long ride." Dan Stuart announced the train ticket price to be twelve dollars, and apologized that he could not let the Rangers ride free. That was all right, explained Adjutant General Mabry to the conductor, a letter from Governor Culberson would suffice. Thirty Rangers boarded the train, pistols and Winchester rifles as their provisions. Captain Rogers and more than half of his company were on board, with several left behind in El Paso to maintain order there.

The train, two engines and ten passenger cars long, headed southeast through the dark of night. As dawn came, the two fighters—situated in separate cars, would leap out at the regular water stops and sprint up and down the tracks to keep limber. At Marathon Fitzsimmons spotted a big black bear chained to the corner of a house not far from the tracks. With his reputation for "rasslin" on the line, this was too tempting. He leapt off the train, dashed at the bear, which began to backtrack away from his attacker, and managed a few moments of entertaining bear hugging to the delight of the folks on the train and the dismay of Dan Stuart.

At Sanderson the train stopped long enough presumably for the passengers to disembark and seek meals, there being no dining car on Stuart's fight train. But the trip was running late to meet its designated arrival in time for a boxing match before dark, and the conductor announced that only ten minutes would be allowed. All hell broke loose as passengers scurried to the few restaurants and impatiently ordered food. In the next few moments one of the great and legendary incidents of the entire escapade was said to have taken place.

As the legend would be told and retold for years thereafter, Bat Masterson had made the trip as Stuart's head of security and sat now in a too-busy restaurant with a too-slow Chinese waiter at his table. The place was packed with gamblers, promoters, El Paso merchants, and Texas Rangers, among them Captains Bill McDonald and John Rogers. Masterson, frustrated with the slow response of the waiter to his demands, picked up a castor from the table leg where he sat and struck the waiter on the top of his head as he passed by. Several folks at the table chuckled. The two Ranger officers did not.

McDonald stood up from his chair nearby and reached for Masterson's still-raised arm, gripping it just above the gunfighter's wrist. The packed room fell instantly silent. McDonald spoke in a steady voice, "Don't hit that man." The two locked eyes.

"Maybe you'd like to take it up," Masterson replied, considering a walk outside to settle this matter.

"I done took it up," McDonald said in a calm but sure voice, his hand still gripping Masterson's arm. No one breathed, no one moved. Ten seconds passed as if they were ten hours.

Then Masterson smiled and sat back. McDonald released his grip and sat back down. A collective sigh of relief could probably be heard all the way out into the streets. A face off between these two would have made headlines from San Francisco to New York.

The Rogers family has always related this story differently. According to them it was Rogers who responded to Masterson as McDonald gripped the gunfighter's arm, "He done took it up." Masterson himself wrote a response to the tale years later in a New York newspaper: "We never saw a Chinaman from the time we left El Paso until we got back. We never at any time had an argument with Capt. Bill McDonald. The whole Paine [Albert Bigelow Paine wrote McDonald's biography and told this tale] story is a brazen, cowardly lie and we'll not forgive this mean, cowardly slanderer for that." Either way it is a most dramatic moment and a great story, even if it is fiction.[23]

Rain showered down on the passengers as they ran back to the train. At three-thirty on the afternoon of February 21 the train pulled into Langtry. Two hundred folks from Eagle Pass and beyond had already arrived by another train. Judge Roy Bean stood at the depot greeting the dignitaries and then conferring with Stuart. Everything seemed in order and soon the crowd was making its way toward the river. A young Canadian teenager named Jimmy White had already scoped out the site and now led the large crowd along a rocky path to the banks of the Rio Grande. A wooden bridge on pontoons had been constructed with lumber brought a few days earlier, and it led out to the sandbar where a ring had also been put up. Surrounding the ring was a large canvas wall in a more or less circular stand, dedicated to keeping the nonpaying customer away.

However, the high bluffs on the Texas side of the river afforded a spectacular view of the ring far above the constrictions of the canvas, and there many observers set up, including most of the Rangers who had come along. Rogers and his men made themselves as comfortable as they could on the rocky precipice, having decided that no Texas laws were being broken with the fight taking place out on the sandbar. But about 100 men gathered up against the ring to watch, including a filming crew sent by Thomas Edison's company with the latest Kinetoscope equipment. Unfortunately, a deep cloud cover made it too dark for the filmmakers to utilize their machine.

Referee George Siler introduced the principals, briefly went over the rules of the fight, such as they were, and the fight began with a whistle and a ringside helper shouting, "Time!" Maher never got into it. Ninety seconds into the first and only round he was struck by a blow that sent him into an extended daze. He hit the canvas and barely heard Siler count him out. The championship fight, months in the making and controversial in at least three states and two countries, was over in less than two minutes.[24]

The *Dallas Morning News* duly reported that Dan Stuart had somehow won the day despite the brevity of the fight itself, noting that "it was amusing to see the flower of the frontier guard [the Rangers] sitting on the crags above with their rifles lazily on their laps while that great and unpardonable crime, the big glove contest, was taking place a few hundred yards away." On the other hand, Mabry received a letter of commendation from the governor's office thanking him "on behalf of the law-abiding citizens of Texas for the active and successful effort of yourself and command in enforcing our laws and protecting the honor of Texas in preventing the prize fight from taking place on Texas soil."[25]

For his part Mabry wrote glowingly of the Rangers' contribution to the entire escapade in his bi-annual report to the governor: "I desire to express my approbation for the intelligent and efficient manner in which Captains Brooks, McDonald, Hughes, and Rogers executed every order and performed every duty. The rangers conducted themselves in such manner as to reflect additional credit upon the name of a ranger—always a synonym for courage and duty well performed, quiet and orderly in manner, determined in mien, fearless and vigilant, to the displeasure of the law-breakers everywhere."[26]

The Rangers made their way back to the train and eventually back to their camps across the state. The logjam of passengers out in Judge Roy Bean's country wasn't cleared out for a day. So anticlimactic was the fight that Captain Rogers' terse recording of the event seems almost an afterthought: "With my command in company with Genl. Mabry and other Rangers I left El Paso on same train [with] the Pugilists. We came on together to Langtry. The contest being pulled off in Mexico opposite Langtry. I proceeded on to San Antonio arriving there on the 22nd."

Of greater concern to Rogers than the prize fight, his in-law and fellow Ranger Will Burwell had taken ill in El Paso and the rain and the long train rides had made his condition worse. A cold had turned into pneumonia and Rogers took Burwell to a hospital in San Antonio immediately upon their arrival. After a day or so the captain rode on to Alice, but returned a few days later to sit beside his friend and relative. The doctors told Rogers later that Burwell had nearly died; Rogers' vigil and prayers had sustained the Ranger private in the two weeks before his recovery. Some strong medicine may have helped, too. In his March report Rogers apologized for the company bills being "high but altogether unavoidable. The whiskey bill seems especially large but he [Burwell] was kept alive almost altogether on it— we gave it according to the doctors directions."[27]

The rest of 1896 was anticlimactic as well for Company E. New recruits C. B. "Charlie" DuBose and A. Y. "Augie" Old joined up in the spring, and Will Burwell returned to work in the spring only to be discharged along with DuBose in August. Murders, mule and horse thefts, and assaults dot the monthly reports. Captain Rogers worked in Duval and Encinal counties, and he and Tupper Harris cooperated in the arrests of Tom and Bill Edwards charged with a Nueces County murder in November. The captain tracked down one of six members of a cattle-rustling gang and brought him in at the end of the year. 1897 was likewise routine and calm, with an Encinal fence-cutter being one of the few highlights.[28]

In the official bi-annual report of the adjutant general for 1895 and 1896, W. H. Mabry notes Rogers and Company E had made eleven arrests for murder, nine for assault, and forty-nine for cattle and horse theft as part of a total of 124 arrests. The Frontier Battalion as a whole had made 671 arrests. Company E had made 111 scouts during those two years and recovered seventy-eight stolen livestock (as compared to Hughes' Company D and over 2,500 head returned). Rogers and his men recorded 36,210 miles of official travel.

Captain Rogers and Company E had had plenty of excitement in El Paso: A relatively calm two years had been earned and was heartily welcomed. The peaceful months afforded Rogers an opportunity to spend more time with Hattie and the two children, and to spend more time in the Presbyterian church pew with his wife nearly every Sunday. When the captain found himself on the trail on the Sabbath, he continued his long-standing habit of attending the closest church he could locate, often attending morning and evening worship there and voluntarily teaching a Bible class as well before moving on. His testimony, sometimes just by his presence in the congregation awed by the sight of a Texas Ranger in earnest prayer—and occasionally joined by fellow Christian Augie Old, produced an untold harvest of disciples, for it was a habit that Rogers maintained the rest of his life.

But the Texas frontier never remained calm for long, and the extended time of administrative duties and only the occasional criminal's trail to follow certainly could not last. Another confrontation awaited John Rogers, one that would nearly take his life, one that would test his faith and his strength to live.

CHAPTER 7

The Streets of Laredo

AS CAPTAIN ROGERS STARED DOWN at the infant boy, he marveled at the wonder of new birth and beamed as a proud father. It was January 5, the beginning of the new year 1898, a wonderful beginning at that. His and Hattie's second son was healthy, even though born on this cold wintry day in the Rangers camp home outside of Alice. Four-year-old Lucile and two-and-a-half year old Pleas would enjoy their little brother. His name? Only weeks before the Presbyterian Church had taken up another special offering for Reverend Samuel N. Lapsley, a man of faith who had been called as the first Presbyterian missionary to Africa. The Rogers' had made a significant contribution to his expenses. It was Providential, the captain decided. They would name their new son Lapsley. His middle name, Harris, extended the Rogers kin one more generation.

Yes, all in all a great start to the new year, a sign perhaps that it would be another relatively calm one as 1897 had been. That, however, was not to be.

On February 16, Captain Rogers read the shocking bold headlines in the newspaper—"Battleship *Maine* Explodes!" The day before, far away in Havana harbor, the article declared, Spanish terrorists had planted a bomb against the hull of the American battleship anchored in the Cuban port. During the night the bomb had detonated, sending the ship and over two hundred of its crew to the bottom of the sea. After several years of following the Cuban rebellion, the United States would soon be involved in a war that traversed two oceans and reached as far as the Philippines. President McKinley's call for war in April led to a short but furious confrontation with the Spanish on that Caribbean island, at Santiago Bay, and on Kettle and San Juan Hills. Occupying American troops marched onto the island of Puerto Rico. After seizing the Spanish-held islands of Midway, Guam, and Samoa in the Pacific, the U. S. Navy sailed victoriously into Manila Bay. The war was over almost as it began, but not without it reaching into Texas. Adjutant General Woodford Mabry resigned in order to fight in the war; he would succumb to malaria in Havana. He was replaced for nine months by A. P. Wozencraft who then gave way to Thomas Scurry. For the Rangers, concern for activities on the Mexican border led to an increased vigilance; namely, U. S. troops stationed in Texas were being considered for redeployment to Cuba, thus diminishing the law enforcement capacity in the Valley. On May 12, Rogers received a copy of a telegram sent earlier by Governor Culberson to Texas Senator Horace Chilton in Washington: "Authorities at Fort Ringgold, Brownsville, Rio Grande City and others wire that it is dangerous to withdraw regulars from those places as is being done. Secretary of War does not reply to my protest. Indications are that the object is to give regulars chance in the war and put our troops on the frontier and is objectionable." In a postscript Culberson wrote to Rogers: "Wire number of men you have and where they are." The legislature made provisions for the Ranger force to be increased with each company enlisting a total of twelve men by the end of May.[1]

Five days later Culberson wrote Rogers to update him on the troop redeployment situation. "President Diaz has written Culberson on May 13 that his detachments 'on right side of the Bravo' are to assist American authorities if there is any trouble 'injured by robbers' on left side, and would Culberson do the same.

"If you [Rogers] give your detachment similar orders, I believe it will be impossible that any Alarm should be felt on the dividing line, especially if the respective chiefs on both lines should put themselves into accord when they have to make any prosecution. Believing the course suggested will assist in the purpose to maintain order, you are directed to act in accordance herewith."[2]

With heightened awareness of the war footing, Company E remained on alert. From April to June the companies were increased to twelve men each. Otherwise law enforcement seemed fairly routine and on June 15 each unit was again reduced to eight Rangers. Kid Rogers re-enlisted on April 23 following his latest leave. Several men from the company were sent east to Wharton County to track a gang of cattle rustlers, some of the first truly "detective" work accomplished by the Texas Rangers. In Cotulla in May W. J. Bowen was assassinated and the case turned over to Company E. Back in Alice on June 10 the captain arrested brothers Henry and Paul Perkins for "being intoxicated in a public place," and put them in jail for the night.[3]

Then things got frantic. Heavy rains came to south Texas in mid June, flooding Alice and destroying many of the homes and businesses of the town whose population had just reached the 1,000 mark. The Ranger camp also felt the brunt of the flood with much equipment ruined and supplies floating away.

In July, as a result of a combination of the war's alarms, trouble on the border between Laredo and Del Rio, and probably the flood damage as well, Company E was ordered to move back to Cotulla. After five-and-a-half years in Alice it was not easy to pick up stakes and head west once more; for Rogers it was doubly hard with a wife and three small children to make the adjustment with him. For Tupper Harris and Kid Rogers it was simply too much to ask to go back to Cotulla: they resigned from the force in early September. The captain's little brother joined the federal government forces as a treasury agent for a year, although he did return to the Rangers briefly in 1899.[4]

In Cotulla one of those who objected to the return of the Texas Rangers was a saloonkeeper named George Reed who apparently thought himself sufficient law enforcement on his end of the street. Captain Rogers had not been in town a week when word came that Reed was causing trouble. Rogers went to investigate. Reed had gotten drunk, scaring all of the patrons out of his saloon as he swung a loaded shotgun around, and had then marched out into the street shooting the gun off and hollering that the Rangers weren't needed in his town and they could all go to hell. He then stumbled back into his saloon and shut the front doors.

Rogers stood at the corner of the building for a moment. Years later he told the story in his own words. "I tried the side door but he had locked it, so I went back around to the front. I looked in the door and saw him with his gun to his shoulder. He had it leveled on me and both barrels cocked. My first thought was that maybe I best not try to go in the front way. I naturally figured that he might shoot and that I had better try to get in the back way.

"But then I realized that such a step would be showing weakness and that it might cause trouble," the captain explained. "There was but one thing to do and that was go in and get him right then and there. He had been getting by with his gun play too much and it would not do to let him think he had anybody bluffed.

"Praying, I walked in the front door. I knew if I hesitated a second he would shoot. Something just told me to keep walking right to him, so I did." The Ranger walked right up to Reed until the muzzle of the

Captain Rogers and Company E in Cotulla, 1898. Courtesy Curren Rogers McClane, Ft. Worth

loaded shotgun pointed inches from his head. As he took each resolute step he talked in a calm but firm voice to the drunken barkeep.
"You know better than to shoot," Rogers said. "You've been getting by
with this stuff too long. You'll have to cut it out."

The saloonkeeper froze in his deadly stance as the Ranger stopped
right in front of him. In one smooth motion Rogers lifted the gun
barrel toward the ceiling with one hand while catching Reed's collar
with his other.

"Come out of here," said Rogers, never raising his voice. "Come
with me." Reed let go of the gun and accompanied the officer outside and to jail. When he got home that afternoon and told the story
to Hattie, the captain concluded, "I wonder why I did that." In his
monthly report, Rogers' only notation lists the name George Reed
after the date, July 8. In the next two columns are the words "assault"
and "Cotulla."[5]

Two weeks after the incident in the Cotulla saloon Captain Rogers
took his wife and three children and rode the train to Kingsbury to
visit with family and, naturally, show off the children. While there he
was called to business. A horse thief named Will Hewitt was wanted in
Karnes County and had been spotted a few miles out of Luling. Rogers
picked up Hewitt's trail, caught up with him, and escorted him to the
Karnes City jail. Rogers returned to retrieve his family and they headed
back to Cotulla.[6]

Augie Old's brother W. A. joined Company E on September 19
just as Kid Rogers and Tupper Harris left. With a reduction in force
that fall, Company E ended 1898 with eight men. Rogers commanded
just-promoted Sergeant Harry DuBose and Privates Augie and W. A.
Old, Frank D. McMahon, Jim Moore (a relative of the Ranger of the
same name who had died in the Conner Fight), Eugene Bell and
John McMurry. The company traveled thousands of miles in the last
quarter of the year, from San Angelo to Encinal, and from Medina
County to Caldwell County. The captain himself arrested Frank Burris
in Cotulla on October 15 on murder charges and returned him to
the Dimmit County sheriff.[7]

Word of a possible prizefight in Galveston reached Cotulla in the
form of a straightforward telegram from Governor Culberson to

Rogers dated November 26: "I will need you and two or three men tomorrow morning. Be ready." No doubt the company remembered the recent incident and prepared for another long bout with sports promoters and gamblers. The fight never came off. Rogers does not record if they were actually called into action.[8]

The captain managed to be with his brother for a family Christmas celebration and with pleasure handed him his gift, a pocket New Testament. On the flyleaf it read: "From J. H. Rogers to C. L. Rogers, Dec. 25th, 1898. May God help you to read and obey the teaching of this holy book." For the next three-and-a-half years Kid Rogers kept the small Bible with him at all times, wearing its cover frayed and thin from the days and nights on the trail poring through it.[9]

The adjutant general's bi-annual report to the governor of Texas for 1897-1898 lists a remarkable 411 scouts recorded by Rogers' company E, more than any other company and covering 29,067 miles. And 212 arrests had been made, including fourteen murderers captured and fifty-nine thieves.

Company E began 1899 expecting another fairly routine year; at least there was no longer a war going on that involved the United States. Captain Rogers found himself in San Antonio on January 20 to stop a prizefight that had been promoted there; the fight never took place. On the night of February 18, Tom Warren (a.k.a. Tom Burke) escaped from the Cotulla jail by digging a tunnel under the outside wall and making his way into the night. Rogers and another Ranger were awakened and went after him. They found Warren walking along the road about two-thirty the next morning some twelve miles south of town. The criminal wanted in three counties was back in the repaired jail cell by dawn.

Captain Rogers arrested Cotulla resident Bob Lewis on February 27 for public drunkenness, but not without a struggle that landed the citizen in jail for an additional charge of resisting arrest. This was one of many opportunities for the earnest Ranger to do a little preaching at and praying over a captive audience, a ritual that had by now become a steady practice whether in town or out on the trail. Many a crook—and not a few Rangers and deputies—listened with rapt attention to the calm, soothing testimony of John Rogers. And although no count was ever kept, certainly more than a few changed their lives around after that experience.

The next day after his tussle with Lewis, Rogers records his activities: "I left Cotulla for Ballinger in Runnels County for the purpose of interviewing a prisoner in jail who claims to know who assassinated W. J. Bowen in Cotulla in May 1898. I failed to get from him the name of the assassin or any testimony that we could use at this time. Yet he claims if liberated he could furnish sufficient evidence for a conviction, but I seriously doubt the truthfulness of his statement.

"I returned to San Antonio March 5, met Sheriff (and brother-in-law Will) Burwell and together we taken [*sic*] A. J. Poteet from the Bexar Co. jail where he had been kept for safe keeping. We carried him back to Cotulla."

On March 10 Rogers made a day trip to Pearsall. On March 13 he was in Encinal and two days later traveled to Carrizo Springs with Burwell to search for more evidence on the Bowen murder case. They found nothing substantial and headed back to Cotulla. Winter in south Texas was making its subtle changeover to spring and everything continued to be typical and routine. March 18 may have dawned just as normally as any of the previous days, but the next three days would be far different, far more dramatic, and, for Rogers, deadly to the point of being nearly fatal.[10]

La Viruela. Just those words alone raised the hackles of citizens across south Texas and along both banks of the Rio Bravo. Smallpox, The Plague as many called it, came all too frequently to the small villages and even large towns in nineteenth century Texas. In Laredo the disease brought tragic memories to families each time it snaked through the streets and into innocent homes. In early October, 1898, local physicians began treating what they first thought was an outbreak of chicken pox. But when a Mexican child died on October 29, their fears were realized; smallpox had struck. By the end of January more than 100 cases had been treated and the disease spread, devastating whole neighborhoods in Alice beginning that February.

Laredo's mayor Louis T. Christen ordered an investigative committee to begin dealing with containing the spread of the disease. In the meanwhile Christen wired the state health office in Austin and

Rogers and Company E just before the Laredo Quarantine, 1899. Courtesy Charlie, Lauren, and Carley Reeves, San Antonio

asked its director W. T. Blunt to come to Laredo to supervise a quarantine and arrange vaccinations for the residents. Blunt arrived on March 16 but the situation was beginning to careen out of control as panicked citizens hid in their homes or worse, headed out of town for refuge—many of course carrying the smallpox with them. Laredo claimed a population in 1899 of nearly 13,000 people, a dramatic rise from the sleepy little border town of 3,500 just a few years before. An influx of onion farmers, coal miners, and railroad workers had taken the town by storm. The population was overwhelmingly of Mexican descent, especially through the eastern neighborhoods, and the poor sections along Zacate Creek had been hit hardest by the epidemic.

Dr. W. T. Blunt went into consultation with Mayor Christen, City Marshal Joe Bartlow, and Sheriff L. R. Ortiz. The situation seemed dangerous, according to Ortiz, whose inspection through the eastern part of the city showed the citizens to be uneasy about reports that a quarantine might be put into effect. There had never been an immunization program there and it brought additional fears to the community. Instead, Blunt indicated his intention to carry out a massive fumigation program across Laredo. First he wanted any patients already sick to be transported to the one hospital in the city. Next he would place smoking camphor cans in the homes where the smallpox had been most prevalent. At the same time, the immunization plan would also go into effect. He would need all the assistance he could get from city law enforcement.

Bartlow and Ortiz agreed they would not likely be able to control the crowds with the deputies they had, especially for the expected resistance as they tried to evacuate people from their homes. Some later reports indicate that the Mexican deputies in fact refused to assist. Mayor Christen decided to call in the Rangers. On March 18 he wired the adjutant general's office in Austin requesting the assistance of Company E out of Cotulla. Captain Rogers received his orders later that same day. Although there are several published versions of this story, it is best left to Rogers himself to give most of the details. His official monthly report outlines the next forty-eight hours beginning on March 18:

"By order of Gen. Scurry I took Private A. Y. Old and went to Laredo, reported to State Health Officer Blunt to assist him to enforce quarintine [*sic*]. On 19th we proceeded to move small pox patients to the Hospital. The Mexicans manifested a disposition to riot but we moved patients until Noon without any serious trouble. While eating dinner I received information that there was a shooting affray downtown. I took Private Old and went to investigate same. I found the City Marshal and his assistant were in the eastern part of the City and while attempting to disperse a crowd became involved in a difficulty with the Mexicans in which shots were exchanged between officers & Mexicans."[11]

In fact over 100 citizens had poured out into the streets to protest the immunization program which they feared. Although Bartlow reported that several guns were in the mob, most of the problem was a lot of shouting and threats along with a few rocks thrown at the officers. Rogers writes, "In this row the assistant Marshal [Idar] received a severe wound by being hit on the head with a stone. When we reached the City Marshal in the eastern part of the city," Rogers continues in his extensive report, "hundreds of Mexicans were crowding around him and the town was wild with excitement. I accompanied him to his office. Several arrests were made by the city officials. I assisted in making one." There was one injury as a protester named Pablo Aguilar was shot in the leg resisting arrest. Rogers was now in the thick of it.

"My force was deemed insufficient to remove the small pox patients and we suspended operations until the morning [Monday, March 20]. In the meantime [U. S. Army] Captain Dodge wired Gov. Sayers to take steps to secure the assistance of the U. S. soldiers stationed at Fort McIntosh on the 20th." This would have been the 10th United States Cavalry, a troop of Black soldiers with a long and storied history reaching back to 1866. Rogers also wired his sergeant back in Cotulla to come to Laredo right away.

"Sergt [Harry G.] DuBose and 4 men arrived from Cotulla." These were Creed Taylor, W. L. Wright, Will Old and Jim Moore. Special Ranger Thomas Ragland came along as well. "In Company with Dr. Blunt I met them at the depot and directed them to go to the Hamilton Hotel and wait for further orders. Dr. Blunt and I returned to the City Hall to see Mayor Christian [Christen, but an interesting misspelling by the captain] and other officials about moving out to the small pox patients. Just at that time Dr. Blunt received information that guns & ammunition had been bought and were stored in certain houses in the eastern part of the city for the purpose of making a fight against the officers to present them from removing small pox patients." The Deutz Brothers Hardware Store had received a telephone order on March 18 for 2,000 rounds of buckshot to be delivered to a certain house in the southeastern part of the city. The authorities were notified; at least that ammunition was never delivered but there was plenty still out there. The ante in this already tense situation had just been raised.

"Sheriff Ortiz decided to go at once and search said houses to see if the report was true. He procured a search warrant. I asked him if I had not better call my men. He said, 'No, the fewer the better. Just you and I will go. If we meet with any opposition we will not try to force our way but return for assistance.' As we were leaving he called 3 Mexican officials who accompanied us to the first place we searched. We met with no opposition. It was here that Ranger Private [Augie] Old & Special Ranger [Tom] Ragland joined us."

The action began to pick up immediately. Rogers continues: "The second house we went to was that of Agapito Herrera." Herrera was an acquaintance of the captain's, for he had served some time earlier as a deputy sheriff there in Laredo. "The sheriff told him our business and produced the search warrant. Herrera desired to speak to the Sheriff privately and they stepped a few steps away. I did not understand their conversation but supposed Herrera was refusing us admission to his house and Ortiz was trying to persuade him to submit to the search. During the conversation of Herrera & Ortiz two or three Mexicans were nervously pacing around in Herrera's yard." According to eyewitnesses these were relatives of Herrera, growing increasingly uncomfortable as was the Ranger captain who kept his eye on their every move.

"Ortiz & Herrera walked back towards us. Ortiz caught Herrera by the shoulder as if to restrain him," writes Rogers, "and as I understood, he called his Mexican Deputies to assist him." The sheriff's movement brought an instant response across Herrera's yard. "At this time the men in the yard bolted for their Winchesters. They ran up to the fence near us with their Winchesters in a shooting position." At least two of the men had run inside the house to grab their rifles, while another—indications are that this was a young boy - ran around the side of the house. The three Rangers had brought only their holstered pistols on this search, fearing that carrying rifles would further alarm an already unruly citizenry. They wished for those rifles at this moment, but pulled their pistols and readied for the fight.

"I fired on one of them with my pistol and they disappeared and took shelter behind a wall," writes Rogers. "I then faced about in a different direction [as] Herrera escaped from the sheriff & his deputies [and] then reappeared in the open street with a Winchester apparently aimed directly at me. I fired at him, pistols being the only weapons we had. I wounded him in the breast. The shooting then became general, being participated in by Old & Ragland and Herrera's Mexican friends."

A shot rang out from just above and to Rogers' right, apparently from someone firing from an upstairs window or Herrera's rooftop. The bullet entered the captain's right arm just an inch below the shoulder, shattering the bone in his upper arm and rendering him almost instantly disabled. Another bullet grazed Rogers' thumb and bloodied it. Augie Old returned fire at Herrera, shooting him in the chest. Old then walked up to the wounded Mexican and fired two bullets at close range into his head, killing Herrera instantly. In the ensuing fire that lasted another minute or so, Herrera's sister Refugia was wounded in the arm and a neighbor, Santiago Granaldo [Grimaldo], was shot in the stomach.

"Private Old & Ragland after emptying their pistols retired and went to the Hotel," Rogers wrote later, the Rangers putting down protective fire as their captain walked as steadily as he could away from the fight, holding his bloodied, lifeless right arm with his left hand. Rogers described it later as holding it "so that it wouldn't fall off." On the way back up the street Rogers commandeered a horse-drawn hack and boarded it carefully, ordering the driver to get him to the Hamilton Hotel. A moment later Rogers spied Dr. Blunt on the street and hailed him. Blunt took a quick look at the captain's wound and escorted him to the hotel to administer aid. The two also came upon Marshal Bartlow who was informed of the shoot-out.

Upon arriving at the hotel, Rogers apprised Sergeant DuBose of the situation. DuBose immediately headed for the trouble spot accompanied by Creed Taylor, W. L. Wright, Will Old, and Special Ranger O. N. Wright. "I told Sergt. DuBose what had happened and to keep cool and handle the trouble the best he could," wrote Rogers in his report. Rogers was attended by Blunt and several others including a Laredo doctor named McKnight.[12]

DuBose and the other four Rangers strode down the street headed for the neighborhood where the shooting had occurred. They were soon joined by Augie Old and Tom Ragland who had retreated from the battle to reload their guns. The others held Winchesters at the ready as they walked the dusty street side by side. According to various reports they then encountered between fifty and one hundred Mexicans hovering over Hererra's body which still lay where he had fallen. [Rogers wrote that twenty of them were well armed but he had second hand information.] Some of the armed men turned and drew their guns as the Rangers steadfastly approached the scene.

The Rangers drew pistols and lifted rifles to their shoulders, firing as they walked. Creed Taylor shot practically from the hip, hitting every target at which he aimed. Years later Captain Rogers said, "young Creed Taylor could shoot unerringly without taking much time to aim. He was one of the best shots I ever saw."[13] The Ranger bullets found their targets as at least eight men went down wounded. The firing became general as the mob scattered and ran for cover. The Rangers stood in the middle of the street and returned fire, finally moving purposefully for cover. A bullet whistled through DuBose's pants leg but missed flesh. A spent bullet ricocheted against O. N. Wright's groin, doubling him over and leaving a serious bruise. One Mexican rifle continued to fire as the others quieted. Taylor stepped from his cover and dispatched the sniper with a single shot.

With the last volley the shootout was finally done. The crowd had dispersed, leaving several down, wounded on the street. The only other fatality besides Herrera was a man named Gonzales who apparently escaped across the Rio Grande and died in Mexico. There were shots heard in the streets of Laredo during the night, but the Rangers had retired to Market Square away from the scene of the gun battle.[14]

The next morning, March 21, the Tenth U. S. Cavalry arrived from Fort McIntosh under the command of Captain Charles G. Ayers. They fanned out through the town and patrolled the streets as Dr. Blunt resumed his vaccination program. Some twenty arrests were made over the next few days of those thought to be involved in the March 20 shoot-out. By March 27 the small pox patients had all been moved, camphor cans had smoked out dozens of homes, and the vaccinations were nearing completion. Company E returned to Cotulla. The quarantine was lifted on May 1.[15]

As for the badly wounded Rogers, he spent the night in a room at the Hamilton that was quickly converted to a medical facility. On March 21 he was transported by train to San Antonio, his injuries beyond the scope of the Laredo physicians and their facilities. He was accompanied as far as Devine by another Laredo doctor named Wilcox and taken with great care to Santa Rosa Hospital. There he was placed under the responsibility of Dr. Marvin Lee Graves, a thirty-two-year old surgeon who was currently serving as superintendent of the Southwestern Hospital for the Insane.

The first diagnosis of the wound, which had left the upper arm in ragged pieces, had been made during the night in Laredo and recommended amputation. Rogers sought a second opinion from Dr. Graves. The young but experienced physician admitted the difficulty of the situation, his only suggestion being surgery to remove the mangled pieces of bone. This could save the arm but would result in its being shorter than the other and with no guarantee as to the recovered strength and use of the arm in the future. For the captain this was a better alternative than losing it altogether. Either way the operation was urgent to literally save Rogers' life.

By five o'clock that evening of March 21 Rogers was in surgery. Graves removed an inch and a half of the upper arm bone and cleaned out the wound. Sutures tied the arm back to the shoulder. The operation was a success. Rogers lay in the bed without moving his arm for the next six weeks, Hattie joining him a day after the surgery and staying at his bedside through the ordeal. He did manage to scribble his monthly report from his hospital bed on May 1st, addressing it to Captain Sieker from the Santa Rosa Infirmary.

During the second week in May the captain was allowed to be taken to his mother's home there in San Antonio, where she had moved some years before. He convalesced there for three more weeks. On the last day of May, he returned to Cotulla to resume his duties as a Texas Ranger. Later that summer a gunsmith fashioned a rifle with a curved stock that fit comfortably in the crook of Rogers' shoulder. The gun would become a famous identification of the Ranger captain for the rest of his days.[16]

On June 23, 1899, John H. Rogers signed his reenlistment papers for yet another stint as Ranger captain, prayerfully thankful that he was alive and able to continue on. His faith and his family and friends had seen him through the deadliest encounter of his life. As the new century loomed ahead, the quiet-spoken but earnest Christian man resolved to accept whatever his Lord had in store for him; after all, he had cheated death once more. His life's mission as lawman and man of God wasn't done yet.

Rogers' bent-stock Winchester .351 rifle. Courtesy Pat Halpin, Pioneer Memorial Hall—Pioneers, Old Trail Drivers, Former Texas Ranger Association Inc., San Antonio

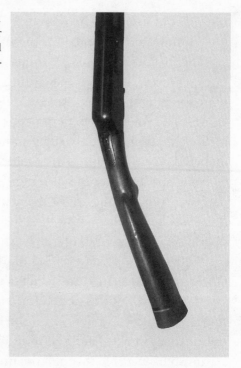

Hardly had the ink dried on his reenlistment signature before Rogers and trusty Augie Old took a train to Columbus in Washington County to settle down an unruly feud between the Townsends and the Reeses. The violence in that area "rivaled the Taylor-Sutton Feud," according to Ranger W. W. Sterling. On August 3, 1898, Larkin Hope was killed in Columbus during a heated election campaign. Jim Coleman, a friend of the Reeses, was suspected but never charged. Six months later Sam Reese was gunned down and friends and relatives of Hope were prime suspects of the reprisal. A bystander was also killed and a young boy wounded in the gunfight. The Columbus community was frustrated and afraid, and business on the unruly streets was even being jeopardized.

One of the interested parties, young Light Townsend rode into town a day or so after Rogers' arrival. Townsend carried a pistol under his coat, a violation in Columbus instituted by Captain Rogers to prevent future shootings. Having just dismounted, Townsend was approached by a kindly gentleman who he took at first to be a local preacher.

"You're Light Townsend?" the man inquired in a soft voice, a smile across his face.

"Yes, sir," replied Townsend.

"I'll need that pistol you have there under your coat," Captain Rogers said in the same motion disarming the young man and whisking him off to the jail.

Although the feud continued for nearly eight more years, and no one was ever convicted of any of the killings, Light Townsend related years later that the experience with Rogers that day so impressed him that he turned his life away from frivolous violence and pursued a career in law enforcement, becoming a Ranger captain himself.[17]

CHAPTER 8

Getting Gregorio

NEARING HIS SEVENTIETH BIRTHDAY, ALEXANDER Gilmer stood with his hands on his hips, fists clenching, as he watched the fire consume his sawmill. The Irish born shipbuilder turned Texas lumber magnate stared in anger and disbelief at this, the fourth time his Orange County-based mill had gone up in flames. The other three times it had been accidental; this time it was deliberate. No more building here, he thought to himself. His next sawmill would be in Lemonville a few miles away.

The Texas Rangers had arrived in Orange County a few days earlier when the race riots were determined to be beyond the control of the local authorities. In fact, it was roundly thought that local law enforcement was behind the violence. Roving gangs had controlled the countryside all summer, running off the Black families, beating up a number of them. In early August a mob had opened fire on a house, killing one of its residents and wounding several others.

Some of Company E arrived in Orange on August 18. Two days later Captain Rogers, in his first activity since the Laredo shootout and accompanied by Augie Old, arrested Jack Morris, Doug Harris, and Frank Weatherford for disturbing the peace and suspicion of involvement in the recent killing. The Rangers stayed in Orange

County into September. The three men arrested were released and on September 16, 1899, Frank Weatherford was causing trouble again. Rogers faced him in the streets of the little east Texas town and the two men wrestled on the ground until the Ranger got the upper hand. Weatherford landed in jail once more, this time to stay.

But Rogers had re-injured his arm in the scuffle, the wound opened and bleeding. The tough Texan chose to stay at his post and supervise the return of order along the lower Sabine until he and his company were eventually replaced by Bill McDonald's men. But by early October, his company briefly stationed in Comstock, Rogers could barely function, his arm for all practical purposes useless at his side. In fact over the years that followed the photographs of Rogers show quite clearly his holding his right arm very gingerly. In his November report Rogers listed six months of medicine he had been taking since the Laredo fight.[1]

Midway through the year Rogers inventoried the weaponry of his company and it is an interesting list: "4 Winchester carbines Model 1873, .44 caliber; 2 Marlin rifles Model 1893, .30-30 cal; 1 Marlin rifle in .38-42 caliber and another .32-40; and two Winchester shotguns, a 10 and a 12-gauge." He noted that every man wore a .45 Colt pistol on his hip. In October he reported that the company wagon was "playing out" as was the packsaddle, and that in September a stray bullet during target practice had killed the company's mule. He implored the adjutant general "not to send any more smokeless pistol cartridges. They don't penetrate," Rogers wrote after recording that the spent bullets had been found no deeper than the outer layer of the tree bark they had targeted. The mule had indeed been unlucky.

In November, with his captain recuperating at home in Cotulla, Sergeant Harry DuBose took two privates with him to track three men wanted for robbery in Sonora, Sutton County. On November 8 they confronted the fugitives in an old abandoned farmhouse. A shootout ensued and one of the fugitives was killed, the other two arrested.

Captain Rogers recovered enough by December to be back on the job, helped by the transfer of his company from Comstock back to Cotulla. On December 8 there was a murder in the streets of Cotulla, possibly a marital disturbance turned tragic. The captain investigated and Clara Centoya was arrested and put on trial for the murder.

The new century dawned in Cotulla with Company E split between camps there and west in Del Rio. Augie Old was recalled to Orange where he spent much of the spring. The Rangers were dispersed over thousands of square miles over the first months of the new year, from Houston to Millett in northern La Salle County, where Rogers tracked down a thief, and to Langtry where new recruit Private Ed DuBose, Harry's older brother, made an arrest in April.[2]

On January 10, 1900, Rogers filled out a questionnaire from the adjutant general's office in which he listed the significant skirmishes thus far in his career: "fence cutters in Brown County—2 killed caught in the act; Conner Gang on the Sabine; horse thief shot near San Angelo." And of the Laredo quarantine: "We met with opposition," wrote Rogers of the latter and with typical understatement, "and had a brush with Mexicans resulting in the death of one Mexican—in this engagement I received 2 wounds one serious and one slight wound." He also noted with some satisfaction that the Cotulla station (his own home) now had a telephone.[3]

In May the state legislature cut back on the Rangers budget and forced a reduction of the companies from twelve to eight men, and then to only six as of June. About the same time Augie Old's brother Will was discharged from Company E for, as Rogers curtly noted, "making unbecoming talks about his superior officers."[4]

Curren Rogers left the Treasury Department post and rejoined the Rangers on June 1, promoted to Second Lieutenant and assigned to Company A. Under "Occupation" he wrote candidly: "Ranger off and on for 13 years." His promotion was the result of a politically charged controversy that swirled around the Rangers that year related to a technicality in the law that addressed their authority to make arrests. An earlier question during the Jeff Milton trials years before had become a legal loophole for critics of the Rangers' authority to attack the Frontier Battalion if not destroy it altogether. The 1874 law that incorporated the Rangers said that "officers of the law had the power to make arrests." Now the question of what constituted an "officer" in the Rangers was raised again. In a startling interpretation, Texas Attorney General Thomas S. Smith ruled on May 26, 1900, that the term meant only commissioned officers and not just any Ranger as had always been the common understanding.

In response, Adjutant General Scurry attacked the narrow ruling by reorganizing the four active companies into six, thus adding two more captains, and allowing for another level of officers—lieutenants—in each company. Now, with a captain and two lieutenants in every company, eighteen Rangers could make arrests legally instead of four. Harry DuBose from Company E received such a promotion as did Kid Rogers—DuBose was also moved to Company A—and at least for the time being the restrictive interpretation of the attorney general had been circumvented.

But the proverbial handwriting was on the wall and the fate of the famed Frontier Battalion was at hand. Scurry cautioned his men in an order sent out that summer: "Company commanders will instruct their men to keep within the bounds of discretion and the law under all circumstances," he wrote, "and should there be any men now in the service who make unreasonable display of authority or use abusive language to or unnecessarily harsh treatment of those with whom they come in contact in the line of duty, or who are not courageous, discrete, honest or of temperate habits, they will be promptly discharged." It is certain that Captain Rogers would have agreed wholeheartedly with Scurry's moral directive, and also possible that Will Old's discharge may have been related to this issue.[5]

The Rangers carried on. Company E worked southeast Texas as far north as Pearsall in the summer, and returned to east Texas in the autumn. Rogers was back in the piney woods of San Augustine where he arrested Frank Sparks on September 12 and Theodore Vorters in Nacogdoches a month later.[6]

Two of the last recorded deaths involving the now-fading Frontier Battalion took place in October as well, with the death of Ranger Tom Fuller in Orange and the killing of a drunk and disorderly J. R. Davenport outside of a Cotulla saloon by Private Will Wright. Wright was young and new to the Rangers and left in charge of the town this night, but proved his mettle on October 24. "When Davenport resisted," wrote Rogers in his monthly report, "and drew his pistol, he fired at Wright, the ball passing through the latter's coat. Wright immediately shot and killed him. Davenport," the captain added, "had been wounded by Rangers once before when arrested for murder. While in Cotulla he had frequently been arrested for drunkenness and for firing his pistol and for carrying concealed weapons." Will Wright would become one of the great Ranger captains of the next generation.[7]

In November Company E moved to Laredo and established a headquarters there. A mob scene off in Hempstead, however, brought Rogers and three of his men by train to guard several prisoners being held there. The presence of the Rangers discouraged the mob from further action. A month later Company E was called to restore order in the streets of Marathon, a small railroad town of less than 200 people but the second largest community in Brewster County. The far west Texas county had originally been carved into three and Marathon had been designated county seat for Buchel County, an arrangement that never materialized. Marathon became a lawless town with rough and tumble ranch hands facing off against Mexican miners from Boquillas after long hours at the local saloons. The Rangers settled the town down by the end of the year and returned to Laredo.[8]

With Company E making arrests along the Rio Grande Valley and kept especially busy right there in the streets of Laredo, 1901 seemed to be a routine year for law enforcement on the surface This certainly gained John Rogers' attention what with the deadly confrontation of one-and-a-half years earlier that had nearly cost him his life. Sgt. Ed DuBose and Privates Will Wright, Creed Taylor and Augie Old took on the brunt of the longer distance tracking work, but the captain made arrests about once a month through May—all in Laredo. Will Burwell rejoined the Ranger company on April 16 after his stint as sheriff, and Kid Rogers contemplated leaving the Rangers as the summer approached.[9]

Beneath the surface, however, politics in Austin drove toward a confrontation that had the Frontier Battalion at the epicenter. With the "civilizing" of the frontier and a new century as clarion, more congressmen joined the bandwagon to eliminate or at the very least further diminish the power and authority of the Texas Rangers. Despite the efforts of its vocal supporters and Scurry's constant public relations efforts, a growing majority now spoke of a new day of law enforcement in Texas, one that did not necessarily include the Rangers.

On the eve of that decision, one of the most remarkable manhunts in the history of Texas law enforcement placed its own exclamation point on the controversy.

> *Decia Gregorio Cortez*
> *Con su pistola en la mano,*
> *"Ah, cuanto rinche montado*
> *Para un solo mexicano."*[10]

> Then said Gregorio Cortez
> with his pistol in hand,
> "Ah, how many mounted Rangers
> against one lonely Mexican!"

On June 12, 1901, Karnes County Sheriff W. T. "Brack" Morris rode up to the W. A. Thulemeyer Ranch ten miles west of Kenedy. Deputies John Trimmell and Boone Choate rode alongside in a rickety buckboard wagon. Trimmell jumped off at one of the gates near two ramshackle tenant cabins and set up there as security in case trouble started. Morris and Choate approached the second cabin and the sheriff walked the last few yards to the porch alone. A mustachioed Mexican stepped from the front doorway. His name was Gregorio Cortez Lira, twenty-five years old, a native of Matamoros and, some said, a notorious horse thief. He was one of the men whom Morris was looking for; Morris had been called to the area by Atascosa Sheriff Matthew Avant after reports that Cortez and his brother Romaldo had ridden there after stealing fifty horses from Avant's jurisdiction.

Sheriff Morris spoke to Gregorio in English, but the Mexican shrugged as if to say he did not understand. Out of the corner of his eye Morris saw movement at the side of the cabin. Romaldo Cortez stepped from the shadows. "*Te quieren,*" Gregorio said to his brother ["Somebody wants you"], his eyes never wavering from Morris. Morris motioned with one hand and Boone Choate slid down from the buckboard seat and walked toward the confrontation. "Translate for me," Brack Morris said calmly without looking away. Choate nodded, but no one saw.

"Did you trade for some horses?" Morris said. Choate translated in broken Spanish and used the word for stallions.

"*No, senor,*" replied Gregorio, "*no caballos.*" He smiled. But he had some *yeguas,* [mares] all right, he thought to himself.

"Can we look around?" asked Morris through Choate. Gregorio shrugged again. Morris glanced to the edge of the cabin, then knelt down on the ground. The small house sat some 20" off the ground on stilts and blocks and one could see through the dark space beneath to the back yard. The sheriff immediately spied the legs of two, maybe three horses at the back of the house.

"You're under arrest for stealing those horses," Morris announced as he stood up. Choate struggled through the translation. Gregorio smiled beneath his mustache, but there was nothing friendly about the grin.

"*No me puede arrestar por nada* [You can't arrest me for nothing]," he said, his arms outstretched, palms up. Morris turned to Choate who frowned as he translated, "He says no White man can arrest him." Morris tensed, his hand reaching for the holstered pistol at his side.

Romaldo reacted at the same instant, brandishing a long-bladed knife as he leapt at the sheriff from the shadows. Brack Morris, a former Ranger and noted gunman, had his gun in his hand in a flash. He pulled the trigger as Romaldo descended upon him, the bullet catching the Mexican in the mouth and exiting through the back of his throat. Romaldo crumpled to the ground, bleeding profusely.

Choate froze in place, and Gregorio pulled an unseen pistol from his side and fired off a shot at the sheriff, striking him in the right arm. Morris' gun fell to the ground and he went to his knees, lifting the pistol with his left hand. Before Morris could aim, a second bullet from Gregorio's pistol slammed into the left arm, totally disabling the wounded sheriff as he fell forward onto the step of the porch.

Choate broke and ran. Morris rose to his knees, weakly attempting to gather the gun in both hands for another shot. He arched his back to raise himself up. Gregorio, now at nearly point blank range, shot the sheriff in the stomach. Morris collapsed. Gregorio stepped over the mortally wounded man's body and knelt beside his brother, who was still breathing. Cortez shouted and two women appeared from the cabin. They began to administer medical aid to Romaldo as Gregorio sputtered instructions.

Meanwhile Boone Choate had run to where Trimmell waited, told him what the gunshots meant, and the two of them made their way towards Kenedy to get help. Gregorio helped the women stanch the bleeding from his brother's wounds and lift him into a hay wagon. Covering him with hay, Gregorio told the women to take his brother to relatives some miles away and care for him there. This they did, eluding at least one posse who never thought to look in the passing hay wagon as they rode in pursuit of Gregorio. Both Brack Morris and Romaldo Cortez died from their wounds. Morris was found the next day at a tank where he'd crawled for water, hundreds of yards from the cabin.[11]

And so one of the longest and deadliest manhunts in Texas history began. Over the next ten days Gregorio Cortez would crisscross seven counties, cover hundreds of miles, some on horseback and some on foot, and manage to escape from more than one hundred peace officers and their deputized posses. His zigzag course took him northeast first, then slowly but surely he began to make his way for Mexico, tracking across Atascosa and La Salle counties and along the northern line of Webb County toward the Rio Bravo.

In western Gonzales County near the town of Belmont, Gregorio paused at the home of Martin and Refugia Robledo, tenants who lived on the property of Henry Schnabel. County Sheriff Richard "Dick" Glover, a boyhood friend of Brack Morris and now leading a posse after Cortez, received word that the fugitive might come to the Robledo place for refuge. On June 14 a posse approached the ranch, surrounding the cabin where they believed Cortez was hiding. But Cortez, too smart to be caught so easily, was hiding on a small rise just rifle distance away, watching as the posse attacked.

Accounts differ as to what happened during the next few minutes, but it appears likely that the posse, most of them volunteer townsfolk who had bolstered their courage before the hunt with several shots of whiskey, emptied their rifles and pistols at the house, firing indiscriminately. Cortez may have joined in the shooting as well from his hiding place one hundred yards away. When the shooting stopped, half a dozen of the posse nursed gunshot wounds. Dick Glover and Henry Schnabel lay dead; no one could tell whose bullets had done the damage.[12]

Cortez escaped, working his way back southward, stealing a mare at the Atascosa River and riding her nearly to death past the Frio and the Nueces rivers. Approaching Cotulla and skirting the ranch of Thomas Atlee Coleman—the fugitive knew that some of the best horses in Texas were corraled at Coleman's place but was unable to get to them—Cortez now proceeded due west on foot headed for the safety of Mexico. As the days passed, newspapers across the region kept the citizens aroused and on alert. Rumors abounded, rewards escalated, and at least a dozen Tejanos were shot by edgy ranchers or angry posses.

The Texas Rangers received urgent messages two days into the manhunt to spread out across the region and track Gregorio down. Captain Rogers, interrupted once again while attending Sunday morning services at a Laredo church, sent his men out from camp in pairs in several directions across Webb and La Salle counties, and then narrowed his focus when he got word that Cortez may have been spotted near his friend Coleman's place. Rogers figured Gregorio would try to steal a horse from Coleman. He knew then where Gregorio was headed, and remarked to his officers that the fugitive would attempt to cross the Rio Grande up from Laredo.[13]

Midway into the ten-day hunt one of the most respected trackers in south Texas, Manuel Tom, was hired to track Gregorio down. At his side rode Ranger Will Wright who had been at home in Wilson County when the incident began and now joined the hunt. Tom quickly found the fugitive's trail after reports came in of sightings near the Atascosa, and the distance narrowed.

John Rogers rode north out of Laredo on June 20 accompanied by Deputy U. S. Marshal William Hansen, U. S. Customs Mounted Inspector William Merriman with whom he had worked trails before, and several other deputized Laredo citizens. About forty miles up the

The capture of Gregorio Cortez, 1901. (*Front row, left to right:* Rogers, Cortez, Manuel Tom). Courtesy Texas Ranger Hall of Fame and Museum, Waco

Rio Grande from Laredo, and ten miles out of the little hamlet of Palafox, the Ranger-led posse split into three groups, Rogers and Merriman going on together to the Las Tiendas Ranch about ten miles from the border. Next to this property was Don Abran de la Garza's goat ranch named Las Mesas. Rogers was familiar with the territory and knew there was an often-used crossing of the river west from there. Reasoning that Cortez would need food and shelter in this otherwise empty stretch of arid land, the captain awoke on the morning of June 22 and prepared to make for de la Garza's goat camp.

As it happens, June 22 was Gregorio Cortez' twenty-sixth birthday. He was tired and hungry, having traveled nearly one hundred miles on foot after a week of elusive but equally exhausting riding. He had crawled into the lean-to at a goat camp near the trail he followed, knowing he was only half a day from freedom, and slept hard during the night.

Captain Rogers heard a horse riding into his camp just past dawn. Jesus Gonzales, a *mestizo* nicknamed "El Teco" by those in that area who knew him, informed the Ranger that a tired Mexican on foot had dragged into his goat camp earlier and that he thought it was the wanted man, Gregorio Cortez. The growing reward had certainly garnered El Teco's attention. Rogers instructed the *vaquero* to lead him there as Merriman rode alongside.

They arrived near the goat camp where Gonzales pointed to the tiny shack situated next to a roughly executed corral. El Teco watched from the brush as the two lawmen crept to Gregorio's hiding place. Rogers motioned as he went to the front end of the shack, and Merriman raised his Winchester at the back exit.

After ten days, hundreds of trackers and thousands of square miles, the end was anticlimactic. Cortez was so sound asleep that Rogers had to prod him awake. Sitting up, Gregorio gave a fictitious name when asked to identify himself but did not possess the strength to put up a fight. His pistols hung in a bag on a nearby tree limb, a handful of bullets left in the bandolier. Unarmed and utterly drained, he gave up quietly.[14]

The captain's entry into the official records is likewise without drama. "Gregorio Cortez, June 22," Rogers wrote, "arrested for murder in Webb County, returned to sheriff in Karnes County." Rogers escorted the prisoner to Laredo where a coal train took them to Karnes County. Arriving next at the San Antonio depot, the captain paid trolley car fare for him and his prisoner on the way to jail. Rogers stayed with Cortez until he saw him safely in the hands of San Antonio officers as he awaited trial. Rogers and Manuel Tom and fifteen others who had come to San Antonio for the arrest paused long enough for a now-famous photograph with Cortez seated at the center of those who had brought him in.

When it came time to discuss the reward, Rogers was typically modest about accepting extra bounty for a job he was already paid to do, and he suggested that El Teco and Merriman get the money. "No special credit is due me for the capture," he told a reporter for the *San Antonio Express*. "Somebody else would have got him if I hadn't."[15]

Though far from the end of Cortez' story—he would survive several trials with hung juries and at least one lynch mob, serve time in prison but ultimately be pardoned by a Texas governor in 1913, and capture the imagination of the Rio Bravo people in legend and *corrido*—it was the end of this chapter and, ironically, the end of the activities of the famed Frontier Battalion of the Texas Rangers.

> *An Act to provide for the organization of a "ranger force" for the protection of the frontier against marauding and thieving parties, and for the suppression of lawlessness and crime throughout the state; to prescribe the duties and powers of members of such force, and to regulate their compensation.*

On July 8, 1901, the state legislature effectively eliminated the battalion and reorganized the Texas "ranger force" under much tighter scrutiny and with constrained law enforcement authority. The six small companies that had existed in a precarious state for a year now became just four. Each captain was given authority to hire up to twenty men in his company, but only eight privates and a sergeant were budgeted for in the initial legislation. That number would change but in the years that followed each company usually rode with less than a dozen Rangers. Captains and the quartermaster were appointed for two year stints by the governor, and the entire force was directly accountable to the governor. The quartermaster now took on the responsibilities of commissary and paymaster as well. Each Ranger brought his own horse but would be supplied with "one improved carbine and pistol at cost" by the government. Daily rations were spelled out to the ounce for both ranger and mount.

Section 11 of the new law stated that "this force shall be clothed with all the powers of peace officers, and shall aid the regular civil authorities in the execution of the laws." The Rangers had broader jurisdiction over the whole state than sheriffs, and could deputize "volunteers" as necessary. Arrested felons were to be returned to the appropriate county authorities.

Captains would receive one hundred dollars monthly wages, sergeants fifty dollars and privates forty dollars each, the new pay scale to take effect on July 9, 1901. In an addendum the Legislature noted that "members of the Ranger Force will keep within the bounds of discretion and the law under all circumstances," and be discharged for "unreasonable display of authority, abusive language or unnecessary harsh treatment." Each Ranger was expected to take an oath "to faithfully perform their duties under the law."

The law was passed in the House by voice vote and twenty-three to three in the Senate. The Frontier Battalion ceased to exist on July 8, 1901 and the Ranger Force was born the next day.[16]

John Rogers' Company E now became Company C, still headquartered in Laredo. John Hughes of Company D in Fort Hancock, John Brooks of Company A in Alice, and Bill McDonald of Company B in Amarillo rounded out the ranger captaincy. The legendary "Four Captains" now led the new "ranger force" into the twentieth century.

Lam Sieker became the quartermaster of the Ranger Force, a position he helped transfer and remake from the Battalion days and until his retirement in 1905. Lambartine Pemberton Sieker was born in Baltimore in 1848 and came to Texas in 1873. Promoted to Ranger captain in 1882—the same month John Rogers enlisted—Sieker served as quartermaster from 1885 to 1893 as well, and as assistant adjutant

Ranger Force Commanders, 1901. (*Front row, left to right*: Lam Sieker, Major John Armstrong, Bill McDonald; back row: John Brooks, Rogers, W. H. Mabry). Courtesy Charlie, Lauren, and Carley Reeves, San Antonio

general. He taught the four captains the ways and means of the new paperwork, from vouchers to the new monthly reports. Honest and disciplined, Sieker was highly respected by the Ranger Force and counted as friend by many.

Some of old Company E's most trusted lawmen continued to serve under their captain: Sgt. Ed DuBose, Will Wright, Creed Taylor, Will Burwell, Kid Rogers, and Jim Moore stayed on the trail. Oscar Latta and Charles Sandborn joined up.

Captain Rogers would begin his eighteenth year as a Ranger; a whole new decade as a Texas Ranger now opened up before him. His faith and his dear family would be his foundation. He would face death at least once more, and would be forced to test his faith twice in the midst of deep personal tragedy—the loss of his brother, and the loss of a son.

CHAPTER 9

Hill Loftis and the Sand Dunes Shootout

JOHN ROGERS SAT IN A stiff-backed wooden chair next to the hospital bed, his head buried in his hands as he prayed. Santa Rosa Hospital, where John had recovered from his Laredo wounds, was sweltering in the desert heat of this July day, and no breeze stirred outside. Hattie stood nearby leaning against the bare wall, wiping tears quietly from her cheeks. The man in the bed breathed unsteadily as if struggling to inhale. The breaths came unevenly and more shallow as the minutes dragged by. Two doctors stopped by intermittently and a nurse stayed in the room as helpless as the others to do anything.

Kid Rogers had become seriously ill while working at Tom Collins' ranch outside of Alice. Having resigned from the Rangers in the fall of 1901 he had spent almost a year working for Collins. They had rushed him to the hospital on July 15 and removed his gall bladder in an operation that had at first seemed to go without complications. The captain and Hattie had been by his side since the day of his surgery, ten days now, hardly ever leaving the hospital. After several days of recovery Curren had taken a turn for the worse, internal bleeding perhaps, or an infection. Now he was at the end.

Only thirty-three years old, Kid left behind a wife, two daughters, and a son he really never got to know. After a lifetime of adventure and excitement as a Texas Ranger, "off and on" as he liked to say, Curren Lee Rogers was buried at the Odd Fellows Cemetery in San Antonio with the honors due him as a peace officer. Family, friends, and a large company of Rangers looked on, but it was a bitter personal loss for his older brother, whose faith once again severely tested withstood the tragedy.

The year 1902 found Rogers' company of Rangers roaming literally all across Texas. With the constricted organization now, a few men were required to cover thousands of square miles. During much of this year Rogers divided his company in order to cover the vast west Texas country, traveling himself between Laredo and the small town of Fort Hancock up the Rio Bravo near El Paso. Although the old fort itself had long since been abandoned, the town served as a railroad stop that allowed the captain and his men to make connections from the New Mexico border all the way to Brownsville and San Antonio. Jim Moore found himself patrolling Val Verde County, while Ed DuBose—before his resignation in October—made arrests in Pecos, and Oscar Latta did the same as far away as Menard. Will Wright traveled throughout the expansive country. On March 12 Rogers arrested Charles Smith for murder in Lockhart and returned him to the sheriff of Guadalupe County. He was attending court in Rio Grande City later that summer and arresting a Starr County cattle thief in October. When the railroad workers went on strike in late summer along the Laredo to Corpus Christi line, Rogers and Wright kept the peace.[1]

A popular though apocryphal anecdote may have arisen from this period when Rogers found himself in the valley with his company. With potential trouble staring them in the face, Rogers was said to have asked his men to join him in prayer whereupon he lifted these words: "Lord, if you'll just stick around for a few minutes you'll see the golldangdest fight you ever witnessed. And Lord, if you can't see fit to help us, just please don't help them."[2]

Ranger William W. Sterling retells a favorite Rogers family story as having happened in Cotulla about this time. "When Captain Rogers was absent from Cotulla, Rangers [Ed] DuBose and Woodlief Thomas went into Capp's Saloon for a few drinks. They had gotten pretty well organized," writes Sterling in his inimitable style, "when County Judge Knaggs, who wore the only stovepipe hat between San Antonio and Laredo, walked in front of the saloon. The target offered by his two-story headpiece proved irresistible. The roistering pair ventilated it with .45 caliber bullet holes, against the peace of the state and the dignity of the judge.

"Captain Rogers was in San Diego [Texas] attending district court, and Ranger DuBose knew him to be an exponent of the axiom, 'Liquor and six-shooters won't mix.' DuBose resigned from the Service by wire [before Rogers returned], packed his outfit and rode back to Alice where he had lived for several years. He enlisted in John Hughes' Company D shortly thereafter." Captain Rogers had earned his reputation which brought to mind another old axiom about "putting the fear of God in a man."[3]

Will Burwell was promoted to First Sergeant in November upon Ed DuBose's untimely resignation. That same week Rogers found himself in the lower Rio Grande valley keeping watch over particularly vitriolic elections in Zapata and Maverick counties. Others in his company kept watch over the Pecos elections. In his monthly scout report the captain noted that "when the local political factions waxed warm, trouble of a serious nature might have occurred [but] for the appearance of the Rangers."[4]

In December, 1902, Company C was reassigned to Colorado City, the place where John Rogers had first enlisted in the Texas Rangers. The town had changed dramatically in the twenty years since he left. Rogers brought his family to Mitchell County and bought a home there that became the company headquarters. They would live in Colorado City for the next five years, although the company still maintained unofficial outposts in Amarillo—Will Burwell took charge there—and Fort Hancock. In 1903 Fort Hancock had lost all but fifty of its citizens and only the hotel and the general store stood alongside the tiny train depot. Trouble in Hutchinson County also kept at least one Ranger there throughout the year.

In January of 1903 and again in October Rogers was also in Hutchinson County, keeping the peace in Plemons "when it looked like trouble and maybe bloodshed over the contention for the sheriff's office," and returning as bodyguard for a state witness testifying against local thieves. The captain noted that there was "no legal sheriff at that time, although there were two men claiming the office."

In June Captain Rogers found himself traveling even more miles than usual, most by rail. In the east Texas town of Hempstead he mediated between prohibitionists and antiprohibitionists—the "dries versus the wets"—and maintained an uneasy peace there even though he was quite openly a "dry" himself. By the end of that same month Rogers was in Amarillo alongside Will Burwell investigating the death of a Black man who, as it turned out, had been unjustly accused of a heinous crime. Rogers and his in-law came down hard on the men who had fashioned themselves into "a mob or secret order or society" bent on their own brand of justice. "An inoffensive Negro was shot and murdered at night," reported the captain, "by the element of *worthless hoodlums*." The members of the lynch mob were summarily arrested and prosecuted.[5]

Late in August Captain Rogers rode the Texas and Pacific rail to the small town of Thurber seventy-five miles west of Fort Worth. Thurber was a tried and true railroad "company town" created by a T&P engineer named William Whipple Johnson in the 1880s and named after one of its founding investors, H. K. Thurber, a New Yorker and organizer of the Texas and Pacific Coal Company. In the late 1800s a large brick plant was built there, and trouble soon followed as the unions tried to wedge themselves in.

The Knights of Labor and the newly organized United Mine Workers [UMW] had already made several unsuccessful attempts to get into Thurber as early as 1890 but both were soundly rebuffed by the coal company's tough president Colonel Robert Dickey Hunter. Again in 1894 the company town faced the threat of a strike by workers sympathetic to a union there. Both times the Texas Rangers were called to keep order; both times the union organizers left but always with a promise to keep trying.

In 1899 Colonel Hunter retired, handing over the very powerful reins of the coal company operations to his son-in-law Edgar Marston and a career railroad man named William K. Gordon. In the next three years the unions made great headway across the Southwest and into Texas, with a union camp situated as close to Thurber as Bridge-port. The company town was now squarely in the sights of the UMW and activists began to work their way into and among the workers. Gordon held fast, confident that two of the largest ethnic groups in his employee—the Irish and the Mexicans—had long been anti-union. In fact, late in August, 1903, a company announcement was posted in four languages criticizing the attempts of "agitators" to infiltrate Thurber.

On September 3, 1903, the company posted a notice inviting any pro-union employees to "get your settlement at any time," assuring everyone that Thurber would remain closed to the unions. Rumors that a Mexican organizer had been murdered the night before swelled the crowds and spread a dangerous alarm.

Word quickly traveled throughout the region that a union rally would be held in Thurber on Labor Day, September 5. All the ingre-dients were present for violence. Gordon wrote Governor S. W. T. Lanham on August 30 warning of trouble and indicating that "UMW activists are endeavoring to create discontent amongst our people." Lanham responded by instructing the Texas Rangers to maintain or-der there, and Rogers got the word the next day.

Men from Company C arrived in Thurber on Labor Day morning in time to see competing company picnics facing off. The coal com-pany had arranged for a barbecue to begin that Monday hosted by the usually private and elitist Thursday Club: all company workers were invited. The picnic was held behind the intimidating steel fence that had been erected around the mining area. Not to be outdone, the UMW agitators also had set up a three-day barbecue picnic nearby with sixty just-signed union men giving testimonials. Monday passed peacefully but Tuesday things heated up. Mineworkers listed a set of demands for Gordon and his managers, including one that the fence come down. Gordon refused. That night some fence-cutters made quick work of one section.

On Wednesday hundreds of the nearly two thousand mineworkers went on strike and seven hundred of them joined the UMW in a very public showing. A second union meeting was called out at the Palo Pinto Bridge on Thursday. The crowds were growing restless. Fist-shaking and shouting matches were headed for open violence. Rogers prepared to step in.

On Friday nearly eighteen hundred men and women gathered at the bridge outside of town to hear rallying speeches from the UMW leaders including international speaker William M. Wardjon and Texas Federation of Labor secretary C. W. Woodman. Rogers and several of his Ranger company were in the crowd. As the noise increased, Captain Rogers very calmly spoke with Wardjon and Woodman, asking them to keep the crowd peaceful and to not agitate the situation by detonating the traditional blasting powder fireworks as part of the celebration. The union men complied.

Hundreds more signed up with the UMW and another confrontation seemed imminent. Again, negotiations by the calm peace officer defused the situation. The company management agreed to settle up with those who wished to join the union and allow them to leave Thurber unmolested. For their part the UMW would also leave town and take their new converts with them. Ultimately over 500 men picked up their tools and other belongings and moved on. In his report Rogers wrote: "It is believed that this is the most quiet and orderly strike ever had, or that is of record anywhere; hundreds and hundreds of men simply walking out and quietly leaving for other coal fields without causing any trouble; the general manager of said mines gives the rangers much credit for bringing about this orderly conduct of such a rough lot of coal diggers."

Most of those who remained maintained the strike for the remainder of the month, forcing the crippled coal company to accede to several of the laborers' demands. Over the next two decades the trouble came and went with no clear winners: Thurber was virtually a ghost town by the 1930s. The Rangers under Captain Bill McDonald were called back at least once more to keep the peace.[6]

The Rangers of Company C returned to their routine as the year moved to its close. Captain Rogers spent some of the fall working out of Fort Hancock, arresting three cattle thieves in mid-October up in Pecos County. Will Burwell and Jim Moore worked out of Amarillo, Private T. B. McMeans kept especially busy making arrests all across the region, and Moore was promoted to First Sergeant on January 1,

1904. During this time near El Paso, and again when stationed in Alpine, Rogers took several travel opportunities to the large west Texas city to invest in land in that area and near Fort Hancock. Over the years that followed he accumulated a more than respectable amount of acreage, land that later would be sold off in order to support his family, send his children to college, and establish a comfortable bank account long after his death.

In January Captain Rogers went to Bridgeport north of Fort Worth to investigate "the alleged stealing of an express package by a member of the State Guard as they were on route to Fort Riley, Kansas; failed to locate for sure the identical man who did the stealing," Rogers reports, "but found out beyond a doubt that it was stolen by one of the soldiers." Twenty years later Rogers would once more be involved in the investigations of packages being shipped by the American Express Company, but from a different point of authority.

Near the end of February, 1904, a Fisher County rancher named Ross Millsap was brutally murdered just northeast of Colorado City in the town of Roby. Rogers spent the first two weeks of March investigating the homicide culminating in the arrest of Millsap's son-in-law Ross Green. Rogers returned to the district court in Roby in August to testify at Green's trial, but watched helplessly as a grand jury failed to indict a man whom the newspapers heralded as a "model citizen and a popular defendant."[7]

The spring of that year found Company C still ranging to all corners of west Texas, from Stonewall and Kent counties to the north, and to Deaf Smith County and even east to College Station. In May the company captured "several men who had been burglarizing the depot at Bryan," Rogers writes, "and also a party who attempted to wreck a train by placing an obstruction on the track at Calvert." But an incident in June caught Rogers off guard and he was nearly killed as a result.

One of the most vicious criminals on the Texas frontier throughout the 1890s was George "Red Buck" Waightman. He traveled from Indian Territory across the Texas Panhandle and into New Mexico with his gang always a step ahead of law enforcement and posses who chased them. Their reputation for wantonness exceeded the legendary Dalton or Doolin gangs, and one of those who rode as a young gunman was Hill Loftis, alias Tom Ross. In 1896 Captain Bill McDonald sent Sergeant W. John L. Sullivan in hot pursuit of the Red Buck Gang. The Dugout Shootout near Doans Crossing on Christmas Eve became the basis for legend and lore decades after. Waightman was wounded and another gang member killed, but Loftis got away.[8]

Hill Loftis's name now made it to the Rangers' Fugitive List, the frontier version of the Most Wanted. "Wanted for highway robbery, Hill Loftis," it read in the "Black Book" carried by all Rangers. "Age about 32 (in 1900), 5 feet 9 inches, weight 160 pounds. He has a very peculiarly shaped head, being very long behind with a high forehead. Occupation, cowboy. Probably in New Mexico. Indicted in 1896. Reward by sheriff of Wilbarger County." His unusually long hair and the odd shape of his head prompted Ranger W. W. Sterling to refer to him as "Buffalo Head." The reward was twenty-five dollars, dead or alive.[9]

Loftis remained on the run for the next six years, embarking on ruthless jaunts across the Llano Estacado then escaping into Indian Territory when chased. Word came to law authorities in 1904 that Loftis, under the name Tom Ross, may have settled down, married, and was operating a ranch east of Hobbs, New Mexico on the Texas border. Local sheriffs and posses of deputized gunmen went looking for him throughout the spring but without success. A report in early June indicated a sighting of someone matching his very distinctive physical description working roundup on the Halff Ranch in Gaines County, and John Rogers rode the train west from Colorado City with the Mitchell County sheriff to look for Loftis.

Rogers met briefly with Sheriff Charles Tom of Martin County who accompanied the captain on horseback the last 100 miles to the vicinity of the Halff Ranch. In this area are the famous sand dunes that spread across the landscape as a geographical oddity; in and around these high dunes danger could be hiding at every turn. On June 17, eight days after he had left Colorado City and now riding exhausted and "inferior" mounts they had borrowed from a nearby rancher, Rogers and Tom spotted Loftis as he disappeared into the dunes to make his escape. Rogers got off at least one shot with his

Winchester, aiming for but missing the fugitive's horse. "He ran out of shooting distance from me," Rogers reported later, "thereby avoiding arrest." The two peace officers returned to the nearby ranch house, ate supper, and returned to the trail by early evening.

According to at least one version of this story, Sheriff Tom had convinced Rogers to ride without his rifle so that they might look like two innocent ranchers and thereby sneak up on Loftis without alarming him from any distance. It is hard to imagine that Rogers would have left his Winchester behind, or for that matter that the seasoned Charlie Tom would even suggest such a thing in the first place. Whatever the case, both men now rode the trail into the sand dunes without rifles at the ready, perhaps holstered in their saddle scabbards.

The captain moved ahead some distance from the sheriff as they came to the edge of the dunes and was just out of sight of his companion. But Hill Loftis had John Rogers dead in his sights. He fired a shot from his rifle, the bullet grazing the jaw of Rogers' mount and popping the reins in two. The horse reared in alarm and Rogers slipped from his saddle to the ground. He landed hard and was momentarily disoriented as the outlaw walked up. Rogers tells the story now himself: "I felt confident that I was ruined [to be killed]. He kept me covered with the Winchester, giving me no opportunity to draw my pistol or even to get a hand on it. Advancing with the Winchester coming all the way to me, I lay on my back with my hands up, and in spite of all I could do or say it looked as though he would kill me, saying that I had tried to murder him one and one-half hours previous." In another report Rogers added, "This party [Loftis] is an old time robber of a hard gang."

Speaking in as calm a voice as he could muster, Captain Rogers told the outlaw that the killing of a Texas Ranger would only bring more trouble and that he should think about the consequences of his next decision, for vengeance by the Rangers would be swift and sure. Loftis ordered Rogers to hand his pistol over to him, which the Ranger did, carefully. Rogers remembered later that he commented upon the personal significance of that pistol, it being a gift from his company. It seemed a trite plea, sitting there in the sand facing sure death. Later he wrote, "I was completely in his power." It may have been in that moment that Rogers also called on the higher power upon which he had relied for most of his adult life, a prayer escaping his lips.

As the evening shadows closed in, Loftis heard the steps of Sheriff Tom's horse just around the high dunes from where he stood with the drop on Rogers. For whatever reason racing through Loftis's mind in that instant, the fugitive emptied the bullets from Rogers' pistol, tossed the gun off into the sand, and vanished into the landscape and the enveloping darkness.[10]

To the adjutant general Rogers wrote, "It is very humiliating to me, this being the first report of this kind in 22 years of service, but I feel that to have made the fight under the conditions, being out of range of effective work with my pistol and [then] having a man with a Winchester thrown down on me, I would have better attempted suicide."

Three days later Rogers sent four of his men into the sand dunes to track Tom Ross, but they returned without success. The end of Hill Loftis's story stretches over another two decades. Having cleared himself of the Wilbarger County charges, "Tom Ross" returned to Gaines County and settled down as a rancher for nearly twenty years. In one of the trials, for a double murder committed in Lubbock, Captain Rogers was subpoenaed to testify against Hilary Loftis. Morally convicted by the fact that Loftis had spared him there among the sand dunes years before, Rogers refused to speak against the defendant. It was a strong but controversial stand that the quiet captain had made.

In the 1920s Loftis was on the rampage again, however, and was chased all the way to the broad Montana Country. In 1929 Ross killed a cattle inspector during a brief but heated exchange, then walked back into his cabin and shot himself.[11]

After Rogers' brush with death, the next twelve months must have seemed strangely routine and eerily calm. The power of his Christian faith had escalated to yet another level with his absolute belief that he had been saved in that dire moment by the hand of God. A rededication of his life to his family, to his church, and to the Texas Rangers brought a sense of peace that neutralized the humiliation he had confessed to his superiors. He carried his Bible everywhere he traveled now, even on the trail of desperadoes, and took even more opportunities to witness to outlaw and peace officer alike, reading Scriptures in his calm voice while sitting around trail campfires, and leading company or congregation in prayer.

Rogers worked out of Colorado City into the late spring of 1905, making arrests in and around Odessa, a bulging railroad town that had more than its share of street trouble at that time. He was also on the trail in Cottle, Dickens, and Kent counties that winter, Crane and Upton counties in the spring, and Midland. His company now included George and Tom McMeans, Jim Hinnant, future Ranger captain J. J. Sanders, and the trusty Jim Moore. Tom Goff, who had worked under Rogers years before, reenlisted in his company on May 1, 1905. Colorado City went "dry" in 1904 and Rogers reports at least one arrest he made himself, of a J. L. Hinchen for "selling whiskey."

Late in May, Captain Rogers received word that the Mitchell County camp was to be removed farther west to Alpine, a twenty-five-year-old town at the edge of the Davis Mountains in Brewster County, boasting just under four hundred citizens. The family packed and moved with him and his company. They would live in and work out of Alpine for two years. The Rangers kept an outpost at Fort Hancock, and Rogers mentions many visits to the El Paso area both on Ranger and personal business. The captain tracked down and arrested two Mexican train robbers near Odessa in late July, but spent the rest of the summer patrolling the streets of Alpine and taking care of administrative duties while attending to his wonderful family.[12]

Before the end of 1905, however, John Rogers and Company C had lost two good men, a serious depletion of forces, as well as a tragedy for one Ranger. Fiercely supportive of the rules of Ranger conduct, an incident occurred in the fall that required a harsh but sure decision by Rogers. In Amarillo Sergeant Jim Moore found himself in a situation that may have involved excessive drinking in public. Moore had been a fine peace officer and dedicated to his captain and company; however, this incident could not go unnoticed, exacerbated by the fact that Moore had attempted to hide it by lying to Rogers when asked about the report. On November 30 the captain wrote into the monthly file that Sergeant Moore had been "reduced to ranks [private] for unbecoming conduct of an officer and then concealing the fact from me." Unable to overcome the shame of his punishment, Moore was discharged on March 31, 1906.[13]

The tragedy occurred on September 14 when Private Tom Goff was ambushed by a Tejano outlaw named Augustine Garcia, "murdered," wrote Rogers, "in the discharge of duty." It appeared that Goff had been unseated from his horse while escorting Garcia to jail, and that the felon had used the Ranger's own gun against him. Goff was one of the first Rangers killed in the line of duty since the 1901 reorganization of the force and the first lost by Rogers. Goff's home was in Throckmorton and Captain Rogers retrieved the body, accompanied it by train to Goff's hometown, and stayed to pay his respects to the family at the funeral held on September 19. A warrant was immediately issued for Garcia's arrest and several Rangers went on his trail. Garcia managed to elude the authorities for the remainder of that year. The killer had escaped into Mexico.

Captain Rogers sent a telegram to the Governor's office requesting help from the state or from Washington, D. C., to have Garcia detained and extradited. Governor Lanham wrote Rogers on October 9: "In compliance with your telegram *and* letter, I have asked for the provisional arrest and detention of Augustine Garcia in Chihuahua, Mexico through diplomatic channels in Washington and to the governor of Chihuahua. If the arrest is made you will be notified to forward the application for requisition at once." On December 5 Lanham let Rogers know that permission had been granted by the Chihuahua authorities and that the Ranger captain should "get a Mexican consul in San Antonio, El Paso or Laredo to attest to the signatures first." Eleven days later similar permission from Washington was also forwarded to Alpine.

Papers were in order, however, the Mexican authorities were unable to produce Garcia after all. At one point, the day after Christmas, Rogers traveled to El Paso to interview a man who knew Garcia after word had come that a man matching the felon's description sat in a Tucson, Arizona jail. Rogers and the witness went by train to Tucson, but the prisoner there was not Garcia. Garcia had made good his escape into Mexico.[14]

Thus, 1905 ended—with a murdered Texas Ranger and friend taken, and without justice, and with another fellow Ranger demoted. On an upbeat note, though, Rogers wrote on January 25, 1906, that "everything is very quiet throughout my entire district. The presence of Rangers in the Big Bend country is very beneficial and I feel that the ranch men and myself and men understand each other."[15]

The quiet was about to change.

CHAPTER 10

*"The Lord Giveth;
the Lord Taketh Away"*

ON AN OCTOBER AFTERNOON IN 1905 a young cowboy sat alone in the main house of the Carr Ranch out near Fort Stockton. His boss was away in El Paso on business and the trustworthy young man had been left nominally in charge while he was away. A telephone sat on the desk nearby and the young man picked up to listen casually, not maliciously, to a conversation on the party line. Sheriff Dud Barker was speaking to his former deputy Charlie Witcher about a horse thief who had been spotted near Fort Stockton. Witcher was declining to go on the trail at Baker's request when the young cowboy interrupted the phone call. "I'll go get him, sheriff!" he exclaimed with excitement in his voice.

"Who the hell are you?" asked the sheriff, obviously disturbed that his conversation had been eavesdropped upon.

"I'm Frank Hamer," replied the cowboy.

Getting over his anger the sheriff agreed to let Hamer go on the trail. Within twenty-four hours the thief had been captured by Hamer and turned over to Sheriff Baker. "You did a mighty fine job of catchin' this man, Frank," said Barker, who then added, "How'd you like to be a Texas Ranger?"

A new era was born in that moment, a next generation of Rangers who would continue on well into the 1930s and carry on the vast and deep tradition that would be handed to them by the Four Captains.

On February 23, 1906, Sheriff Barker wrote the adjutant general's office recommending the young cowboy for service. Captain John Rogers arranged for the interview in Sheffield two months later and on April 21 Frank Hamer enlisted as a private in Company C. He was twenty-two years old and a strapping six foot, three inches tall.[1]

In April John Rogers lost his mother Mary Harris Rogers Crier. He took a leave absence from April 5 to 13 to make arrangements and attend her funeral in Del Rio, where she had moved some years earlier to be closer to her son and his family. She was sixty-one when she died and had outlived two husbands and a son.[2]

Captain Rogers kept busy in the months that followed with activities in El Paso for most of the month of May and again in September. Several of the arrests he made there were smugglers moving horses

Rogers *(seated center)* and Frank Hamer *(standing to his right)*. Courtesy Charlie, Lauren, and Carley Reeves, San Antonio

and contraband across the border. A team made up of Rangers, federal customs inspectors, and New Mexico sheriffs worked together to make the arrests. One arrest proved at least interesting when Jerome Fisher was picked up for harassing the local ranchers. Rogers described Fisher as "a crazy man" in his report.

When customs inspector Frank Chapman was murdered on September 23, Rogers took Will Howell, John Dibrell, and W. M. Hudson on the trail of Dick Riggs and caught him two days later. Chapman and Riggs had engaged in a bitter fight over a young woman at a Mexican *fandango* resulting in Chapman's death. Fourteen Tejanos were also detained as accessories when they refused to give Riggs' name to the authorities.

Late in October Rogers traveled to Del Rio to "quell a hot political fight" that was brewing there the week before election day. He sent Private C. J. Roundtree to Hempstead in November to shut down a gambling ring; Roundtree arrested twenty-three gamblers and nine other "rowdies" in a three-day period. Rogers himself remained along the Rio Bravo where he arrested three Hispanics for murder on October 22, and two Anglos for another homicide just five days later. W. M. Hudson and Frank Hamer assisted in the Del Rio arrests.[3]

On November 15 Rogers learned over the telephone that John A. Brooks, one of the four famed captains of that day and a friend of Rogers, had announced his retirement from the force. The first of the four legendary officers had bowed out. Brooks had already purchased land near Falfurrias, where he moved and went on to spend an illustrious career on the bench in district court. Brooks County was later named after him.[4]

In the Shelby County seat of Center, Texas, a Black preacher named Dick Garrett had been accused of breaking some law in that town where race relations had deteriorated to the point of street violence. He went to the home of Judge Short for counsel and was hidden there while the judge tried to calm things down. Mike Paul learned of the fugitive's whereabouts and headed to the judge's home to negotiate an end to the tense situation. But the preacher panicked when he saw the man approaching his door and fired at Paul, using a borrowed gun. Mike Paul died of his wounds and the townspeople immediately called for a hanging. Local authorities wired for outside help and Captain Rogers responded along with the local Timpson National Guard unit.

The protection of Dick Garrett lasted only through the trial. The preacher was found guilty, sentenced to die, and hanged; the whole process took just three days. Witnesses remarked later as they told the story that the trial itself had been unusually noisy because of the hammering and sawing on the scaffold outside the courtroom window.[5]

November had been extremely active, but December would prove more deadly. While Private Roundtree was arresting thirty-one more gamblers back east in Hempstead, Captain Rogers joined Hamer and Duke Hudson in a dangerous shootout near Del Rio. A criminal named Ed Putnam, alias Ed Sibley, had murdered Box Springs sheep rancher J. W. Rolston in November and stolen his herd with the idea of "selling" it to someone else. Putnam rode to the Del Rio area where he convinced another sheep man named B. M. Cauthorn to put up $4,000 for the flock. As they left town with the money withdrawn from the bank, Putnam shot Cauthorn in the back. But when an eyewitness to the crime appeared, Putnam took off.

On the north side of Del Rio near the railroad tracks the killer ducked into the house of Glass Sharp and his family, all of whom were there when he arrived; they became his hostages. The eyewitness meanwhile had ridden into town and informed Captain Rogers of the whole incident. Rogers, Hamer, and Hudson rode out to Sharp's place. As Rogers calmly tried to negotiate with the man Glass Sharp's daughter Georgia came out of the house and told the captain that the man inside "says he won't come out. He's got a funny look in his eyes," she added, "and says he won't give up." While the rest of the family made their escape, Putnam opened fire on the peace officers, running from window to window as the Rangers took cover and returned his fire. The shootout lasted nearly an hour. Finally, as Putnam appeared at a window one time too many, Hamer fired his Winchester. The bullet struck Putnam in the face, careened down into his shoulder and came to rest in his heart. The killer was dead before he hit the ground. The authorities estimated that over three hundred shots had been fired and that Putnam had enough ammunition to have continued the battle.[6]

At about this same time, Captain Rogers wrote a concise and strictly enforced "Rules and Regulations Governing Company C, Ranger Force." It had four components:

> 1: Men, upon entering the service, are required to procure a good outfit consisting of horse, saddle, Winchester, six-shooter, rope, and bedding. It shall be maintained in good order continuously as long as they remain in the service.
> 2: Each ranger is required to perform his full amount of camp duty, such as cooking, herding horses and any and all of the regular routine camp work. This must be strictly observed and any complaint substantiated shall be sufficient grounds for a dismissal from the service.
> 3: Each member of the ranger force is expected to look out for and care for and take interest in the preservation of all State property; and especially the pack saddle, pack blankets and pack rope must be kept hanging together and not be molested by the men for their own use in any way, but in some designated place understood by the men it must be kept so that it may be readily found any time even of a dark night when we might be leaving in haste.
> 4: Men are expected to keep their quarters, at least, in a reasonably clean and neat condition. No one need even apply for a position in this company that is not sober, honest and of a good moral character."

John Rogers finished 1906 in Jeff Davis County in the little rail town of Valentine about a hundred miles west of Fort Davis on the Southern Pacific line. Railroad strikes there had brought violence that the local sheriff couldn't handle. Rogers could and did.[7]

The year 1907 dawned bright with hope out in west Texas as most new years do, fresh and innocent and unblemished. The first four months of that year were fairly routine for John Rogers and Company C, with activity in almost every direction out of Alpine. The most

Rogers and mount at Alpine, 1906. Courtesy Charlie, Lauren, and Carley Reeves, San Antonio

Company C in informal pose at Alpine, 1907. Courtesy Charlie, Lauren, and Carley Reeves, San Antonio

surprising news had to be the resignation of Captain Bill McDonald, one of the already fabled "Four Captains." The gregarious and colorful "Cap'n Bill" had made quite a name for himself among friends and foes, and his leaving the Ranger force left only Rogers and John Hughes to carry on the transition from the old Frontier Battalion days.[8]

Captain Rogers leaned heavily on the work of his most trusted men at that time, Frank Hamer, Goff White, W. M. Hudson, Sgt. John L. Dibrell, and C. J. Roundtree—the latter finally returned from his gambling arrests in east Texas. Rogers made several trips to El Paso, investing in more land and in late February arresting a thief there in the city.

But in mid May Rogers was ordered by the newly appointed adjutant general J. O. Newton to remove the company's headquarters to Austin. This was a significant move, leaving the wide-open and empty land of the still-wild west Texas frontier for the capital city itself. In fact their jurisdiction would include an area almost exclusively east of Austin. Rogers may have had some mixed feelings, but Hattie and the children were certainly thrilled at the prospects of city life. The company took two weeks in May to make the move and were rewarded with a complete outfitting of provisions for their efforts and for their new post. The list included new cots, fresh ammo and a stove. Apparently the only one who had trouble with the transition to city life was the redoubtable C. J. Roundtree, who resigned from Company C on June 22. He was replaced by J. T. Laughlin who was soon promoted to sergeant and later served with distinction as a deputy U. S. Marshal.[9]

The day after Roundtree left the service, Captain Rogers was on his way to Moulton, not far from his old homestead, where he arrested two residents for making threats against another and assaulting him, and a third for "whipping his wife."

On the first of August the Ranger companies were reduced to six men, making their work doubly difficult and not for the first time. To make matters worse, in the eight weeks after moving his company to Austin Rogers grew impatient with the peace officers he had met in his new jurisdiction. The stories he heard from citizens not only in Austin but across central Texas chilled him to the bone. What he had witnessed already bothered him enough to make an official comment. On August 20 he vented some of his frustration in a letter to the adjutant general in which he noted that "the lawless element of this section has absolutely no fear of the law. They break out of jails and are taken out of jails by their friends or enemies, it seems almost at will." He continued, "In trials, in the vast majority of cases, the criminals go unpunished."[10]

What John Rogers likely needed was a few days off. He had been traveling thousands of miles almost without let-up for the past three years. He had moved his family twice, just bought a house at 2406 Lampasas Street (also known as Speedway Street) in Austin, moved his own office into the state capital building, and was having limited success adjusting to his new surroundings. A day off with his family would be a pleasant respite.

On Tuesday, August 27, Captain Rogers came home from work before noon. He and Hattie had planned an afternoon of recreation for the whole family. Fourteen-year-old Lucile had her friend Ann Baines from San Marcos in tow, and Pleas had invited a friend named Edward Lincoln along as well. Rogers' son, nine-year-old Lapsley, looked forward to an outing at the old Austin dam. In 1893, three miles west of downtown Austin on the Colorado River, the dam had been constructed of Burnet County red granite and limestone. It had collapsed under the rush of floodwaters on April 7, 1900. Two hundred feet of the middle of the dam had washed down river and the power house adjoining it on the north banks had been severely damaged as well. The structure still stood in its broken state seven years later as city funds had been inadequate for reconstruction.[11]

But a deep-water pool formed just above the dam and shade trees covered the banks on both sides where the hills rose quickly from the water's edge. A bluff of no more than ten feet ran about eighty yards along the banks from the power house and, when the river was high, provided an excellent jumping spot for daring young boys.

Carriage packed with blanket, food, and refreshments, the family headed out from their Lampasas Street home for the thirty-minute gambol to the dam site. Pleas and Edward shared rides on Pleas' pony, racing ahead in the flat areas, returning to joke about the slower wagon. The captain and Lapsley walked some of the way alongside the carriage while the demure young ladies sat for the ride. It was a typically hot late August day in central Texas, a slight breeze struggling to cool the temperature already in the 90s. The breeze seemed to win out as they neared the shaded hillside and the deep green waters of the Colorado.

As the girls helped Hattie arrange the blanket above the bluff the boys took off immediately for the pool above the dam. It was mid afternoon already and the water was refreshing if not all that cool. The two teenage girls sat along the lower banks down from the dam dipping their bare feet in the slow current. The captain and his wife watched from the shade, occasionally rising to walk about and speak to the children as they played.

Lapsley watched the older, bigger boys splashing in a pool out near the middle of the river, the water eddying up around their chests. Not one to admit being younger and smaller he waded out to join them. None of the boys realized that they stood on a gravel shelf that reached out toward the middle of the river. Lapsley took an errant step as he approached his big brother, and suddenly disappeared beneath the surface.

Pleas saw him go under and was at the spot only seconds later. He reached beneath the murky waters, both hands flailing as he tried to grab some part of Lapsley's clothing, or an arm, or anything. But nothing was there. Edward joined in, both of them hollering for help. The captain was in the water in an instant, no time to shed shoes or vest or coat. He waded out to where the two boys splashed about in vain, feeling his way along hoping to bump the soft flesh of his vanished son. Hattie and the girls came to the edge of the river, sobbing and hugging one another, wishing they could do more.

The Captain called for Edward to swim quickly ashore, take Pleas' pony and ride into the city for help. As Edward bounded up the banks Rogers called for him to make for his office and summon the Rangers who might be there, and to send anyone along as he rode for assistance. Edward was on his way in a moment, his alarm sending several men and boys he mnet along his route to the dam. He finally reached the city, and from there a crowd of men on horseback came to the desperate scene.

The heavy weight of wet clothes began to take its toll on Captain Rogers as he searched for Lapsley, and he tired to the point of going under briefly himself. Reluctantly he forced himself to the banks to rest. Hattie met him there and embraced him. They stood that way for what must have seemed an eternity, joined in prayer, joined in diminishing hope.

Then Pleas went under! Hattie screamed and her husband struggled to his feet. But the two girls were faster, stepping out hand in hand into the river. Lucile pushed her way through the slow current to where Pleas had disappeared. She reached under the surface and grabbed a struggling arm, pulling Pleas back to the surface. Her hand firmly gripping her brother, she began to step backward toward the bank. Ann took her best friend's hand and pulled. Then the captain was there, his last strength pulling the three to shore. At last, Pleas lay exhausted on the bank.

Two police officers and two men from the sheriff's department arrived at a gallop, stumbling their way down the bank to the water. Another young man had also arrived and he leapt into the water and swam with strong strokes out to the middle of the river. Repeatedly he dove under and felt about in the shadowy current.

Six o'clock. It had been nearly an hour since the boy had gone under. The young man—one of the sheriffs called him Lloyd, gave a shout. Edward Lincoln was a stride away and slipped underwater. They came up together with Lapsley's lifeless body held between them. There was no hurrah from the banks, only silence. Everyone stopped where they were, frozen with the realization no one had dared even whisper.

Captain Rogers moved first, wading out into the Colorado, still in his soaking wet suit. He took Lapsley in his arms, turned and carried him slowly, reverently, to the river bank. No one made a sound. Hattie stood a step away, grief overtaking her. Rogers laid his dead son's body on the ground, paused for just a moment to issue a silent prayer, then stood straight and looked at the gathered crowd. In a voice gripped with horror and yet deep with serenity, he said:

"The Lord giveth, and the Lord taketh away."

As doctors broke from the crowd and knelt beside the boy, Rogers walked away, never turning back to look on the tragic scene. Hattie finally broke down in uncontrollable sobbing and was carried back to her home by the girls. Pleas and Edward walked alongside the ambulance wagon that had been sent out from the V. O. Weed funeral home and now carried Lapsley home, to Lampasas Street. Young Lloyd vanished from the scene before anyone could thank him for his efforts. The rest returned to the city to spread the terrible news.

The next day the *Austin Daily Statesman* carried the story with bold headlines: Drowning Near Dam. Twenty-four hours after Lapsley had vanished beneath the Colorado's waters a private funeral service was held in the Rogers home, Dr. Josepheus Johnson of First Southern Presbyterian Church officiating. A large crowd of Austin citizens stood outside in the yard and along the street to pay their respects. All of the lawmen who were in Austin at the time were there to support the Ranger captain in this tragic moment. Lapsley was buried in the Austin cemetery. On a tombstone engraved and laid there later are these words beneath Lapsley Harris Rogers' name: *Our darling boy Safe in the arms of Jesus.*

As far as family and friends recollect to this day, Captain Rogers never spoke of the incident again for the rest of his life.[12]

The death of his youngest child dealt a terrible blow to John Rogers, one that severely tested the resilience of his faith. No one would ever know what thoughts careened through his mind, what shudders broke his heart again and again. Hattie never spoke of his having nightmares, the other two children never related any remark that their father might have made about the tragedy. On the Sunday that followed Lapsley's funeral the Rogers family sat in the Presbyterian Church pew and worshipped. The captain continued to teach a Bible class when he was in town and led the congregation in prayers when asked. On the trail he carried a small Bible given him by a Christian men's organization called Fishers of Men; perhaps he held it closer to his breast as he rode. He read the Scriptures to convicts and peace officers alike by the flickering campfire light or in a hotel room in any anonymous town. Some called him "the praying Ranger." A

Del Rio men's Bible class wrote years later that Rogers "never missed an opportunity to testify to the saving grace of his Saviour, his influence a real blessing and a heart to heart talk with this Man Unafraid like a soft spoken benediction."[13]

This life-changing experience, compounded by the loss of his brother at too young an age, and his mother recently as well, perhaps even an unwitting reminder of the untimely death of his father so many years gone by, rather deepened his faith by all accounts. Whatever churned inside him never broke the surface of his calm attitude. He never wavered in his resolve to be a man of the law and a man of God in his every waking moment. The depth of his faith overmatched the depth of the river that had taken his boy.

Within two weeks of Lapsley's death Captain Rogers rode the train out to Trinity County where word of a gambling ring deep in the Piney Woods had alarmed local authorities. Nearly the entire company went along and within a few days the ring was shut down, its leaders arrested and jailed.

On October 1, 1907, an Anglo citizen of Nacogdoches was murdered and a another local citizen, a Black man named Doc Bailey, was arrested. Bailey's trial began immediately and reached its second day with the jury's decision a foregone conclusion. Racial unrest inside and outside the courtroom turned quickly to mob activity—who saw no reason to wait out the trial nor the thirty-day waiting period for a hanging. Authorities sent word and the Rangers were called in. The situation seemed potentially more dangerous than just simple guard duty, so Adjutant General J. O. Newton went there with Captain Rogers. Several sheriffs from neighboring areas also joined in. Ranger John Dibrell accompanied his captain and a young recruit named J. C. "Doc" White went along as well.

On the evening of October 5 the three Rangers stood guard outside the jail as a mob swelled into the streets and headed their way. Rogers cradled the specially built bent-stock rifle in his arms, his demeanor calm as ever on the outside, yet alert to every movement. Dibrell and White stood at his shoulders, their rifles at the ready. The others created a cordon around the jail where Doc Bailey sat in the gathering darkness.

John and Hattie Rogers, Pleas, Lucile, and little Lapsley. Courtesy Texas Ranger Hall of Fame and Museum, Waco

The noise grew as the crowd reached the front porch of the jail-house. None of the Rangers had moved a muscle, their eyes set on the trouble that faced them. A. J. Hadley, a former sheriff in Nacogdoches, stepped out of the swirling mob and on to the first step of the jail porch. The crowd behind him bolstered his courage for this confrontation with the Ranger captain. Hadley said in a voice loud enough to evoke cheers from his supporters that he intended to march inside that jail and retrieve the Negro who needed hanging right then and there.

His voice so alternatively quiet to Hadley's that only the two Rangers could hear what he said, John Rogers told Hadley that he needed to stop right where he was. But Hadley had come this far and the mob was urging him on. For a moment he lost his presence of mind, and stepped forward past where Rogers stood.

In a motion so smooth that no one caught its significance, the captain had his Winchester over in his left hand, his six-shooter out of his holster and in his right hand. Rogers snapped the butt of the revolver on the crown of Hadley's head, drawing blood, and the mob leader sprawled onto the porch. The mob gasped as one and some moved forward. The two Rangers calmly pulled their Winchesters into a position directed right into the crowd. The mob halted, then began to step back.

Rogers gave an imperceptible nod and his men dragged Hadley inside the jail, depositing him in a cell next to where a shaken Doc Bailey sat. The captain asked, in a remarkably polite voice, that the crowd to go home, and they did. The other peace officers kept their station as Rogers stepped inside the jailhouse to look after his new prisoner. Young Doc White met him at the cell door. Hadley sat against the stone wall moaning, his legs sprawled out on the floor, blood from the skull wound tracing tiny rivulets down his face.

"Hm," Rogers mused. "I only meant to tap him."

Private White shook his head. "Cap," he said, "if that's what you call tappin' a man I would hate to see one who was really hit."[14]

CHAPTER 11

End of This Trail

Not only have yourself and your men received the universal commendation of the citizenship of this county, but the entire Ranger service has been greatly raised in the estimation and good will of the public here by the examples furnished by the deportment of yourself and men.

District Judge James Perkins to Captain Rogers, Center, Texas, September 1, 1908[1]

But it had not been easy. Company C found that it could hardly get out of east Texas for the trouble that continued to start up there, more and more of it racially motivated. Just a few weeks after the incident in Nacogdoches, Rogers reported that he and members of his company had tracked three men "who were hunting Negroes" after an incident near San Augustine in which a White man had been gunned down. The Rangers captured the three assailants and put them on trial, but a biased jury of their peers and several perjured witnesses ended the proceedings with a hung jury. The men were released.[2]

Late in June, 1908, Frank Hamer made his way to Beaumont where racial attacks had escalated beyond the scope of—or perhaps with the assistance of—local authorities. Two Black men had been arrested and put in jail but a growing mob gathered in the Beaumont streets to take justice into their own hands. Hamer secreted the two prisoners out of the jail after dark and hid them in a barn. Some of the crowd actually poked around in the barn during the night, with Hamer and the two men hidden and quiet, and then moved on. The Black men were safe, the trial went on without incident, and Rogers commended Hamer's "presence of mind, coolness and courage" during that dangerous incident.

Company C registered investigations, arrests and other activity in Angelina County, Lufkin, San Augustine, Floresville, and Hempstead during the first half of 1908. Rogers was in Beaumont in June and arrested three men for perjury including a local judge. That same month Oscar Latta and Frank Hamer brought down a San Augustine gambling ring with the arrest of twelve men.[3]

On the downside of all this activity, Rogers could hardly afford to lose any of his men. There were only seven in his entire company, thanks to the tight legislative budget and continuing suspicion in Austin that the Rangers had become antiquated and no longer useful. But on September 1, 1908, John Dibrell resigned from the force and three months later Frank Hamer left the Rangers to become Navasota's city marshal. His appointment actually came from Dibrell's recommendation; the city of 3,000 had experienced nearly uncontrolled violence for three years with over a hundred citizens killed. When the most recent of many inept or scared marshals hung up his badge after only one week on the job, Hamer took over and eventually brought law and order to the town. It was a tough loss for Rogers and the Rangers, but Hamer would wear the Ranger badge again.[4]

Captain Rogers left the haunts of his east and central Texas jurisdiction briefly in November, 1908 when he was called to San Diego to oversee the elections there. Peace reigned during the week with his presence, although he did make one arrest of a drunk for disorderly conduct.

Back home by the middle of the month, the captain was honored at the First Southern Presbyterian Church in Austin, his family's house of worship for the year they had lived in the capital city, with the title of ruling elder. This was a prestigious leadership position that Rogers took very seriously and included his stewardship of a campaign drive that resulted in the purchase of a new parsonage for Pastor D. N. McLauchlin and a new Sunday School building as well. When Dr. William A. McLeod became the church pastor in 1912 he wrote about Elder John Rogers: "He was a man of singular devotion to the Master's work. Any preacher who had ever had him as an auditor could not soon forget the eagerness with which he caught every word. He was a man of unflinching courage in the line of duty, but tender and gentle in his dealings. He and his devoted wife and children made a strong force in the church." Bestowed with the same title of church elder that Sunday morning was Thomas Watt Gregory, a friend of Rogers, fellow "dry" Democrat and future attorney general of the United States.[5]

In February of 1909 trouble seemed to be concentrated in San Antonio where word of a huge gambling ring in the Mexican neighborhoods brought Company C to investigate. Rogers came along on this one with his new sergeant J. T. Laughlin and Goff White. On February 13 after several days of investigation the Rangers were ready to bust the ring. That evening they walked into the neighborhood and to the saloon and warehouse where the gambling was just starting up for the night. The three peace officers surprised sixty members of the ring and proceeded to shut down the festivities. At the point of their Winchesters, they ushered the large gang of prisoners out into the street. It was some ten blocks, however, to the city jail and trouble began almost immediately. Crowds of Mexican citizens began to gather around the scene, marching alongside the wary Rangers, shouting and bumping and finally enveloping some of the prisoners.

By the time the Rangers reached the main streets of San Antonio and the city jail, only twenty-seven of their prisoners were still in custody. The rest had simply disappeared into the sympathetic crowd along the way. One who hadn't been so lucky was Planton Sanchez, the ringleader of the gambling operations. He would stand trial. But in August another report of illegal gambling brought M. E. Bailey, Hall Avriett, and J. L. Anders from Company C back to San Antonio. Disguised as innocent farm boys looking for a good time, they found themselves in the midst of a gambling party being held upstairs over the old Washington Theatre. Pulling their guns, the three Rangers arrested thirty-six more. They managed to get all of them to the jail that night.[6]

In between the two gambling raids Captain Rogers had been busy as well. In May with the rest of his company engaged all across east Texas, Captain Rogers spent ten days in Tyler guarding prisoners at a trial being held there in district court. In late July Rogers took an extended leave of absence to be with his family in Austin, but on August 7 he was on his way to Galveston on business. There he met Adjutant General Newton and four other Rangers to investigate reports that the Sunday closing "blue laws" were being ignored by many of the local merchants on the island. Whether they cleaned up their act when they heard the Rangers were coming, or whether it had been a rumor, the lawmen found no evidence of that crime being committed. A local gambler, however, was arrested and eventually sent off to state prison for running a ring on the island city. Never one to miss an opportunity, Rogers attended the Presbyterian Church there on the Sunday he was in town.

On September 1 Rogers took the train to Trinity County, where he had been on several occasions before, this time to investigate an incident involving a man named W. E. Collins. Bailey, White, and Avriett went along. On September 5 Rogers and his men confronted Collins and his seventeen-year-old son at their cabin. The two men refused to come out when called by the Rangers and a dangerous standoff ensued. At the calm entreaties of the Ranger captain, the two suspects came out, but with their guns raised and ready. A brief shootout took place, Rogers' Winchester spitting fire and bringing both men down. Collins was dead, his teenage son badly wounded.[7]

On October 12, Rogers received a rather startling telegram from the governor's office. President William Howard Taft was traveling to El Paso to meet with Mexican President Porfirio Diaz and a security escort was needed. Rogers took the train out west and spent four days alongside the entourage which included the Texas governor and the adjutant general. It was a brief encounter with two heads of state but a foreshadowing of things to come, both for the two nations and the Ranger captain. Brewing rebellion all across Mexico had caught the

Ranger Force, Company C, in Austin, 1909. Courtesy Charlie, Lauren, and Carley Reeves, San Antonio

attention of both countries and this meeting was intended to show a good faith relationship between Diaz and Taft. But its objective would not come to fruition. Revolution south of the Rio Bravo was now only months away. And Rogers himself, and the Texas Rangers as a whole, would be at the center of much of this controversial period for the next decade.[8]

Captain Rogers finished the year 1909 somewhat anticlimactically with a December 20 arrest of Bill Adams up in Jasper where the captain reported the man had been "making himself very disagreeable in the hotel." In fact, the drunk Adams had been firing off his pistol in the hotel lobby all evening and scaring the daylights out of its patrons and staff.[9]

The news of an upcoming Austin celebration to be held on April 6 no doubt brought tears, not smiles, to the family residing at 2406 Lampasas. Reconstruction of the old Austin dam had been completed after nearly three years of work and an all-day party was planned. Thousands came to see the new edifice that stretched across the Colorado River three miles from the city. Souvenir programs were distributed and refreshments were plentiful. Games and races for the children took place in the nearby park; the fifth race of the day was for boys between ten and fourteen years old. Without the tragedy of 1907 the dam might not have gained enough attention to be rebuilt at all. And young Lapsley Rogers might have enjoyed that spring Saturday with his family.[10]

But life moved on. With Dibrell and Hamer gone, and Laughlin becoming Austin's city marshal, as well as the resignation of Goff White and the promotion of M. E. Bailey to captain of Company B in March, 1910, Rogers was left with a company with very little experience. J. L. Anders was promoted to sergeant. Thankfully the first quarter of the year passed rather quietly, but in April things heated up once more for Company C. In Austin Rogers arrested two burglars, one vagrant and an escaped convict, all in a period of only a few days. The next week he was in Rosebud where equipment and supplies stolen from an Elgin warehouse were being "auctioned" off by the thieves. Rogers arrested them and several members of a local gambling ring at the same time.

Before April was over, however, Rogers was on his way to Hempstead to help Waller County Sheriff J. J. Perry quell a very dangerous situation. The captain got there only hours too late. A "sensational shootout," as he described later, had occurred at the Hempstead depot leaving three men dead and three others wounded. One of those injured was the sheriff's younger brother. At Perry's request, Captain Rogers escorted the young man by train to Abilene after he received medical care in Hempstead. The wounded man suffered from epilepsy and had been visiting his big brother during a brief furlough from the epileptic colony out in west Texas. Rogers does not report how the younger Perry became involved in the gunplay. [11]

In mid July, 1910, street riots in Navasota took place after Frank Hamer had left that area. Captain Rogers went with Hall Avriett to restore order. On July 18, two Italian immigrants stole a horse and buggy during the melee and made a break for it out of town. Avriett commandeered an automobile on the main street and took out after them. Twelve miles south of town the Ranger caught up with the fugitives. A gunfight erupted on the dusty road and one of the escapees was killed by Avriett, the other captured and returned to the city jail. It may have been the first recorded car chase in the history of the Texas Rangers.[12]

In late July racial violence erupted in Palestine in northeast Texas and the Rangers were called in three weeks later. A Black man named Abe Wilson had been accused of killing a White man and was now a fugitive somewhere near the town. Mobs roamed the countryside hunting him. While restoring order and reining in the mobs, the Rangers' investigation turned up a White man named Budge Wyse who was the actual murderer. Wyse was arrested by Rogers on August 2 and the violence died down. O. N. Rogers, a Palestine citizen but no kin to the captain, joined Company C a month later as a result of these activities and became a steadfast lawman at Rogers' side in the year that followed.

The next two months were somewhat quieter. Rogers took a leave of absence and spent nine days in El Paso "on personal business," as he reported. This likely included the purchase of more property but may also have been an opportunity to visit with U. S. Marshal Eugene Nolte, a long time friend who had grown up in Guadalupe County not far from the Rogers homestead. Such a visit may have included conversations about the growing dissension just across the border where President Porfirio Diaz' government had suddenly found itself on precarious ground. There might even have been talk of a future situation that might include Rogers working with or for the marshal.

Back to work after the extended leave, Rogers arrested T. J. Tumlinson in Pleasanton on September 29 for being drunk and carrying a concealed weapon. In October the captain took another brief leave to be in Guadalupe County and back at the old homestead for six days. But in November the Rangers' duties became active and dangerous once again.[13]

Captain Rogers stayed in Brownsville for the first week of November to keep order during elections. By November 13 he was in Crockett attending and testifying at a trial against a defendant from the Palestine troubles earlier that year. From Crockett Rogers traveled by rail on a long journey out west to Rock Springs in Edwards County to investigate the mob murder of a Tejano named Antonio Rodriguez. He took two of his men with him. What they found at Rock Springs must have shocked them, an incident of mob violence as sickening as any they had seen before. Preliminary reports of the viciousness of the original crime and the subsequent attack against the perpetrator were such that Adjutant General Newton requested a detailed report from the Ranger captain.

"I find that the mob which committed this crime consisted of a crowd of Americans estimated at from fifty to one hundred men," wrote Rogers on December 3, "and that possibly seventy-five men stood near and about the jail when the [alleged murderer] was taken out, and that twenty-five actually participated [in the retribution]."

"On November 2 at about 4:00 P.M. the Mexican Antonio Rodriguez hitched his horse at the front yard gate of L. K. Henderson's ranch twenty-eight miles north of Rock Springs, took his Winchester off the saddle, taking same into his hands,—went to the back yard of the house where Mrs. Henderson was on the back galley of said house. It is believed that he asked for something to eat, but Mrs. Henderson not understanding the Mexican language, and being alone, was naturally alarmed, and a small child who was there said her mother simply told him to *bomus* [*vamoose?*]—"Go;" whereupon he shot [Mrs. Henderson] twice, killing her instantly. His actions proved he was of unsound mind."

A Mexican woman in the vicinity heard the shots and saw Rodriguez ride into the woods. She went to the authorities and reported what she saw. A posse went out the next morning in search of the killer. Eighteen miles south of the Henderson ranch Rodriguez stopped at a house to ask for food. The rancher pulled a rifle and held the suspect until others arrived and took him back to Rock Springs. When asked at the jail why he had killed Mrs. Henderson, Rodriguez is purported to have replied, "She talked ugly to me."

"About 4:00 p.m. that afternoon," Rogers continues in his report to Adjutant General Newton, "the mob crowded around Sheriff Pope, seized hold of him, overpowered him, took his pistol and jail keys, overpowered or overawed his deputies also, - unlocked the jail, took out Rodriguez, marched him about one-half mile south of the court house, tied him to a tree with a chain, piled wood around him, each member of the mob putting a stick of wood so as to be implicated together, [and] sent for Mr. Henderson."

At that exact moment L. K. Henderson was attending his wife's funeral at the town cemetery some miles away from the mob scene. When the messenger arrived the service was temporarily suspended and Henderson rode to the scene where Rodriguez was chained to the tree. Rogers continues, "[Henderson] poured the kerosene oil and touched the match which burned to death Antonio Rodriguez. After that he returned to the grave of his wife and the final burial services."

Later in the report he wrote that Henderson was "finally in the last analysis responsible for the burning of Rodriguez. The mob was simply carrying out his wishes and according to my best information [he] could have stopped it with a word." Justice of the Peace J. L. Lockley's findings, however, were less sure: "The deceased [Rodriguez] came to his death by burning at the hands of persons unknown to me. The body was found by me in a bed of red-hot coals, still burning." Rogers' subsequent statement sums up the frustration of his investigation being thwarted by a righteously indignant mob and its leaders: "It is wonderful," he writes sardonically, "how universally the crime is endorsed." The Ranger report finishes with a list of nearly fifty names of those who most likely participated in Rodriguez' death, none of whom were ever prosecuted.[14]

A thousand miles away events were creeping toward Texas that would soon change forever the borderlands as well as the Texas Rangers. The four decades long rule of Mexico's Porfirio Diaz was on even shakier ground, and a mild-mannered man from a wealthy Chihuahua family was advocating a democratic form of government for Mexico. His name was Francisco Madero. With his philosophical leadership and his San Luis Potosi Plan as an inspiration, people began to flock to his ideals. A revolutionary army, of sorts, emerged under the command of Venustiano Carranza, Alvaro Obregon, Abraham Gonzalez, Pascual Orozco, and Francisco "Pancho" Villa. Widespread violence was only weeks away and the borderland communities would find themselves on the front lines.

At Nuevo Laredo a band of guerrillas gathered in the name of Madero's revolution in mid-November. They crossed into Texas and set up camp. The authorities in Laredo called for the Rangers to keep the peace. John Rogers never had a chance to get home following the Rock Springs incident, and instead took the train directly to Laredo arriving on November 22. There he met with Calvin G. Brewster, U. S. Marshal of the Texas Southern District since 1906, and also with Francisco Mallen, Mexican consul for the Diaz administration. U. S. troops were on hand as well.

Scouts indicated that the revolutionaries' camp was situated at or near the Minero coal mines about thirty miles up the river from Laredo. Brewster, Rogers and a company of troops made their way to the vicinity but the army had no orders to engage the guerrilla soldiers. Word came on November 24 that Pancho Villa and his men had now camped across the Rio Grande and not far away. Captain Rogers, at the behest of the other authorities, rode into the *villista* camp and paid a visit to the revolutionary leader. Reports of their conversation are no longer extant but the gist of the meeting was to promote peace along the border. Gathering anti-Diaz troops would be counterproductive to good relations in that region, Rogers no doubt insisted. Villa, on the other hand, was hardly sympathetic to any plea for peace.

Later that evening the American authorities rode on to Minero without the army, arriving at an abandoned camp just past sundown. The guerrillas were gone, having moved on. A report that Madero himself had been spotted only fifteen miles up the river sent scouts that way but without success. Of more importance came a report that some of Diaz' troops were now in the northern Mexico area hunting Madero and Villa. Again Rogers took the lead, riding over to Hidalgo to visit with a Mexican army Colonel Molino stationed there. Nothing came of the meeting. Rogers spent one night in Palafox and then returned with Brewster to Laredo. By November 29 he was on his way home.[15]

The captain had not been home but two weeks when word came that the Mexican consul Mallen had been assaulted while traveling in El Paso. J. O. Newton wanted Rogers there right away. The fourteen-hour train ride deposited the weary Ranger in El Paso on December 19. He spent six days investigating the incident and much of that time soothing the irritated Mallen who was threatening to sue the U. S. government for not protecting him. The situation finally in hand, Rogers headed home, missing Christmas with his family.[16]

But 1911 presaged even more revolutionary activity with or without Rogers on the scene. Abraham Gonzalez came to El Paso in January and set up a front for the revolution on the fifth floor of the Caples Building downtown. His primary goal was to purchase arms for Madero's growing army. There were plenty of merchants in west Texas eager to help. The Bannerman Arms Company out of New York shipped supplies through the Shelton Payne Company in El Paso, where guns and equipment were secretly sold to Gonzalez and then smuggled across the border.

The revolution was edging nearer to American soil. U. S. Army Brigadier General J. W. Duncan reported that "in a conservative census eighty percent of the Mexicans on both sides of the river and a majority of Americans along the border were insurgent sympathizers" supporting Madero. Marshals Brewster and Nolte for their part reported a figure of ninety percent but noted it was "impossible to procure evidence that they are rebels." Whatever the precise percentage, the ingredients for foment were more than sufficient to boil over, and soon.[17]

In Austin an exhausted John Rogers contemplated his future. A dedicated Democrat and devoted prohibitionist, he had actively supported Judge Cone Johnson of Tyler in the just-completed gubernatorial campaign. But Johnson had lost to Oscar B. [for "Budweiser" some opponents wagged] Colquitt in the Democratic primary race and Colquitt's subsequent election over the nominal Republican candidate greatly disturbed the tea-totaler Rogers. Support for the "dry" stand would now be in jeopardy in Texas. More importantly the criminal element would be even more difficult to constrain if Texas did not prohibit the sale of whiskey. "Whiskey is to blame for the majority of all crimes," Rogers was wont to say.[18]

Of no surprise but aggravating nonetheless was the continuing lack of family time for the head of the Rogers household. With Lucile getting ready to turn eighteen and Pleas two years behind her, Hattie needed her husband nearer if possible. College decisions were not far away either.

John Rogers had served in the Texas Rangers since 1883 and as captain for nearly two decades. He had just celebrated his forty-seventh birthday. Perhaps it was time for a change. And perhaps a series of conversations with Marshal Nolte over the preceding months had made an impact as well.

On January 9, 1911, the captain traveled by train to Bellville to attend a trial and give testimony if called upon. He returned home two days later. On January 20 he reported that he had sent three men to meet Captain Hughes in Post City between Lubbock and Snyder to give testimony at a "white cappers" trial. *Las gorras blancas* came out of a secret order of Mexican laborers in New Mexico, lately San Miguel County, organized in response to the incessant and massive land grabbing schemes of Anglos across the Southwest. Although they claimed a loose connection with the national Knights of Labor organization, the white cappers associated with the fence cutting and livestock thievery in the Texas Panhandle were often no more than common criminals.[19]

On January 29 Rogers was called to San Antonio to investigate an incident involving an armed and dangerous fugitive. When he arrived he was told by local authorities that the man had barricaded himself in a building at one of the army posts. Rogers went to talk him out. The fugitive was armed with a shotgun and swore he would use it if anyone tried to come in after him. Surely the captain recalled the Cotulla saloon keeper in those next few moments. But he went in, talked the man into surrendering, and stepped outside with the man disarmed and handcuffed.[20]

It was the captain's last action with this company.

Two days later, on January 31, 1911, John Harris Rogers resigned as captain of the Texas Rangers. And hardly skipping a beat or missing a day's work, he accepted a position as deputy U. S. Marshal under his old friend Eugene Nolte out in the Western District. His responsibilities would be primarily to deal with the revolutionary activities brewing along the upper Rio Grande and to assist the local authorities curtailing the smuggling that was on the increase.

He would be officed in El Paso and his family would soon move there with him. Rogers rented two rooms in the home of widow Margaret Merrill at 1108 North Florence where he and Hattie and Pleas lived for just over a year. They then moved a few blocks to a home at 304 East Rio Grande in 1912.

Lucile Rogers did not go to El Paso with her family. She went to college instead. The Texas Presbyterian College for Girls opened in 1902 in Milford, a small community between Hillsboro and Waxahachie that had put up a twenty-five thousand dollar bid along with ten acres of land for the privilege of having the school. By 1911 the school proudly claimed four buildings and nearly forty acres of campus. Every young woman was required to take two years of Bible classes along with her other studies under the auspices of the school motto: "Christian Women for Christian Homes." Unable to pay its own way with tuition alone, the school depended on the subsidies provided by various synods of the Presbyterian Church. Some of these substantial gifts came from Austin's First Southern Presbyterian Church and individuals like Ranger Captain and Mrs. John H. Rogers. They, of course, were immensely pleased that Lucile chose to attend college at Milford, even though they surely missed her during the two years in El Paso.

A new era of law enforcement had opened for John Rogers and new environs for his family.[21]

CHAPTER 12

Deputy U. S. Marshal

Perform, in conjunction with the military forces stationed along the Mexican border, such patrol duty as may be necessary to prevent violations of the neutrality laws, and in proper cases to arrest persons caught in the act of violating such laws. . . It is proper for your deputies and the military forces to make appropriate inquiry in connection with the arrest of persons engaged in violating the law, or where it is believed that the law is being violated at or near the place where such deputies or military forces are operating.

This February 21, 1911, directive from the U. S. attorney general's office instructed the marshals along the Texas-Mexican border to be pro-active in their watch over the escalating border troubles. It granted them broader powers than they had before, but still the protection of the 2,000-mile line was nearly impossible. Even with the addition of customs inspectors and armed forces, and deputies like former Ranger John H. Rogers who knew the territory so intimately, the challenge was formidable to keep the peace, stop the smuggling, and intervene in the coming revolution.[1]

Upon taking his new position working for the federal government in law enforcement, Deputy Marshal Rogers knew he was walking right back into the heat, this time the heat of a revolution. The great west Texas historian C. L. Sonnichsen put the borderland passions into his own words: "They rose. The first to do so were easily suppressed, but the movement spread across the country like a prairie fire. First Chihuahua was a focal area. Then El Paso moved into the center of the revolutionary picture. It could almost have been called the headquarters of revolutionary Mexico and the Sheldon Hotel was practically the capitol building. South El Paso—*Chihuahuita* [Little Chihuahua] they called it then—sheltered dozens of organizers, agents, undercover workers, exiles."

Marshal Nolte kept a close eye on the movements of the revolutionaries. Only one month before Rogers had taken on his duties in El Paso his boss reported, "My representatives along the border are alert, closely in touch with the situation, investigating all rumors of gatherings of supposed revolutionists. We have found no evidence of any violation of neutrality. There is good reason to believe that many Mexicans have crossed the border from this side, but not in large bands."[2] That was about to change.

On February 1 a report came to Nolte that Colonel Rabago was marching government troops into Western Chihuahua while rebel leader Pablo Orozco, himself a native of that state and absolutely confident within its environs, had been spotted only ninety-four miles south of Juarez. In less than forty-eight hours Orozco and his troops were on the outskirts of the city. Merchants and citizens of Juarez, fearing the inevitable confrontation, poured across into Texas by the hundreds. For their part many El Paso citizens began to line up along the river's edge to get a glimpse of what they thought would be a glorious battle.

But this battle would not take place, not now. The *federalis* marched to the smelters at the edge of town but then retreated from the site. The *insurrectos* found themselves low on ammunition and unable to get into the city for supplies, and Orozco moved his forces off to the south after a brief skirmish. John Rogers arrived in El Paso during this interlude and assisted law enforcement in keeping order among the now-disappointed El Paso crowds who had come to see something more. Francisco Madero arrived in the city at about this time as well, secreting himself there for several days before crossing into Mexico on February 14 to join his revolutionary army. For the next two months the uprising slowed, with several minor engagements in the mountains of Chihuahua that resulted in some casualties, including the wounding of Madero.

On April 15 word came that Madero was headed for Juarez once again. This time he had the troops and the supplies to lay siege to the Federalist forces garrisoned there. But before a battle could erupt word came from Washington, D.C. that a truce was being offered to negotiate a peace between the main parties of the escalating conflict. The truce took effect on April 23 and lasted for two weeks. Diaz sent Judge Francisco Carbajal as his representative, Dr. Francisco Vazquez Gomez arrived from Washington to participate, and Pino Suarez joined Madero at the peace commission. Most of the meetings took place along the Rio Grande near Hart's Mill in a lush valley that thereafter became known as Peace Grove. Madero and Suarez stayed at the Sheldon Hotel in El Paso during much of the negotiations. Rogers and several others alternated as security for all of the principal parties. Hordes of the curious and the international press crowded the city streets forcing additional law enforcement. The U. S. army remained in the vicinity.

On Sunday, May 7, the negotiations broke down over the issue of Diaz' immediate resignation prior to any new election. Madero left. Orozco and Villa took this to mean that the battle was on despite Madero's later entreaties. By Monday noon a forward company of revolutionaries had attacked at the edge of Juarez. The Battle of Ciudad Juarez lasted three days with the rebels soon overwhelming the Federalist garrison. General Juan Navarro surrendered the city on May 11. Porfirio Diaz was soon on his way out of the Mexican presidency and off to Europe, to be succeeded by Francisco Madero. This stage of the revolution had been victorious.

In El Paso the battle across the border caused chaos in the streets, necessitating twenty-four hour work by Rogers and peace officers of every rank and station. Hundreds of families from Mexico surged into the relative safety of the Texas town. But hundreds of El Pasoans again sought a front row seat to watch the battle in Juarez. Stray bullets whizzed overhead, striking walls and chimneys and even the boxcars upon which many of the witnesses sat. At the Union Depot near the Madera lumber plant the crowds came directly into the line of a crossfire. By the end of the three-day battle five American spectators were dead and fifteen wounded.

Escorted with the tightest security by the U. S. Marshal and his officers, the triumphant Madero entered El Paso after vanquishing the Federalist troops and took up temporary residence once more at the Sheldon Hotel. Dignitaries from both cities hosted a victory banquet at the Toltec Club as Rogers and others kept close watch over the proceedings and the eager crowds that milled about outside. On May 20 Madero assembled his troops, gave a rousing farewell address, and headed for Mexico City. The first phase of a protracted war was over. El Paso was quiet again, but not for long.[3]

Intrigue in San Antonio during 1911 kept law enforcement vigilant as General Bernardo Reyes conspired to lead his own army into Mexico where he believed himself to be as popular as Madero. He was wrong on several counts in his plan and after several futile efforts gave up any thought of pursuing his objective.

Of more concern was the infighting of now-President Madero's confederates, especially Orozco, Villa, and Victoriano Huerta. Unable to get along with each other except in battle, and feeling unappreciated and unrewarded for their efforts to put Madero into the presidency, the loose association broke down. Madero for all of his idealism and grand principles proved unable to operate the Mexican government with any success and the necessary diplomatic support from the United States began to unravel. Ambassador Henry Lane Wilson made little effort to conceal his lack of confidence in Madero and both the Taft and Wilson administrations kept their distance.

On February 9, 1913, the "Ten Tragic Days" began, a bloody coup that ended with the execution of Madero and the emergence of Huerta as Mexico's president. Huerta proved to be incontestably worse than either Madero or Diaz, and the revolution that had shown such prospects in 1910 became a ruthless battle of war lords for two more years. Venustiano Carranza's triumph, and the immediate recognition of his coalition government by U. S. President Woodrow Wilson's administration, brought an uneasy peace to Mexico City by 1915. Pancho Villa carried on his own peculiar brand of revolution—or was it banditry?—along the Rio Grande until 1917, necessitating the futile intervention of U. S. troops under General J. J. Pershing.

El Paso had seen some of the worst of the fighting from the perimeter, had played host to presidents and aspirants and media alike, and had overworked its law enforcement agencies throughout the ordeal. Merchants and gamblers, photographers and mercenaries, diplomats and smugglers, all had found a place to stay or pass through during the revolution waged just across the river.

Refugees from Juarez and a dozen small villages along the border made their way into El Paso during that time. In Chihuahuita conditions deteriorated to abysmal levels, with disease and crime heightened by the overcrowding. This *barrio* became essentially unmanageable by city authorities and the Second Street boundary with the Anglo neighborhoods became fixed, the refugees and poor on the South Side forced to contend for themselves amidst abject poverty. Perhaps its only silver lining was the writing of one of the refugees, Mariano Azuela, whose novel *Los de Abajo (The Underdogs)* became the printed clarion of the Revolution.[4]

The U. S. marshals in Texas worked under the special provisions of legislation passed by the Taft administration to protect the borderlands during the trouble in Mexico beyond the standard and often vague neutrality statutes. The Act of March 26, 1910 provided for the deportation of conspirators and provisions to "prevent the territory of the United States being used as a base for a military expedition against the established government in Mexico." In March, 1912, the Congress passed a law prohibiting the exportation of arms and munitions into Mexico. This allowed federal authorities to go after smugglers with much broader powers of arrest and deportation. In Arizona as in Texas this still didn't solve all of the problems, however, as one authority noted: "The exporting of any arms or ammunition is not generally done through any port of entry, but is generally carried over by small parties miles away from the towns and where there is no deputy stationed." Cavalry units soon took up the patrols instead of the infantry.[5]

In tandem with these laws was the U. S. Criminal Code which made illegal any activity that "provides or prepares the means for any military expedition or enterprise to be carried on from thence against the territory or dominions of any foreign province or state or people . . .with whom the United States are at peace."

Additional legislation provided for a cooperative effort of border patrols involving marshals and U. S. troops. In south Texas Marshal Calvin Brewster added customs inspectors and deputies to his staff, with his men "cooperating with the military in the capacity of guides, and continually working as an independent body patrolling the river front from its mouth," an area of over 600 miles.

The Texas Rangers participated in the border activities as well, although there was some concern that the politically charged "Special Rangers" might be inadequate to the task. The adjutant general received one letter that claimed these Rangers had been "recruited from the parlors and colleges of Texas" and "were of the picture show variety and used for politics only, unfit to be trusted with firearms [and] unable to follow Indians on trail unless it was as broad as an improved automobile road." Such criticism was generally unwarranted and specifically untrue when related to the regular force.[6]

On October 7, 1911, Deputy Marshal John H. Rogers brought one Guadalupe Gonzalez in after a patrol along the river. In his report Rogers noted that Gonzalez had been detained while "unlawfully returning to the United States after deportation under 'Section 3. Act of March 26, 1910.'" Several months later Rogers recorded the arrest of a smuggler named Luis Luna Villalobos, again arrested under the new and broader provisions of the law.

The headlines in the November 17 El Paso *Herald* celebrated the arrest by the marshals and customs inspectors of smugglers caught near Douglas, Texas, in possession of 2,500 opals that had been brought in at the El Paso point of entry. Evidence proved that the jewels were to be used for the purchase of munitions intended for the revolution.

On April 13, 1912, Deputy Rogers arrested the De Leon bothers for "unlawfully hiring men to enlist as soldiers in service of a foreign people." Only four days later Rogers arrested Allen Rogers [no relation] and John Thomas for attempting to "smuggle munitions to the war in Mexico." These two turned out to be leaders of a ring of smugglers and by the end of April, the deputy had reported the smashing of the ring including the arrest of eight more arms smugglers. In addition and as a result of his continuing investigation, Rogers arrested three Tejanos on April 18 for bringing Chinese laborers into the United States, a violation of the Exclusion Act.[7]

The jailhouse filling up because of Rogers' activity, the federal judge ordered some of the alleged criminals sent to the federal prison in Leavenworth, Kansas, until their trials could be scheduled. Rogers escorted four of the men, including one Frank Green who had been arrested for forging federal documents, to Leavenworth in May.

At the same time Rogers was performing his duties with aplomb and the veteran expertise of a former Ranger, there were abuses along the border patrols as well. An article in the April 10, 1912, El Paso *Herald* reported that L. E. Ross, an operative for the U. S. Secret Service cooperating with the local authorities, had been employing Mexican spies on both sides of the river who were "using harsh and harmful tactics" in their attempts to gain information about smuggling activities. With complaints from citizens in both countries as well as local mayors and sheriffs, the article reported that Ross and his superiors had agreed to "let up" on their practices.[8]

Rogers was busy again in the fall of 1912, breaking up another ring of munitions smugglers and arresting thirteen in late September, hauling in five more smugglers on October 5, and jailing Canuto Leyva on October 10 for recruiting mercenaries. A second trip to Kansas in mid-October resulted. Rogers left on the train with his prisoners in tow on October 17, one day after arresting Blas Noche for transporting - not munitions into Mexico but prostitutes into Texas.[9]

"There are more liars in El Paso than in any other place I ever saw." So said Mayor Charles Morehead in reference to a squabble over gambling laws in his city in 1904. The opposing sides on the gambling and drinking issues had proven to be resilient and constant in their bitter dispute that still simmered when John Rogers came to El Paso in 1911. When he wasn't chasing smugglers or patrolling the vast territory of the upper Rio Grande, the deputy had his hands full with the politically charged domestic issues of the growing west Texas metropolis. As an arch-conservative himself on these issues, Rogers intended to be especially diligent in his enforcement of the anti-gambling laws and local prohibition.

On November 20, 1904, the anti-gambling forces won a huge, but as it turned out temporary, victory when over 4,000 denizens of immorality were forced out of town; many crossed into Juarez to take up their business there. The triumph short-lived, gambling and drinking crept back into El Paso three weeks later and stayed. The reformers, led generally by the local ministers and the temperance groups, kept up their struggle to rid El Paso of sin, but they were opposed by a defiant and powerful ring of enterprising Democrats who saw economic opportunity in the saloons and gambling dens.

One of the "Old Guard" Democrats was C. E. "Uncle Henry" Kelly, grandson of an Irish immigrant, raised in Mississippi and owner of a local El Paso pharmacy. Kelly served as the city's treasurer from 1902 until his election as mayor in 1911, after completing the unexpired term of W. F. Robinson who died in a construction accident in 1910. Kelly's years with a political hold on the city's coffers resulted in his leadership not only of the city but of "The Ring," a political machine of which he was Boss. Though never involved in any expressly illegal activity, and unquestionably progressive when it came to city improvements during his tenure, according to El Paso's biographer Sonnichsen, Kelly "ran his show his own way and he believed in controlling rather than suppressing vice." For over a decade Kelly and Morehead represented the two opposing sides of the powerful Democratic stranglehold on the Paseo del Norte. The reformers and the Republicans shouted from the sidelines.[10]

When the Mexican revolution broke out all around him, Mayor Kelly proved up to the task of keeping order, at least to some degree, and admittedly better than most would have been able to do under the chaotic circumstances. Sonnichsen relates a telling episode: "When Pancho Villa appeared at the Sheldon Hotel bearing pistols and announced that he was going to shoot Guiseppe Garibaldi, grandson of the Italian liberator and leader of a group of foreigners in the revolutionary army, the mayor did not send the police. He appeared in person at the hotel and told Pancho to put up his guns and go home. Pancho did."[11]

The gamblers, brothels, and saloons kept up a thriving business with all the newcomers to the city during this time, and Kelly managed to keep the businesses running above board for the most part while at the same time staving off the railing reformers. The two-story Coney Island Club and Saloon stood next door to the Sheldon Hotel and kept a large clientele for years. The Gem Bar and the Parlor Saloon never lacked for customers regardless of the law. Two of the most infamous madams in the city's history, Etta Clark and Tillie Howard, died in 1909 and 1911 respectively, but their houses continued operations at Utah and Second Streets, on "the Line." Opponents of the red light district in the 1913 elections claimed there were 367 "night-life women" operating down on the notorious Utah Street and that "the demand for girls was yet exceeding the supply!"[12]

One of Kelly's loudest antagonists was H. D. Slater, editor of the El Paso *Herald* who had come to the city paper from Washington, D. C., in the late 1890s. The occasional victories of reform championed by Slater, the latest being the removal of the racetrack to Juarez in 1909, kept his voice loud and clear on behalf of cleaning up the city. "If we have to fight the fight all over again," wrote Slater in early 1912, "let's go to it. We can't start any sooner."[13]

One of Slater's supporters was John Rogers. As Ranger captain the conservative Democrat had known the newspaper editor for twelve years before moving to El Paso himself as deputy marshal. The two had become strong allies in the fight against immorality and had sat together at rallies held at the Presbyterian Church on several occasions. One of the local laws that Rogers considered inviolate was the Sunday closing or Blue Law. In the gambling district the Sunday closing of saloons and joints was haphazard at best and not tightly enforced by the mayor's people. In addition, liquor was often sold, albeit discreetly, on the Sabbath as well, a practice particularly abhorrent to Rogers.

In Slater's Wednesday paper of July 13, 1911, there was a news article that reported a fund-raising event, but one of a distinctive nature. The saloon owners were raising money against the prohibition movement. The article said each owner was pitching in fifty dollars to the "cause."

On Sunday morning, July 17, four days later, Reverend Jeff Ray, pastor of El Paso's Trinity Methodist Church, stepped up into his pulpit to face his morning congregation. From beneath his black robe he produced two bottles of whiskey, raising them above his head as the congregants let out a collective gasp. Following a dramatic pause for effect, Ray proceeded to tell the story of the bottles bought just that morning at a local saloon by the preacher himself. He reached beneath the pulpit and produced several more bottles of liquor, identifying the city or county saloon where he had purchased each over the past several Sabbath mornings. It was a remarkable moment, making the papers on a very prominent page and galvanizing the reformers to action.[14]

Throughout the two years of federal service in El Paso John Rogers had maintained his earnest faith, regularly attending church services and men's Bible classes. His reputation for devotion spread across the diverse city and earned him the respect of men and women of every class and station. The polite, quiet-spoken deputy could often be seen in the city streets and business establishments, and was likely often mistaken for a local preacher by new folks come to town. But his demeanor, as always, belied the resolute character beneath the surface, and anyone who thought to cross him or confront him soon found themselves sorry for the effort and usually behind bars.

One of the most important days in all of 1912 for John Rogers was Election Day, the first Tuesday in November. Undoubtedly the deputy marshal cast his ballot right down the Democratic line, with Woodrow Wilson at the top of that list in his run for the presidency. It was a day of surprising victory for Wilson. For only the second time in Rogers' life there would be a Democrat in the White House. The dramatic and highly entertaining three-way race between the incumbent Taft, former President Teddy Roosevelt, and the New Jersey Progressive Wilson had ended with the most unexpected of returns, for few believed that a Democrat governor could unseat a president and beat a former chief executive. But Wilson did just that.

A lame duck president now, William Howard Taft began to "clean out his office" during the sixteen week interregnum. Included on that politicized agenda would be the removal of Democrats in offices held across the national spectrum and replacing them with Republicans before the March 4 inaugural. This age old practice traced back to the Andrew Jackson years and even the Federalists' "midnight judges" scheme, putting political allies in office in the last days before leaving power.

Eugene Nolte, Democrat and U. S. Marshal of the Texas Western District since 1906, was removed on November 30, 1912, and immediately replaced by Republican Bert J. McDowell. McDowell in turn appointed Charles Stevens as his deputy assigned out of El Paso, replacing John Rogers. In the time it took to count votes in a national election, Rogers had helped send a Democrat to the White House and then lost his job.[15]

The unemployment proved short-lived. Except in unusual circumstances, most of the interregnum appointees would be out soon enough as the new administration "set things right." As one scholar put it, "The marshal's office remained one of the last plums, and politicians used it to pay off political debts, reward loyal followers, and earn future favors." In fact, Marshal McDowell resigned on February 25, 1913, succumbing to the inevitable, and was replaced by an interim officer, Rogers' former Ranger sergeant and friend John L. Dibrell. Dibrell had served the Rangers after leaving Rogers' company and also served as city marshal during the intervening years. Dibrell would remain in the office for one month.

Meanwhile Rogers along with several of his colleagues and fellow peace officers worked hard to keep his name in contention for the permanent appointment that would soon be made by the Wilson staff. By the first of the year there were twenty other candidates actively campaigning for consideration. Success would entail a statewide canvass of support, petitions, and letters of recommendation. Rogers took the inside track on the nomination when both U. S. senators from Texas, Charles A. Culberson and just-seated Morris Sheppard, placed Rogers' name on their lists.

Other high-powered names chimed in. When Austin Judge Z. T. Fulmore asked for an endorsement of Rogers from "Colonel" Edward M. House, the presidential advisor and Democratic power broker responded that, although he had already committed to Emmett

White for the position, "There is no man that I admire more than Captain Rogers and if he can obtain the place I shall be entirely satisfied."

Rogers wrote his congressman asking for support, and Uvalde representative and Democratic party whip John Nance Garner wrote back: "We Congressmen are supposed not to interfere in the appointments with suggestions etc., but if [the senators] should approach me for my views, I will have no hesitancy in saying that I believe you would be acceptable."[16]

At the same time petitions and letters went out from Tyler to El Paso and from Amarillo to Brownsville, asking for help to keep Rogers in law enforcement. Edwards County came in with fifty-nine names, and El Paso County added seventy more. Mason County added dozens more and San Patricio County contributed ninety-eight names in support. Rogers had letters of recommendation from the Eckols family in Luling as well as other homestead neighbors such as Robert Jacobs, Clay Nickols, and Robert Payne. Amarillo's chief of police J. F. Speed wrote in, as did Odessa Sheriff S. A. Kelley and Austin's police Chief J. T. Laughlin, a lifelong friend of Rogers.

The list had two hundred names not including those on the several petitions. The postmaster from Millett, the mayor of Alice, and the justice of the peace from Austin wrote on behalf of John Rogers. So did the commissioners of the El Paso County Live Stock Association, a county clerk from Corpus Christi, a professor from Sul Ross College, another from the University of Texas, and Henry C. Evans from Milford's Presbyterian School for Girls where Lucile Rogers was preparing to graduate. Nineteen on the list were attorneys, seven were physicians, and ten were judges. Brigadier General Edward Steever wrote from his headquarters at Fort Bliss. The letters came from Sweetwater, Hico, Snyder, Itasca, Barstow, Eden, Vernon, Center, Yorktown, and Claude.[17]

John R. Hughes, the last of the "Four Captains" serving with Company A out of Ysleta, wrote: "There is no man in this State who is better acquainted with conditions on the Mexican border than Capt. Rogers. As a peace officer his record is that of duty faithfully performed. Under the most trying conditions he has shown good judgment, tact and courage. Added to his splendid qualifications as an officer he is a high minded, honorable, Christian gentleman, and one who has been faithful to every trust confided in his care."[18]

Frank Hamer, already known across the Southwest for his courage and skills in law enforcement since being recruited by Rogers years earlier, wrote: "He [Rogers] has handled many difficult and dangerous situations such as have arisen, and unfortunately for many years to come will continue to arise, on the Mexican border." Hamer added in his January 10 letter, "Capt. Rogers is personally popular, and his appointment if he obtains it will have the universal endorsement of all good people within the state."[19]

Perhaps most telling on the list were the twenty-nine ministers who added their endorsements for Rogers. It is unlikely that any peace officer in Texas would have been able to count on the religious community for support, but Rogers had made a unique and powerful impact across Texas with his Christian witness and constant devotion. Presbyterian churches in every corner of Texas had seen the mustached officer appear on their doorstep, huge white hat in hand and pistol on his hip. His pastor from the church where he still held membership, Dr. William McLeod from Austin's First Southern Presbyterian, headed the list of recommendations. Pastors from Dallas, Beeville, Galveston, Ballinger, Van Horn, Edna, and Mineral Wells contributed letters of affirmation. And J. T. Robertson, chairman of the Presbyterian Home Missionary Conference in Paris, Texas, wrote a recommendation as well.[20]

It was an overwhelming vote of confidence made especially powerful with its distinctive variety of voices. And it had telling effect. On March 22, 1913, word came from Washington, D.C., that President Wilson had appointed John H. Rogers as Marshal of the Western District of Texas. He was to assume his duties on April 3. Oddly, the reorganization of the marshal districts in Texas, from three to four as an Eastern District was added, transferred the headquarters from El Paso to Waco.

John Rogers, who had been the first native Texan of his generation to serve as a Ranger captain, now became one of the first former Texas Ranger captains to serve as a U. S. marshal, his old friend Bill

McDonald being appointed to the Northern District a few days later. One editorial lauded the appointments noting that both men "are known throughout the breadth and length of Texas as fearless Ranger captains . . . and it goes without saying that they will make good U. S. marshals."[21]

A rare photo of a clean shaven Rogers, 1913. Courtesy Center for American History, Austin

CHAPTER 13

U. S. Marshal, Western District

After giving due credit to all loyal friends who stood by me so nobly and endorsed me so unqualifiedly, I nevertheless attribute my success to Almighty God, whose I am and whom I serve and to whom I solemnly pledged if He would favor me for said position, I would use the office for His glory, which pledge I now ratify, relying upon Him for His help and guidance. It is my desire that what additional influence I might have by reason of my office shall be used for Him.

This, the 3rd day of April, 1913, the day I assumed the responsibilities of the office.

J. H. Rogers, United States Marshal[1]

In 1913 the Western District of Texas encompassed a massive amount of land—over 115,000 square miles in a narrow rectangle—and was divided into six subdistricts: Waco as the headquarters, Austin, San Antonio, El Paso, Del Rio, and the new Pecos office added on February 5. As one of his first duties in office Marshal John H. Rogers assigned Charley Burks as chief deputy, J. T. Thompson, J. D. Platt, and C. S. Rogers as his deputies, and added his former sergeant John

Dibrell as well. Burks had a career in law enforcement but was plucked from the state House of Representatives in 1913 where he served as sergeant-at-arms. Fred Peck, James T. Johnson, Early Wilson, and Arley V. Knight would also serve under Rogers in the years that followed.[2]

Rogers moved the headquarters of the district twice during the early period of his tenure in office. By the end of 1913 he had moved from Waco to San Antonio, and a year later he was back "home" in Austin. He commuted between the latter two cities for most of the next seven years—by train since he did not own and never in his life drove an automobile. In Austin, where Rogers preferred to do most of his work near home, the marshal's office was housed in Rooms One and Two of the Federal Building downtown.

Hattie and their son Pleas moved with the marshal from El Paso to Waco, and from San Antonio back to the Austin they loved and where Lucile was residing by that time. In 1915 Rogers purchased the vacant two-story house at 1200 San Antonio—on the northwest corner of that intersection—where his family would live for the next seventeen years. Both Lucile and Pleas attended The University of Austin in 1916 and part of 1917. On April 30, 1917, Lucile married Charles Mills Reeves at the First Southern Presbyterian Church on East Eighth Street. Pastor William Minter performed the ceremony which was one of the social highlights of the spring in Austin.[3]

Significant cases awaited the new U. S. marshal even though most of the work involved bureaucratic paper shuffling and the vapid filing of reports. The office of U. S. marshal had become primarily a coordinating position over the previous twenty-five years, delegating the actual investigations and arrests to deputies. Official job descriptions noted that marshals were "the executive officers of the Federal courts" and "the local disbursing officers of the Department of Justice," hardly exciting for anyone who had been out in the field before. One interpretation said that "marshals simply served process and paid bills."[4] It would have been quite a change for the ex-Ranger and his activities of the previous decades. Still, the opportunity to be closer to home was not without its benefits. And at age fifty Rogers looked forward to at least some slowing in the expectations of his job.

Chief among the marshal's duties in his first two years were actions brought against Mexican revolutionaries who had conspired while in the United States or had recruited fellow soldiers here. Emilio Vasquez Gomez, Francisco Madero's lieutenant and vice-president, was the defendant in a suit brought by the attorney general on January 9, 1913, only days before Rogers took office. The case would drag on for the next six and one-half years despite the efforts of law enforcement on the U.S. side of the border.

Another conspirator, Nicanor Valdez, was named in Case #167 for 1913 for committing acts against the U. S. neutrality laws. This case had originated on Bert McDowell's desk on February 19 and was handed over to Rogers. Rogers filed his first report as a marshal, *United States v. Valdez* on March 17; a second filing is noted that June. Extremely busy with the revolutionaries still active, cases #168-174 are all for the same crime. On October 15, revolutionary General Joaquin Maass, Jr. was brought up on federal charges for "preparing a military expedition in the United States to be used against the sovereign nation of Mexico."

Two years later as the revolution in Mexico continued to spin out of control, Rogers arrested five Mexican nationals in San Antonio charged with "inciting rebellion and insurrection against the United States." Two weeks later Deputy Marshal J. D. Platt arrested Matias Rocha as he fled through Guadalupe County on charges stemming from the same plot.

One of the last of the revolution cases involved none other than Victoriano Huerta himself, who was charged on January 12, 1916, with conspiracy and organizing a military expedition in this country. That case dragged through the courts for two more years. A case involving "conspiracy to sell forged obligations to the Mexican government" resulted in the arrest of five men in June, 1916.[5]

But not all the cases within Rogers' jurisdiction focused on the revolution unfolding to the south. The first case handed over to the new marshal by his boss, U. S. Commissioner R. L. Edwards, was dated April 10, 1913, and brought against an American citizen named William Brady. *U.S. v. Brady* charged the defendant with "the manufacture of opium for smoking purposes." Deputy John Dibrell arrested

Brady in San Antonio and hauled him into the federal courthouse. Brady pled not guilty but could not post bond and was deposited in the Bexar County jail until the next stage of the trial began.[6]

The cases piled high on Rogers' desk and quickly. In the next few months he reported on arrests of alleged criminals on a variety of charges, from interstate prostitution to impersonating an officer of the United States army. Rogers' office investigated an obscene letter that had been intercepted at the post office, and followed the trail of smuggled horses toward the Mexican border. The latter case was certainly a circumstance familiar to the ex-Ranger. Several cases involved peripheral revolutionary-related crimes including the exporting of munitions from the United States, and at least one involved the extradition of a murderer from one federal district to another.

On April 13, 1914, J. M. Hall and Thomas Eagan broke into the post office in Fredonia and stole bundles of letters in search of cash, bearer bonds, and such. Fredonia is a small town located on the boundary of three counties in central Texas—San Saba, McCulloch, and Mason—and about twenty-five miles southeast of Brady. A federal warrant was issued. Rogers sent Deputy James T. Johnson on their trail. The two criminals were apprehended by Johnson only days later and brought in to face judgment. Only a year later M. K. Ross was arrested for robbing a post office in Tehuacana in Limestone County. In an almost identical circumstance two and one-half years after that Deputy Johnson brought Andrew Brooks in after he had absconded with mail from the post office at Marble Falls.[7]

The Mann Act established federal regulations for what was commonly called "White slavery," the placing of women in conditions equivalent to slave labor and prostitution. The White Slave Traffic Act, as it was officially known, passed June 25, 1910, making the trafficking of women "for immoral purposes" a federal crime. On May 18, 1913, Marshal Rogers arrested Floyd Davis in San Antonio charged with such a crime. Davis' trial was prosecuted successfully by District Attorney J. L. Camp. Two years later a White slave ring operating in the San Antonio area was busted by Rogers and his deputies. Five were arrested and later convicted for their organized efforts.[8]

In the off year national elections of 1914, the U. S. marshals kept vigil over any illicit activities to fix elections or voting fraud. Mike Niland was arrested in July, 1915, seven months after an investigation gathered evidence that he had been involved in the fixing of results in Nueces County the previous November. The summer of 1915 also witnessed the arrests of counterfeiters, embezzlers, and several other persons accused of fraudulent practice against the United States government. That year Rogers' deputies investigated crimes in Gonzales, Taylor, San Marcos, Caldwell, Georgetown, and Bastrop.[9]

One of the best investigators John Rogers had ever known was Frank Hamer, the Ranger recruited by Rogers so many years before. In 1916 the Texas Cattle Raisers Association asked the marshal for his recommendation of someone who could assist in the investigation and apprehension of cattle rustlers; Rogers immediately thought of Hamer. "Mr. Hamer is one of the most active [Ranger] officers I have ever known," Rogers wrote in his letter of recommendation. "He is absolutely void of fear, and while he is not an educated man, he is bright and intelligent, very industrious and a splendid detective. He was raised and grew up in the West," Rogers continued, "and when I first enlisted him he was a typical cowboy. The harder the criminal and more dangerous and hazardous the work, the better he likes it. I have never recommended a man for this position that I recommend so heartily and unqualifiedly as I do Mr. Hamer." In something of a postscript Rogers added, "Hamer is a live wire beyond a doubt, and the lawless element stand in awe of him wherever he has worked." Hamer was offered the job and he took it. Rogers had at least one more recommendation he would make for this industrious Ranger a few years later.[10]

In 1916 tragedy visited the Rogers family once more when word came that Emrett Rogers, son of John's deceased brother Kid, had passed away in Alice. Ill with pneumonia on his fifteenth birthday, the young man had died two weeks later on September 2 and was buried in the Alice Cemetery. John and Hattie consoled the boy's grief-stricken mother Bettie and her two daughters.

The Harrison Act was passed by Congress on December 17, 1914, closing down one more of the dependency drugs—morphine—that infested American society during this era. Until this law the manufacture and sale of morphine had been legal; now it required specific prescription from a licensed physician. For federal officers this law increased their duties in the drug dealing community. Over a week's period in late November, 1915, Rogers and his deputies brought a long investigation to a close in San Antonio with the arrest of four drug dealers in possession of opium, heroin and cocoa leaves. Although the subsequent search of the building where the purported sales were taking place turned up no evidence, the case was eventually successfully prosecuted.[11]

The U. S. Marshal was responsible for investigating peonage law infractions as well. Special Agent R. L. Barnes of the Federal Bureau of Investigation office in San Antonio received word in the summer of 1915 of a landowner in Limestone County named Michael Bochs abusing his farm hands as slave labor. On his land east of Waco a young man named George Carroll was employed. Carroll's family in nearby Thornton had written a letter of complaint to the Bureau regarding the treatment of their son by Bochs. The Carrolls were tenant farmers living on the Capps Ranch at the time and had worked the Bochs land in the spring planting ninety-six acres of cotton and eight acres of corn. George Carroll had stayed behind to work through the summer. The letter of complaint indicated that Bochs had driven his farm hands with whips among other abuses. After investigating the situation, Rogers wrote Barnes, "I went over to see George Carroll and he tells me that he is perfectly contented. He is making a crop over there and expects to go to school there this winter. The United States Government cannot help in this matter for if George prefers to stay there he can stay."[12]

Vestiges of the Old West came to John Rogers' desk in May, 1915, when reports of a train robbery arrived at the Austin office. Within a week three men had been brought into jail and were later convicted of the crime. A train robbery of a grander version occurred two years later, the investigation ending with the arrest of a gang of nine men and their prosecution in the district court in San Antonio.[13]

But the vast majority of cases between 1915 and 1918 came because of an event that happened half a world away, an event that changed the history of the United States, and changed the world forever.

On Sunday, June 28, 1914, Archduke Ferdinand, heir to the Austria-Hungarian throne, and his wife Sophie were assassinated in Sarajevo, Bosnia by a nineteen-year-old Serbian nationalist named Gavrilo Princip. Within five weeks, because of the intricate web of political and military alliances formed across Europe over decades, the "Great War" had begun. Every major industrialized nation joined in the worldwide conflict, all except the United States. For nearly three years the U.S. managed to steer a delicate but neutral course away from the world war. President Wilson kept fierce vigil on American neutrality, even through his reelection in 1916, only to have it all collapse with the interception of a telegram. The startling threat of the Zimmermann Telegram, decoded in February, 1917, pushed the United States into the war.

Even before the United States walked into World War I, however, the first alarms were sounding in Texas. The intimidating offensive of the Kaiser storming across Europe brought a xenophobic reaction

Rogers *(second from right)* in U.S. Marshal's office at Austin, 1915. Courtesy Charlie, Lauren, and Carley Reeves, San Antonio

in the states where German-Americans became vicariously suspect. And subversive German activity in and out of Mexico made Texas especially vulnerable and that much more alert.

On May 29, 1915, Marshal Rogers arrested Herman and Otto Schempff in San Antonio for purchasing guns from U. S. soldiers at Fort Sam Houston, their apparent plot to move those guns into Mexico where German agents were at work encouraging a Mexican alliance with the Kaiser.[14]

By early 1917, with American involvement in the war all but inevitable, the U. S. Attorney General's office prepared to launch special provisions for wartime investigations and due process. Rogers' long time friend Thomas Watt Gregory now served as attorney general. Gregory's assistant attorney general Charles Warren reported that the 1798 Alien Act appeared to be still enforceable but that it "was an entirely inadequate way of dealing with this problem. Germans and German sympathizers in the United States intend to commit widespread crimes of violence at the very outbreak of war," Warren continued, and the government needed appropriate legislation to empower the marshals to "arrest all Germans in this country who, from our investigations during the past two and a half years, are known to be leaders, or particularly dangerous or able men, in the German propaganda. . . . We need to break up the German plans at the very outset and in the first two days after war is declared."[15]

Gregory went right to work on Warren's proposal, issuing an alert to all marshals to be vigilant for German activities in their districts and ordering city police chiefs across the country to do the same. Gregory sent a proclamation to President Wilson for his signature, a document giving federal enforcement the right to make "summary arrests" for the purpose of internment or deportation processes as necessary. This proclamation drastically restricted enemy [German] aliens in this country from possessing munitions, radios and ciphers, or from being on or near forts, arsenals, ships or shipyards, and factories. The new regulations were to be coordinated with the War Department.

On April 2, 1917, Wilson addressed the joint session of Congress and asked for a declaration of war. On April 6 he had it. The same day Gregory mailed a letter to every U. S. attorney and marshal. It said in part, "No German alien enemy in this country who has not hitherto been implicated in plots against the interests of the United States, need have any fear of action by the Department of Justice as long as he observes the following warning: keep your mouth shut." By the end of the week sixty-three German aliens had been arrested. By June the number had reached 295 and by November, 600 more. By the end of the war in 1918 over 6,300 German sympathizers had been placed in internment camps around the country.[16]

As an integral part of the clamping down of anti-American activities as the war got underway, a mandatory registration was established for both German and Austrian-Hungarian aliens living in the United States. Failure to register on February 4, 1918, meant arrest and internment. 260,000 men registered on that February day and an extension to foreign-born women added 220,000 more in June. Likewise, the registration of American males age eighteen and older— the draft—went into effect in the spring of 1917. Anyone dodging the draft—"slackers" as they were called—would have a deputy marshal on his door soon enough.

Marshal John Rogers had his marching orders for the Western District of Texas. The war also took on a very personal note when his son Pleas joined the army in the spring of 1917 and marched off to war. Pleas would serve proudly and with distinction in the war and begin what would become a life's career in the military.

The first case to be investigated landed on Rogers' desk two days after President Wilson asked Congress for a declaration of war against Germany, a good example of how prepared law enforcement was to swing into action as the moment arrived. Dr. G. S. Miller of tiny Gause, Texas, in Milam County east of Cameron, gained Rogers' attention when complaints came from an O. D. Baker of Calvert indicating Miller's public conversations of "threatening, abusive and inflammatory language directed against President Wilson and the Federal Government with reference to the embroglio [sic] with the German government." His language had been "particularly abusive, obscene and threatening," Baker wrote to Rogers on April 4. Miller worked at the telephone company out of Gause and his "presence and control of the switchboard might be dangerous to the successful operation of the military forces of the country." As a postscript to his report Baker added, "We must muzzle these loud-mouthed pro-German sympathizers or we will have a good deal of trouble right here in our own state."

Rogers, who was at that time working in El Paso on other district business, wrote Bureau investigator R. L. Barnes five days later: "I suggest that you investigate this matter. In case this man Miller has gone as far as Mr. Baker reports, the telephone company should be advised of his conduct, and he should be removed from the position he now holds." A few days later Baker sent another letter to the marshal's office making additional complaints about Dr. Miller. Rogers wrote a second note to Barnes asking him to please investigate the matter: "The assistant U. S. attorney concurs," wrote Rogers.

Investigator Barnes took the Sunset Central train out of Waco on May 30 and arrived in Calvert to look into the accusations against Miller. He spoke with Baker, who turned out to be Calvert's newspaper editor and admitted that what he knew about Miller was hearsay. Barnes continued on to Gause by automobile that same evening. The next day he spoke with J. T. Fullmer, a local banker, who quoted Miller as saying that President Wilson "was a god damn hum bug and a damn grafter, and was talking war to let those big northern men graft, and that Germany ought to sink every ship that went over there." Sam Spraggins, a farmer out of Gause, claimed he heard Miller say "that bull shit Wilson was keeping down the price of cotton for farmers." A third testimonial, this time from a Henry E. Graham, said he asked Miller if he would enlist to which Miller retorted, "The idea of my fighting for England is a god damn shame, and I wouldn't enlist because I would not fight for England."

Armed with growing evidence, Barnes spoke to seven more residents of Gause, each of whom finally admitted that they knew Miller was against the war but had never heard him say much of anything else about the subject. But Barnes also learned "that Miller was a very peculiar chap, always contrary to everyone else, and not popular. That he also did not pay his school taxes and people did not like him for that." Suspicious of what was beginning to sound like scurrilous claims, Barnes interviewed Dr. Miller personally. "I told him he had been quoted as saying only bums and tramps were enlisting. He said he was a loyal American," Barnes wrote Rogers in his report, "and had recently tried to get into the Medical Reserve Corps but was turned down in Dallas. He said he was a native of this country from Illinois and absolutely against a monarchical government such as Germany has and is decidedly for this country."

Barnes made his conclusions. "Fullmer and Baker owe Miller money. The complaints had been worked up [also] because Miller exposed the graft in the school fund [of which Baker had apparently been a participant] which had been hushed up. It appears that the local squabble has a whole lot to do with this matter, and after talking with the man himself and others, I do not see that this man had done a thing since war was declared with Germany." That ended the matter.[17]

The same day Marshal Rogers received the letter from Baker setting off that investigation he also read a letter from Fred Long, sheriff in Hillsboro. Long was concerned with a small community of Germans who lived in the county and one man in particular named Schronk who seemed to be rousing "the Negroes and the Mexicans to go to Mexico" and work for German agents there against the United States. Long had spoken with a "reliable citizen" of that county who had followed a Mexican traveling between Waco and San Antonio apparently as a courier for the Germans. [Long did not expend much effort over the Mexican's name, which he spelled "Wauloopie Campus."] Two of Long's deputies were "hard at work" doing their own investigation and a plan was being formed. "We are sending a Negro tonight to see Schronk and try to get hold of the papers he wants them to sign." He closed his report, "I am sure that you are worried to death with a lot of dope that does not amount to anything. But I had rather save some of that kind than to let something get by and then be sorry for it." Rogers determined that Long was right; this dope didn't amount to anything.[18]

Of more significance, Rogers sent Deputy Platt to Maxwell, Texas on June 1, 1917, to arrest C. T. Schaine, a German-American on charges of "aid and comfort to enemies of the United States." On August 1 one Henry Schroeder was arrested in Austin for "inciting subordination and mutiny" at an army outpost in San Marcos, and two days later his cohort R. E. Dorris was also brought in.

Draft dodgers—"slackers"—brought out the law enforcement agencies as quickly as German conspirators. Charles Braun, a special agent of the Bureau officed in the Waco area, kept Rogers apprised of such situations in a stream of letters and telegrams especially in the late summer of 1917. Agent Robert Barnes wrote Braun on August 4 inquiring of the arrest of slackers John Brooks and Oscar Shurn [Shearn?]. Braun did not know of their whereabouts and wrote Marshal Rogers two weeks later. "The sheriff at Georgetown informs me that these men were turned over to "Deputy Early Wilson (but) we are not informed just what was done with them." Rogers responded on August 21: "Brooks and Shurn were brought before the U. S. Commissioner, gave their personal recognizance bond in the amount of $100 for their appearance here next January. Just where these men could be found at this time I am unable to state." However he added that both men had indeed registered shortly after being arraigned in district court.

W. F. Lindemann of Bartlett, brother of the postmaster there, was investigated by Agent Willard Utley for making a statement that "the selective draft was unconstitutional and that if he ever had to go to war he would desert the U. S. forces the first opportunity and go to the other side and fight for the Germans." In Agent Charles Braun's investigation he interviewed Lindemann and filed this report to Marshal Rogers on August 30, 1917: "Lindemann stated that he did not believe in conscription to fight abroad; that if the Germans came over here he was willing to do all the shooting possible. Now that conscription was the law, however, he had made up his mind to give his support of it; that he had one son in the draft age who had registered and who would go when the call came." Braun dropped the investigation, noting his last remarks to Lindemann: "I cautioned him to be careful of his utterances and asked that he give his whole support to this government as a true American citizen."

A second Bartlett resident, a German alien named Theo Dowebeit, was also investigated by Barnes' office for "talking against our Government. As German aliens who make improper talks against the United

States cane be handled so much more easily than naturalized Germans," Rogers wrote to Barnes, "I hope that you will cause this investigation to be made as soon as possible." There are no records in the U. S. Marshal papers that indicate the results of this investigation.[19]

John Rogers got a little crossways with Charles Braun that same August when the special agent apparently took three Mexican-American slackers out of the Austin jail without permission and had them duly registered before the U. S. Commissioner. "Although Mr. Braun was in the office several times yesterday and the day before," Rogers wrote Robert Barnes on August 10, "he never at any time before or afterwards mentioned anything to me of his desire or intention of taking my prisoners out of jail to register them, and left without telling me he had done so. All other agents have shown me the courtesy due from one officer to another in all such matters. . . . Perhaps Mr. Braun meant no discourtesy, but I hope he will be more thoughtful and courteous hereafter," Rogers concluded.

One week later Braun responded to the marshal's concern. "I spoke to Mr. Early Wilson, Deputy U. S. Marshal [before taking the prisoners out], showed him a letter of permission to register the prisoners and he gave me instructions as to accompanying them from the jail. Understanding the circumstances I do not see where I have been discourteous to Capt. Rogers in the least." No more was ever said of the incident.[20]

As the war wound down so too did the investigations related to it. Sixty-nine persons were arrested in late December, 1917, for selling liquor to soldiers and several more were hauled in for breaking the war rationing laws, "hoarding and permitting necessaries to waste and deteriorate." There are a scattering of other cases involving German-Americans and German aliens between 1918 and even as late as May, 1920, when Otto A. von Spaugenberg was arraigned for "attempting to incite insubordination." In July, 1918, three German-Americans were arrested for filing false income tax returns, and Willie Rolff went to trial that month for "making statements in favor of the German government." Rolff was found guilty and fined.[21]

But surely the most sensational of the many investigations were two similar cases, one in 1917 and the other a year later. On August

24, 1917, Alice Hamilton was arrested for "setting up and keeping a house of ill fame, brothel, and bawdy house," as Rogers put it, "within five miles of the San Antonio arsenal [Fort Sam Houston]." Eleven months later Irene Miller was arrested for the same crime at what appears to be the same "house of ill fame," found guilty and fined five hundred dollars, which she paid immediately in cash.[22]

As the war came to an end, John Rogers and Hattie lived comfortably in their home at 1200 San Antonio, enjoyed the social occasions now more relaxed and celebratory in the victory over the Kaiser, regularly attended the Austin Presbyterian Church, looked forward to seeing Pleas back from the war, and made frequent visits to see Lucile and Charles Reeves in San Antonio. John turned fifty-five a month before the Armistice but expressed no thoughts of slowing down or retiring from law enforcement.

On his immediate horizon was another kind of investigation, one that harked back to his past as a Texas Ranger, one that would demand his full attention one day in February, 1918, as he defended his own career, the borderlands brand of justice, and the very future of the Texas Rangers.

CHAPTER 14

The Canales Investigation

Up to the time the Mexican revolution started there was never a more friendly people on earth than the Mexicans on the Mexican side of the Rio Grande and the Americans on the American side. . .But since the revolution against Diaz there have been turbulent conditions and complications from a political standpoint.—A Brownsville resident

I think it was German intrigue that they were hoping to keep up strife between the United States and Mexico, hoping to start the war right there. I think it was the Rangers who started it up.—Virginia Yeager, San Diego

It wasn't the Rangers altogether; it was deputy sheriffs and sheriffs and border guards and the immigration agents and the Department of Justice. I don't think the Rangers were any worse than the lawyers.—Kleberg County Sheriff J. B. Scarborough[1]

In 1917 Frank Cushman Pierce published a book entitled *A History of the Lower Rio Grande Valley.* In its closing chapter he catalogued fifty-two incidents of violence in the Valley in a forty-six week period in 1916. There were nearly the same number recorded again in 1917 and once more the following year. These incidents were far and above the ordinary crimes that authorities investigated in any region. The assaults were related to a growing restlessness brought on by a combination of factors, including a migration of Midwest Anglo farmers into the area, after effects of the Mexican revolution, and German intrigue related to World War I.[2]

The Texas Rangers had been divided into two subgroups during this time—the "regular" officers and men who patrolled the state as they had for three decades; and the "special" Rangers who, as generally no more than politically-appointed gunslingers, meted out their own brand of justice outside the bounds of law. The evidence grew by 1918 that at least dozens of Mexican Americans, and perhaps as many as several hundred, had been summarily executed on no more evidence of guilt than the color of their skin.

On January 28, 1918, a company of "special" Rangers commanded by J. Monroe Fox marched fifteen Mexicans out into the scrub brush of south Texas and executed them. The fifteen had been rounded up after a brutal raid at the nearby Brite Ranch on Christmas Day a month earlier.

During the night of October 5, 1918, Ranger John Edds was awakened in his cot by a man in his custody named Lisandro Munoz, so startling Edds that he grabbed for his rifle. The Mexican did, too, and in the ensuing scuffle Munoz was killed. But rumor spread quickly that Edds had murdered Munoz in cold blood rather than take the time to return him to the authorities.

Other stories surfaced naming Rangers William M. Hanson, J. J. Sanders, R. L. Ransom, John Bloxom, Jr., and others as perpetrators of like atrocities. These *rinche pinche, cara de cinche* [those lousy, stinking Rangers, they'll grab you by the tail] seemed to be systematically eliminating what they perceived to be a problem in the borderlands and with the impunity of those considered untouchable by virtue of gubernatorial appointment and Ranger badge. Their activities were staining the reputation of the Ranger force, but most chose to look the other way rather than confront the sordid situation.[3]

Elected to the state house in 1917 out of Cameron and Willacy counties, State Representative José Tomas Canales of the Brownsville area took on this challenge and began an investigation of the stories he had heard from his constituents over the previous several years, including his own eyewitness accounts when he had personally led scouting patrols in the Valley. In late 1918 Canales levied nineteen charges against the Texas Ranger Force for gross and malicious misconduct, and proposed a bill that would dramatically downsize and constrict the law enforcement agency.

The Canales Investigation brought dozens of witnesses to the stand in January and February, 1919, and, along with the federal investigation that followed under Senator Albert Fall, resulted in the reorganization of the Rangers, though not its elimination. New Mexico Senator Albert Fall met from September of 1919 through the following April with the U. S. Senate's Subcommittee on Mexican Relations, moving from Washington, D.C. to San Antonio January 14 to 24, then to El Paso and San Diego and back to the capitol. Dozens of witnesses and testimonials later, they arrived at much the same conclusion as the Canales investigation. Summarized one witness as the investigations concluded, "We cannot get along without the Rangers but we want character with it."[4]

As a result of the combined efforts of the state and federal investigations, José Canales' primary recommendations became a reality for the Rangers. The force was reduced from eighty to sixty men, and a criterion of "high moral character" was instituted as a requisite to enlistment. Salaries were made more competitive to induce a better quality of law enforcement personnel, and most expense accounts eliminated. The governor still maintained a good deal of authority in the appointment of Rangers, but there were now regulated processes by which citizen complaints could be heard. The mistreatment of prisoners in the hands of Rangers now became grounds for immediate dismissal. In this, both a direct result of the abuses of the previous decade and a prelude to one more administrative change only fifteen years away, the Rangers would be forced to "clean up their act."

Marshal John H. Rogers was called to testify before the Canales subcommittee in Austin on Wednesday morning, February 12. He was examined by Robert E. Lee Knight, a high-powered Democrat and Dallas attorney retained by the Adjutant General's office for the investigation. He was interrogated by two of the state senators and

Canales as well. Rogers represented three decades of Ranger history and tradition, and brought his own brand of calm insight—and some objectivity—to the hearings. He and Canales also shared a propensity toward public Christian testimonials during the course of their careers. The transcripts recorded that morning reveal Rogers' thoughts as he responded to the queries, some sympathetic, others hostile.[5] After the opening amenities, R. E. L. Knight proceeded to the issue:

Knight: During the time [as a Ranger] and now as United States Marshal you have had abundant opportunity to know the conditions along the border country?

Rogers: Yes, sir, I ought to know them.

Knight: Captain, give the Committee your views as to the indispensable necessity for the Ranger service in enforcing law and order along the frontier country.

Rogers: Well, sir, I think it is still needed, especially since conditions growing out of the war, and so on, and immediately before the war it was not so bad, but perhaps there has never been a time since it was organized—

Senator R. L. Williford interrupted, "We don't think the Committee requested that."

Knight responded, "I quite agree with you." He turned to Rogers and continued, "You have been familiar with the organization of the Rangers for the last twenty-eight years. Do you consider the general average of the men engaged in the service now up to the standard of former years?"

Rogers: Well, I will tell you. I haven't kept in very close touch with them for the last six years since I have been in the Marshal's office.

Knight: All right. Now, Captain, in the discharge of your duties as U. S. Marshal you have had more or less contact with Captain [W. M.] Hanson and other members of the organization?

Rogers: Yes, sir, I have met him a few times.

Knight: Did you know Captain Hanson while you were a Ranger?

Rogers: Yes, sir.

Knight: How long have you known Captain Hanson?

Rogers: I expect I have known him twenty years or more.

Knight: He was one of your predecessors in your present office?

Rogers: In a different district, the Southern District.

Knight: Oh yes, in a different district. Well, predicated on your observation and knowledge growing from your association and contact with him, as well as what you have heard others say, tell the committee what your opinion is of Captain Hanson as a faithful, fearless officer, and as a conscientious, earnest citizen and enforcer of the law.

Rogers: Well, now, gentlemen, I will tell you at the outset I would prefer not to go into the personalities of these men. Captain Hanson is my personal friend and I should hesitate to say anything against him if I knew anything against him, and I had rather not answer the question, although, of course I am sworn, and—

Knight: I am going to ask you about a number of the captains.

Rogers: I would rather leave that out; of course, if you absolutely force me I would tell the truth. That does not mean that I know anything definite against Captain Hanson but I would rather not enter into personalities for different reasons, but one is this. I have a river front here of six or seven hundred miles and these boys help me and cooperate with me. They are my personal friends, and even if they were not my personal friends they cooperate with me and I want to be friendly with the Rangers. I don't want this Committee to consider this against Captain Hanson, but I would rather not go into it unless you have me to do it.

Knight: Of course. All right, we will not insist. The Canales bill: are you familiar with its provisions?

Rogers: I have read it.

Knight: It provides, for one thing, placing the force under bond—

Rogers: The bond feature particularly attracted my attention.

Knight: What do you think of that in light of your broad and long experience? What effect would it have, putting these men under bond? How would it effect their efficiency?

Rogers: I think it would destroy their efficiency very largely if it almost did not result in destroying the force.

Knight: Do you think there are too many Rangers in the employ of the state at this time?

Rogers: How many have you?

Knight: I don't know. About 108.

Rogers: Well, I doubt if there is, owing to conditions on the border at this time.

Knight: Captain, do you think that the efficiency of the service would be improved by paying an adequate compensation to the men, giving them an increased salary?

Rogers: Naturally, I do. Yes.

The answer brought smiles to most in the room. Knight began his response, "Do you think, or not, that the—," then stopped and changed course. "Of course we all recognize that the force is not perfect, that every man in it is not perfect, or any of them for that matter."

Rogers chimed in quickly, "And never have been."

Knight asked, "Have ever been since you have known them?"

"No, sir," replied Rogers.

Knight got to his point. "Do you not think that to give power to the captains to select their own men and place their organization under a stronger, military discipline with the Adjutant General only at the head that it would improve matters, whether or not it would go far toward improving the service?"

Rogers replied, "Yes sir, I do. I have in mind a plan." Senator Williford interrupted and said the Committee would be glad to hear it.

Rogers: I have thought for perhaps fifteen years or more, several years before I left the service, that we had too much divided authority in the Ranger business. We had too many heads, little heads, if I may refer to a captain as a little head. [laughter] I was one of them [more laughter], instead of having the power centralized.

"That's it," Knight said. Rogers launched into the aspects of his plan.

"I have thought for a number of years that this force ought to be reorganized and that we ought to have one Ranger company instead of three or four, when I was in, and I guess there are a good many more now, and that there should be one captain at the head of it who ought to be a thoroughly good man and to have commissioned officers under him, such as first and second lieutenants, and non-commissioned officers such as sergeants, and perhaps on down to corporals.

"Then, instead of having a half dozen organizations, the power would be centralized, and there should be a big man chosen for the head of it. Let him select all his men and make him responsible for them; even then he might get hold of a disorderly or bad man but he would find it out quickly and fire him out.

"Now, this safeguard could be put in: the commissioned officers appointed under the generalissimo, or head man or captain, would be brought forward to be commissioned as a first or second lieutenant, and the Adjutant General would concur in them or else they would be dropped altogether. The men that the Adjutant General would endorse would be put up to the Governor and if the Governor commissioned them it would be all right. If not, they would have to bring forward another, and keep nominating men until, to get the lieutenant [chosen to be] the captain, the Adjutant General and the Governor would have to concur on them."

Knight broke in, "Well that is exactly the idea I had with regard to separate companies. Your idea of it is one company separated or divided into squads and not separate companies?"

Rogers: And providing, yes, sir, for good, strong, *faithful* men.

Knight and Rogers reiterated the idea for another minute or so, Rogers expanding on the idea of non-commissioned officers being approved by this process. He agreed when Knight suggested that this concept would accomplish the same as Canales' bonding provision. Then the subject was changed.

Knight: Now Captain, there has been a considerable exodus along the frontier of Mexico since 1914-1915. You are acquainted with that situation, are you not?

Rogers: I have heard a great deal about it but most of it in the other district, not mine, down on the lower Rio Grande. . . . Mine is from Dimmit County to El Paso.

Knight turned to the committee and asked that Judge Dayton Moses, Jr., deliver the next question to Rogers.

Moses: Captain, without going into details, there is some testimony here with regard to one of the Rangers killing a man. In fact, he is under indictment in court, the indictment having been lately found, and it was claimed by the Ranger that he went to this party in the night, or about daylight and he was asleep on a cot and that the cot was close to him; that the Mexican who was later killed grabbed the gun of the Ranger, and it is thought that that might be an unreasonable way for one attempting to make an arrest. Now I will ask you if it is not true that you know of instances where, either through inadvertence or carelessness, careful officers have gotten into that same position many times under your personal knowledge or observation?

Congressman Canales rose from his chair and interrupted before Rogers could respond. "That is absolutely improper cross examination of the witness," he declared. "The inexcusable act of one officer does not justify that of another."

"I am not justifying the killing," said Moses.

"Because one officer does wrong does not make it all right for another officer doing the same thing," Canales insisted, his voice raised.

The chairman of the Committee stepped in. "I think the range that the testimony has taken with regard to these matters has been very broad, and we will admit the testimony." Canales stared hard at the hostile Committee, and sat down.

Rogers spoke. "That sometimes occurs, Mr. Moses. It occurred twice when I was in command of the Rangers in my company, and I thought that I had good, careful men, and I know of two mistakes in the nineteen years that I was captain, if not longer. One while I was a sergeant—I suppose over a period of twenty years—I know of two mistakes happening, not exactly as you related but mistaken killings."

Moses: I am not talking necessarily of killing, but in your experience, Captain, did you ever, through inadvertence or whatever the reason was, ever get yourself in a position where you were disarmed, or anything of the sort?

"No, sir," Rogers responded, forgetting or choosing not to mention his brush with death at the hands of Hilary Loftis.

Moses: Have you ever heard of that as to any other Ranger?

Rogers: Yes, I have heard of a case or two of that kind.

"I think that is going most too far," Williford interrupted.

"That is all," replied Moses as he sat down.

Congressman Canales stepped forward and took up the interrogation, intent on getting the issues back on track. "You mean that the men who make those mistakes are justified in doing it? You think they do right?"

"It is very regretful when mistakes are made," said Rogers. "I mean to say the men are trying to do right. Of course, the circumstances surrounding each individual case would have much to do with that."

Canales: Captain, do you think that a man who is armed by law with a Winchester and a pistol and great big belt full of cartridges, going to an unarmed man on a cot, and kills that unarmed man, do you think that man should be trusted to remain—

"We object to that," Moses jumped in. "If counsel is going to ask that question he should state the whole testimony."

Canales proceeded to give his version of the incident, which focused on Ranger John Edds and his killing of a Mexican whom he claimed had wrested the rifle from him while sitting on a cot. Moses interrupted three times, arguing that Canales was telling the story so as to incriminate Edds. Canales objected, then tried to ask Rogers a question. Representative Tidwell spoke up and argued briefly with Canales. Canales answered back and turned once more to Rogers.

Canales: Do you think that such a man [as Edds] is a proper officer and ought to be in the service and to be entrusted with the lives and liberties of the citizens?

Rogers replied, "I think, in considering whether he should remain in the service that you should take into consideration his former record as to whether he was a sober, good man who might be able to take care of himself under one situation and would not in another. You cannot fix a set rule as to how every man would act under a certain case," explained Rogers. "An officer should use only so much force as is necessary to protect himself, and no more. But just how far that should extend is hard to tell from his viewpoint."

Once more the vituperative committee engaged Canales in an argument about protocol for the testimonies, Canales becoming ever more defensive. Rogers sat calmly in his chair and waited for the questions to resume. After several minutes the Brownsville congressman turned to Rogers and asked about his service while in Alice, his relationship with Captains Hughes and Brooks during that time, and his knowing the Canales family, which Rogers readily acknowledged.

Canales: Did you ever hear of any captain then or any of the other men taking a man out of jail or in their possession and after having them in their possession, shooting them?

Rogers: Absolutely not. Such conduct is a blot on the history of this state, such a thing as that.

Canales asked Rogers about his service as a U. S. Marshal, then pressed on.

Canales: Now, do you believe when a condition exists where the constabulary of a state kills prisoners in their possession, don't you think at least some restriction should be made to safeguard the lives of innocent men?

Rogers: Such conditions ought not to be permitted to continue by any manner of means. It may be that bonded Rangers would be better than none but I think it would hamper their efficiency very much. I think they could be re-formed the way I have said.

Canales: I most thoroughly agree with you, because they have six companies now and that is the reason my bill calls for four and I agree with you as to one company. The bill provides for four companies in time of peace and for a certain number, say five or six in time of emergency, and the Governor is the judge of that emergency and the company may be increased to whatever number the Governor sees fit. You think that is a good provision to make?

Rogers: I think it is all right, so far as the number of men, but the bonding business is the thing.

Canales: When the state is quiet and there is no disturbance or anything, nothing much to do, don't you think they should automatically reduce the maximum number?

Rogers: Yes, sir.

Canales: And when an emergency exists the number should be instantly increased?

Rogers: I think that is all right.

Canales: Now, another feature of the bill provides for high class men, God fearing, high class men to enforce the law: You think that is not an unreasonable provision?

Rogers: Yes.

Canales: That it is unreasonable?

Rogers: What do you mean by God fearing men? You mean that every man on the force should be a Christian man?

Canales: No. I mean that every man should be of good character, of good moral character and good habits.

Rogers: Yes, that is all right.

Canales: The third provision of the bill provides for higher pay.

Rogers: Yes, I approve of that.

Canales: The fourth provision is whenever they arrest a man they should treat him like any other peace officer.

Rogers: Yes.

Canales: Should arrest him and not abuse him.

Rogers: It ought not to be necessary to put that in; that should be a foregone conclusion.

Canales: I agree with you. But when the things exist they should be given attention?

Rogers: Yes.

Canales and Rogers then went back over the bonding issue, with the congressman referring to the Pennsylvania State Police, an organization he believed had been patterned generally on the Texas Rangers but with bonding of its officers. In fact, the Pennsylvania police force is historically more closely related to the Royal Irish Constabulary.

Canales: Do you think that a man who is unjustly killed in his own place of business by State Rangers, leaving a widow and children, that that man should have no redress at all against the State? Don't you think that the widow and children should have some right?

Rogers: Yes, it would be very unfortunate indeed. I would be willing to contribute to such a case. [But] I think it would hurt the force to bond it.

Canales: You think it would be better to leave to charity people under such circumstances than to make special regulations to prevent such matters of that kind?

Rogers: I don't know as to the charity. Possibly we hope that nothing like that will occur.

Canales: Yes, I hope so. But it has occurred, and that is the trouble.

Rogers: But a case like that might never occur but once in twenty or thirty years, and to tie up the whole machinery of the state government, the Ranger force, to take care of something that might never happen—

Canales interrupted, "You say it occurs maybe once in twenty years. Now when these things happen once a month or twice a month, don't you think it is time to undertake to regulate it?"

Rogers saw where Canales was headed with this, but spoke his mind. "Yes, I certainly think so." He then added, "And if it can't be done any other way, why, abolish the force!"

Canales thanked Rogers and sat down.

Knight leapt to his feet and approached the witness, in a rush to negate the damage that may have just been done by Canales.

Knight: Do you know, Captain, during your long experience in and around the border, of *any* corrupt practice by the Rangers that is suggested by the vaporous interrogatories of counsel?

Rogers: No, I do not. I have heard a good deal of *complaint* about his section down there, illegal killings.

Knight: There is a good deal of imagination in Mr. Canales' testimony. I will ask you to state whether or not it is possible that Mr. Canales himself is laboring under an obsession or hallucination regarding the extravagant abuses by the Rangers down there?

There was a flurry of responses from all about the room. Canales objected while others chimed in as well. Knight and Representative W. M. Tidwell argued with Canales. The hearings were nearing chaos. After a moment, however, everyone calmed back down and Knight continued with his questions for Rogers.

Knight: Now I will ask you to state, during the troublous times of the last four years on the border, if we had had no Ranger force or anything to take its place of a similar character, if the widows and orphans would not have been infinitely greater along the border than they are with the Rangers?

Rogers: Well, it looked pretty bad down there, with those raids.

Knight: If, as a matter of fact, the bandits across the river learns from this side of the river, not only from alien sympathizers but native sympathizers, the fact that owing to conditions on this side—they are told that this heroic band, who from time immemorial has defended the frontier, has been placed under the anathema of the people of Texas to the extent that it has been handicapped by a bond.

That was too much for Williford, who called out, "Are you asking a question?"

"Yes, Judge," replied Knight. "Don't you understand that? I thought you were a lawyer." The rancor hung suspended in the air, then dissipated. "I will ask you," Knight said to Rogers, "to state whether or not such information, surreptitiously conveyed over there, would not have a tendency to reintensify the smoldering hatred in the breasts of those bandits against the people on this side of the river?"

Canales rose in objection but Knight, having accomplished his objective by putting such a statement into the record, acquiesced to the objection and sat down. Rogers started up from the witness chair, but Representative Tidwell stopped him.

"How many deputies have you in your [marshal's] office and under you?"

"In the office and field I have ten or eleven," said Rogers.

"Do you put all of your deputies under bond?" Tidwell asked.

"Yes, sir," replied Rogers.

"All of them?" asked Tidwell.

"Yes, sir, even my stenographer."

"Is that a matter you do yourself or do the Federal regulations require you to do that?"

"Well, the civil service regulations have forced me to do it," Rogers answered. "I have to bond anyone who is not in the civil service."

"And your deputies are under civil service regulations?"

"Not now. Two or three of my men were when I took charge, but since I have been in the office they have been replaced by men not in the civil service and those men must be put under bond."

"By the Federal regulations?" Tidwell inquired.

"Yes, sir," said Rogers. "And I would do it anyhow."[6]

CHAPTER 15

Chief of Police

After one year from the ratification of this article the manu-
facture, sale, or transportation of intoxicating liquors
within, the importation thereof into, or the e x p o r t a t i o n
thereof from the United States and all territory subject to the
jurisdiction thereof for beverage purposes is hereby prohibited.

The Congress and the several States shall have concurrent
power to enforce this article by appropriate legislation.

18th Amendment, U. S. Constitution (1919)

Anxious to activate the Constitutional amendment before its
scheduled January, 1920 date, Congress passed the Volstead, or National Prohibition, Act on October 28, 1919, prohibiting the sale of
intoxicating beverages over the 0.5 percent of alcohol level, and
"regulat[ing] the manufacture, production, use and sale of high-proof
spirits," while at the same time "insur[ing] an ample supply of alcohol and promotion of its use in scientific research and in the devel-
opment of fuel, dye, and other lawful industries."[1]

Congress applied a generous outlay of funds to the Treasury
Department's Bureau of Internal Revenue for the enforcement of
the Volstead Act, thus bringing up the question of who would actually be in charge—would Justice or the Treasury be the lead en-

forcement agency in the prohibition fight? Assistant Attorney General Guy D. Goff addressed the question: "The duty of enforcing the National Prohibition Act has been placed jointly upon the Commissioner of Internal Revenue *and* the Attorney General, and a much larger appropriation for its enforcement granted to the Treasury Department. The policy of the Justice Department is to assist and cooperate with the Prohibition unit [while] not neglecting its [normal] duties." In practice, the division of responsibility meant that Prohibition agents conducted the investigations, and marshals made the arrests.[2]

John Rogers had been a "dry" for all of his adult life, not to mention his dedication against drunkenness and alcohol-related crimes during a four-decade career, and was more than pleased to have the full brunt of federal law to support his personal conviction of the evils of alcohol. In the Western District files for 1920 and 1921, Rogers' name appears as signator for dozens of arrests under the Volstead Act, most of those carried out by Deputies Fred Peck and A. V. Knight. In addition, Rogers' longtime friend Frank Hamer became a Prohibition agent in 1920, stationed in Austin, and the two worked on several cases together.

One of those cases ended in a dramatic car chase through the Austin streets as recounted at trial by Hamer's partner James C. White. When an informant reported an automobile waiting for a liquor delivery on East Sixth Street, Hamer, City Police Sergeant R. E. Nitschke, and City Detective A. L. Bugg responded. They arrived at the 1300 block of Sixth just before 11:00 P.M. and parked their car. "After waiting about thirty minutes," the report continues, "a Ford car driven by Tom Hamby accompanied by [co-defendant] Leon Koch came out of Sixth Street going east and as it passed the waiting automobile they sounded the horn twice, and stopped near the corner.

"I got out of my car," states White, "walked up to Hamby and Koch and told them to consider themselves under arrest. I saw Hamby with a bottle of Tequila in his hand. Hamby immediately started the engine and started south on the side street. I jumped on the running board of his car and tried to throw the switch to stop the car, again telling Hamby he was under arrest.

"Koch jumped from the moving car, throwing a quart of Tequila as he jumped into the street, which struck Officer Bugg below the knee, probably preventing the bottle from breaking. Hamby struck at me trying to knock me off the running board of the running car; at the same time I covered him with my gun telling him to stop. He immediately grabbed a quart of Tequila and attempted to strike me over the head with it, whereupon I struck Hamby a blow over the head with my pistol"—Captain Rogers would've been proud—"and with the other hand guided the car into the curb. As the car stopped I reached inside the car and picked up two quarts of Tequila. Hamby and Koch were placed under arrest, taken to the City Jail and held."[3]

Stuck behind a desk as U. S. Marshal, John Rogers was not about to let this new law go into effect without personal supervision in the field. On March 8, 1920, Rogers traveled by train to Brenham where he arrested Tom Kendall near the depot "for shipping a trunk of liquor from a joint in Georgia." On June 24 he issued a warrant for Ted Tobin on charges of selling intoxicating beverages in Austin; on July 8 the marshal hauled Tobin to the city jail. The day after issuing the warrant on Tobin, Rogers broke into a warehouse near the Tenth Ward in Austin and arrested Herman and Bertha Schreiber for "manufacture and possession of liquor."

In an interesting juxtaposition of events, Rogers appeared in court on June 28 to hear the jury's findings on three men arrested earlier in the year for train robbery. J. W. Roach was found guilty, but the cases against S. H. Ramsey and J. H. Short were dismissed.[4] Rogers then hurried to the train depot to make his way south to Kingsville, where on June 30 he joined other family members celebrating the double wedding of his late brother's two daughters Margie and Curren.

Into the spring of 1921 the cases piled up against bootleggers. Rogers traveled to El Paso several times that year and made frequent trips to Waco and San Antonio in pursuit of this law's enforcement. On May 23, 1921, Rogers went with Frank Hamer and Fred Peck on an arrest in Austin. They hauled Rosie and Reecie Weathers and Robert Gilmore into jail for the manufacture of hard cider, closing out an investigation that had lasted several weeks.[5]

It was not the most dramatic or dangerous of cases for Marshal Rogers, but it was interesting for at least another reason— it was his last as a U. S. marshal.

On the first Tuesday of November, 1920, citizen John Rogers cast his votes down the Democratic Party line in yet another election that would have significant impact on his career in law enforcement. Rogers voted for James N. Cox that day, but Ohio Republican Warren Gamaliel Harding won the presidency with a popular vote margin of seven million and over four hundred electoral tallies in his landslide victory. It was a campaign made all the more interesting by the strong third party showing of Socialist Eugene Debs who garnered nearly one million votes himself. But the amiable Harding's promise of a "return to normalcy" meant anything but that for the Rogers household.

The office of the U. S. marshal has always been lined with heavy political fringe and the Western District in 1921 would be no different; Rogers had served eight years under a Democratic administration and knew now the likelihood of his being replaced by the Republicans.

In anticipation of that eventuality Rogers looked for other avenues to continue his career. In October, just three weeks before Election Day, the Captain had celebrated his fifty-seventh birthday with family and friends at his home on San Antonio Avenue. Still in good health relative to the years of minor troubles with the old shoulder wound, opportunities in law enforcement were diminishing with each year gone by. Rogers wasn't slowing down but he was thinking more often about retirement and a quieter time with Hattie and the kids and now grandchildren coming along.

The Rogers were stalwarts at the First Presbyterian Church in Austin and the Captain always made his way to a church pew on Sunday regardless of what part of the state he was in. His witness of faith extended in all directions and remained as strong as ever. A beautiful letter he wrote to his ailing friend Tom Roe in Taylor typifies his conviction. "I have often thought it would be so lonely to be confined to one's bed, especially for one who had been blessed with good health and enjoyed so much the Lord's fresh air and sunshine," Rogers writes, reflecting on his own mortality perhaps. "I hope your faith continues to grow stronger and stronger in the Lord Jesus with the passing of years, and that His comfort may sustain you in your illness, and that the consciousness of His love and care for you will bring you daily joy and peace that passes all understanding."[6]

Late in his marshal years Rogers was given to distributing Christian pamphlets laden with Scripture verses and his own personal witness. He was often seen handing the missals to judges, attorneys, and criminals in the courthouse during breaks at trials and hearings. One he had published in early 1920 was entitled "A Sinner Saved by Grace through Faith in Jesus Christ." With quoted biblical verses from Acts and Revelation and Romans, Rogers then writes that "about twenty-nine years ago in humility and weakness I accepted as my personal savior Jesus Christ as he is offered to us in the Scripture, confidently relying upon, and trusting in Him alone, for salvation, endeavoring thereafter to place myself in alignment with, and obedience to, the revealed will of God.

"I then was, and still am, unworthy; but I feel conscious of my acceptance by Him the difference before and after my conversion being simply the difference between a lost sinner and a saved sinner. Certainly if Jesus Christ can save a sinner such as I, none need perish." He adds as a postscript, "It is sincerely hoped that this little folder will be helpful to someone honestly seeking light and truth on this, the most important subject that can possibly engage the attention of man."[7]

Eminently respected across the city of Austin, not to mention the state of Texas, Captain Rogers was encouraged in the spring of 1921 to consider a run for political office given the national circumstances that would soon end his marshal career. In fact, Rogers' duties for the Justice Department came to an end on May 25, 1921, when he was replaced in that heavily political position by Republican D. A. Walker. Rogers announced his intention to run for a seat on the Austin Board of City Commissioners. With widespread support among law enforcement and church patrons in the city, Rogers ran a strong race in his first try at political campaigning, but lost by only five votes to Harry L. Haynes.[8]

Retirement now loomed large for the captain, but a job opening came to his doorstep that summer. The American Railway Express Company (A.R.E.) had formed in 1918 after a reorganization of the larger American Express, and offices had opened in several Texas cities including Austin and San Antonio. Seeking someone to head up their security and investigation team, the A.R.E. invited the esteemed captain to come to work for them. It would mean travel across much of the same area that he had served as U. S. marshal, responsibilities very similar to those he had had as a Ranger captain, and an office in San Antonio.[8]

After consulting with Hattie and with much prayer, Rogers accepted the position. They moved to a house at 129 Weymouth Street in San Antonio, but kept their home at 1200 San Antonio in Austin. Rogers likely intended to work to his sixtieth birthday and then retire for sure, but back in the capital city.

Rogers worked two years for the American Railway Express Company out of San Antonio. He accompanied valuable cargo on rail trips all across Texas. The captain led several investigations for the company during that time, and took his turn behind the desk filing reports and balancing spreadsheets. He made frequent trips to El Paso where he had opportunity to visit with his many friends and former colleagues. He also kept in close touch with his Austin cohorts.

And he stayed politically active on behalf of the state Democratic Party and many old friends who sought his valuable endorsement. Rogers supported Charles M. Cureton on his appointment as chief justice of the Texas Supreme Court and the two of them shared letters of interest in Cureton's leasing the Rogers' house on 1200 San Antonio Avenie in 1922. "Mrs. Rogers and I have thought it unwise to rent as nice a place as ours at any reasonable figure at all," Rogers wrote Cureton on February 13, 1922. "However, I might prevail upon her to lease same to you as we, of course, should feel assured in advance that the place would not be abused." The lease was for one annual payment of one thousand dollars.[9]

Rogers supported Charles Culberson's re-election plans in his 1922 primary campaign for U. S. senator. Even as early as December, 1921, Senator Culberson wrote a "Personal & Confidential" memo to Rogers asking for his opinion on running again: "I will be greatly obliged if you will write me frankly your view of the situation, and what my friends want me to do." In June after weeks of travel and inquiry Rogers recommended to Culberson that "it would be well for you to urge your Fort Worth friends to more active work if possible. Your Austin friends recently organized in your interest, I understand. I am not informed as to your outlook at Waco, which is also an interesting vote owing to its central location and large country vote.

"[Earle] Mayfield and [Cullen] Thomas are going to receive a much larger vote in this campaign than I thought at first," Rogers writes, "but I cannot escape my original opinion that the run-off will be between you and Thomas." Noting that "the KKK issue is the livest issue in the campaign" and that Culberson should receive the largest anti-Klan vote, Rogers concludes that "I may be wrong, but I thought you would be glad to hear from your friends as to how the situation looks from their viewpoints."[10]

Rogers was wrong. Culberson lost in the Democratic primary, but Earle B. Mayfield was in and Captain Rogers switched his considerable influence over. D. E. Lyday, Mayfield's campaign manager, wrote a letter of gratitude to Rogers for his support, noting that "such men as you never could support Jim Ferguson [in the Democratic run-off] and it is indeed a sad state of affairs when a man like Jim Ferguson can claim the serious attention of the citizens of Texas. We are not overconfident, Captain, for this is going to be a hard fight."

It was, but Mayfield won in the run-off and once more against his Republican opponent in November. He wrote Rogers to thank him. "I could not have won had it not been for such loyal friends as you sustaining me. Our victory was a righteous one," Mayfield wrote, "and will live in the political history of Texas because it clearly demonstrated that scalawag Republicans and mugwump Democrats cannot even make a dent upon the true and tried Democracy of old Texas."[11]

Captain Rogers stayed active in local political campaigns as well and had the job that allowed him to travel to many of the election sites. In El Paso he supported W. P. Hawkins in his run for Constable: "As you were one of my El Paso Deputies for some time," Rogers wrote Hawkins, "I know you are heartily in sympathy with law enforcement.

There is a crying need just now for the good old time honest, faithful officer whose heart is in his work. I predict you will make such an officer."

To his old friend and ex-Ranger J. W. Galbreath Rogers wrote an endorsement for Galbreath's run for sheriff of Nueces County. But Galbreath had already bowed out of the race: "After I had announced and began seeing the voters I found that they had lined up so my race wouldn't win," he responded to his former captain, adding, "If there ever was a time when this County need a Sheriff, it is now. Things are torn up terribly. The Klan and anti Klan are fighting one another." Rogers had apparently gotten after his friend for his not being a Church-going man of late. "I read your scripture," Galbreath wrote, "and am putting it away and keeping it. You have a right to get after me, I am one of your boys, Captain. I know I did some wrong things, I drank too much at times, and made some mistakes that way. [But] I often speak of you as being one of the most consciencious [*sic*], clean and best Officers in the World. I prize your friendship more than any other man on Earth."

True to his calling, Rogers kept in touch with state leaders on a personal and religious level as well as a political one. To Governor Campbell he wrote in September, 1922, "I hope in your lonely hours of convalescence you may get much comfort and consolation from the promises of God which comes to those who have accepted Jesus Christ as their personal Saviour. I hope you will soon be restored to health again, and help steer the grand old party [Democrats] in right and safe channels, lest she go on the rocks. Indeed there is much good to be found in it yet, but in my opinion, real leaders are sadly needed such as we had years ago."

When state Associate Justice Thomas Greenwood's mother passed away on October 10, Rogers sent a warm note of sympathy to his good friend, to which the judge replied a week later, "I deeply appreciate your note of the 14th. I am thankful for every day of my mother's life and realize that I never could have given her up without the same shock and grief. We miss you at the Church [in Austin]," Greenwood added, "and hope Providence may guide you back to us." Providence indeed was working on it.[12]

Seventeen months after leaving the marshal's office, Rogers still contended with some untidy bookkeeping that had him in arrears with the Bureau of Internal Revenue, a situation that thoroughly frustrated him as it lingered on. During the Prohibition investigations and subsequent trials, Rogers' office had paid customs officials for their time as witnesses, not an unheard-of activity. However, the funds had become hopelessly entangled in the red tape that knotted up with the Justice Department records and Rogers was being held responsible for some of the monies in question.

In October, 1922, he wrote the comptroller general in Washington, D.C. in an attempt to end the matter. Obviously exasperated, Rogers ended his letter with an extended run-on sentence, quite unlike him but as he said, "assuring you of my anxiety now." The captain wrote: "You can appreciate, I am sure, the hardship and injustice it will be to cause my bondsmen, or myself, any real trouble in this matter, where no dishonesty or moral turpitude is involved, every cent being accounted for, and merely technical differences, the most involved being the payment of Customs Officers as witnesses in prohibition cases, when they should have been paid, it is claimed by another department other than the Department of Justice, although at the time payment was made, we had no notice of this ruling and had always, during my eight years in office, paid these customs officers when appearing as witnesses in all cases other than Customs cases."[13]

Not all was business and politics, however. The captain received an advance copy of J. B. Gillette's still-classic *Six Years as a Texas Ranger* in February, 1922, and wrote a thank-you note in return. "I enjoyed it very much, especially because a number of old rangers, whose names you give, are not only known to me but in some cases were good personal friends of mine. Your book is different from most such books in that it is written in modesty, and relates truths, whether they be favorable or unfavorable, in given cases. In the main the success of this historic old force is simply wonderful and I have but little doubt it has been the most successful small force of peace officers that the world has ever known, and accomplished more bringing about a state of civilization in Texas, and especially the frontier."[14]

John and Hattie suffered the loss of their good friend Thomas Coleman on March 30. The south Texas *don* had been a political ally and religious compatriot, and the two couples had made fast friends from the early Cotulla days. Coleman was buried in San Antonio and the Rogers family comforted his widow Birdie over the months that followed.

Two years of politics and travel had been most interesting and even occasionally fruitful for Rogers, but he and Hattie missed living in their home in Austin. When the opportunity presented itself in the spring of 1923 they took it and happily. Its ending, however, would be anything but happy.

In the Austin city races in 1923 W. D. Yett was elected mayor. The four commissioners and their areas of responsibility were— Harry Haynes (Accounting), the man who had defeated Rogers in 1921; Charles N. Avery (Utilities); George P. Searight (Streets); and Harry W. Nolen (Superintendent of Police and Public Safety). Under the auspices of Superintendent Nolen, Sam Griffin served as Austin's Chief of Police, Robert Nitschke and James Littlepage were his sergeants, and Adolph Bugg was chief of detectives.

As the results of the election were being finalized, Sgt. Nitschke resigned on account of failing health, Adolph Bugg was reassigned, and Chief Griffin returned to his former post as chief of detectives. William Scott served as interim chief for two weeks in April, but by the first week of May the chief of police position became suddenly available and Captain Rogers and several of his influential friends lobbied for his appointment. The effort was a success; Rogers took the oath as Chief of Austin Police and began his tour of duty on Friday, May 4, 1923. Hattie and the Captain delightfully returned to their home on San Antonio Street, renting out their Weymouth Street house to Charles and Lucile Reeves and bidding San Antonio farewell.[15]

A whole new avenue of law enforcement now opened for John Rogers. He had served at every level in the Texas Rangers, both levels in the U. S. marshal's office and as a security agent and investigator for a private company. Now back in the public eye as public servant, and also in a politically charged office once more, Rogers seemed in his element. He was so well known in Austin that both peace officers and criminals knew his reputation, and the citizens would have been most pleased when they heard the news. Austin was feeling some growing pains in the Twenties along with the incessant trouble surrounding the Prohibition laws, the pro and anti-Klan forces in the city, and the usual urban crimes. No one had a stronger background nor greater conviction to enforce the law than "the Captain."

No one would have guessed that his first conflict would come with his boss rather than the street criminals.

The issue was the enforcement of the Sunday Blue Laws in Austin. Guided by a strong conservative tradition in Texas the Blue Laws maintained vigilant protection of the Sabbath, prohibiting most businesses from operating on Sunday and even then not until after noon, as well as a general prohibition of the sale of such as cigars and cigarettes, and the showing of "moving pictures" in the local theatre. The Sabbath was a day meant for worship and for family and its strict adherents refused any labor at the injunction of the Holy Scriptures themselves.

Both Nolen and Rogers agreed in principle with the enforcement of the Blue Laws, and in fact Nolen had run his campaign with a promise to "a strict and air-tight enforcement of all Sunday laws."[16] Certainly his appointment of John Rogers as chief of police would have been in line with his campaign.

On Tuesday evening, May 1, newly appointed Superintendent Nolen met briefly with soon-to-be appointed Chief Rogers. Although the contents of that private meeting were unavailable to the public, there did appear to be some conflict from the start. The newspaper *Austin American* picked up on the problem and interrogated Nolen at a Wednesday press conference. Nolen admitted that he and Rogers had had a disagreement over the Blue Laws but that it had been resolved.

In an interesting turn of events, it seems that Rogers believed a tighter enforcement of the laws than had been pursued in the past would result in an escalation of protest and resistance, thus bringing about more crime not less. In Rogers' estimation, having lived in Austin for the most part since 1907 and after discussion with several police officers, the broader though not necessarily more lenient enforcement of the Sabbath restrictions had been working quite well. He saw little reason to change and had told Nolen as much. The two agreed to maintain the status quo, but this disagreement from the very first days of office may have signaled the trouble that would eventually crop up again between the two men. A much larger showdown awaited.[17]

Chief John Rogers embarked on the next phase of his career in law enforcement with the vigor and commitment everyone who knew him only expected. Scott, Littlepage, and Bugg served as officers and fifteen other men worked the streets of Austin as policemen. The crimes recorded in the city files are typical of a city Austin's size for that period of time. Bootlegging continued to be a major challenge, although it was the primary responsibility of the Prohibition agents and marshals more so than the city police. Still, Rogers proved a valuable asset in continuing investigations and as an expert witness at trials.

Drug rings were busted, prostitutes hauled in, and brothels shut down, usually to open again and repeat the process. Thefts were numerous, drunken brawls became a regular Saturday night event, and assaults and murders were few and far between but not absent from the records. Cars were stolen or chased down after drunken sprees, and dogs were hauled in for disturbing the peace or roaming the streets in dangerous packs, a common problem. Austin had a "no dancing in public" regulation that had been on the books several years and it was tested on several occasions. Trouble in the streets in October brought a one night curfew until calm was restored. On March 23, 1924, a cockfight was broken up near the Tenth Ward and several men arrested.[18]

On Monday morning April 21st Chief Rogers was called to a tragic scene disturbingly reminiscent of one he had been in years before. Brothers Norrell and Choice Platt, ages eighteen and fourteen, had gone canoeing on the Colorado River the night before just a few miles up the river from town. They had not returned home and their parents frantically called the police station around dawn. Rogers immediately ordered a search team to head to the town lake and make their way up the banks. The chief himself assisted in the search as it wore on through Tuesday, likely pausing for a moment as he reached the city dam where his son had died. On Wednesday morning searchers found the bodies of the two boys washed up near Dry Creek off the town lake.[19]

On the Tuesday that the search for the Platt boys continued, Chief Rogers announced a ban on concession wheels and other gambling devices used at the popular traveling carnivals that often came through Austin. In fact there was a carnival setting up to open on May 1. The Texas anti-lottery law would be put into effect, said Rogers, and that included the several games of chance that came with the carnivals and any raffles that might be a part of the festivities. "I deem it but fair and just to give this notice a few days in advance," Rogers declared as quoted in the newspaper article, "as such little violations are being overlooked in other cities and have not been strictly looked after here by this and former police departments as in my judgment should have been. And not desiring to take undue advantage of anyone, I therefore am issuing this notice in advance so all may be fully advised."[20]

John Rogers seems to have moved toward a stricter interpretation and enforcement of the laws than he had for the previous year he had served as police chief, a shift not unnoticed by City Commissioner Harry Nolen. Although this might have been a change that Nolen would have welcomed, there was immediate response from supporters of the carnival and the raffles. An automobile was to be raffled off at the carnival on Saturday May 3, and Harry Nolen had already publicly acknowledged the legality of that raffle. Now his chief of police was apparently banning the game. Nolen suggested that Rogers' ban be put in place, but not until after May 3.

The stage was set for a confrontation at the city council meeting to be held Thursday, May 1. On the day before the meeting, Rogers finished off another investigation that he had been working on for several weeks. A movie was coming to one of the Austin theatres and several of its scenes had been criticized in other cities for being obscene. The movie, entitled "Three Weeks," included what some in those days would have judged "steamy" bedroom scenes. Rogers, not especially pleased with the prospect, had the film set up in the theatre so that he and a few others might preview it before it opened in Austin. After negotiations with the company marketing the film,

"Three Weeks" was allowed to open in the city but without the four objectionable scenes.

Much more trouble loomed with Superintendent Nolen and the car raffle. On May 1 Rogers issued the following notice in the paper: "Yesterday I was told by the head of this department not to interfere with the raffling of an automobile at the carnival to take place May 3. The public can imagine my embarrassment, to say the least, that it caused me not to be able to make good my announced purpose to enforce these laws. I feel that I had better stand this embarrassment and criticism that may follow and obey the instructions of my superior officer."

But the public squabble over this issue was too much for Nolen. He met with Rogers on Thursday evening and the two had a heated exchange according to later reports. At the end Nolen asked for Rogers' resignation; Rogers handed it to him. The letter was read to the city council Friday morning. "In accordance with your request of the 1st inst.," it said, "I hereby tender you my resignation as city marshal, effective immediately.

"I thank you very heartily for entrusting me with the important position of city marshal for one year and hope the standards and ideals of your police force are none the worse for having come under my supervision. With every good wish for you and your police officers, to whom I have become very much attached, and again assuring you of my great appreciation of your favors and courtesies, I am, Yours for law enforcement. J. H. Rogers." The newspaper article added that "in his long service as a peace officer [Rogers] had never been known to back up on anything that he had started and that having set May 1 as the date for stopping open gambling in Austin, he resolved to abide by his decision." James Littlepage was appointed to replace Rogers; he served as chief of police for the next five years.[21]

Captain Rogers was sixty years old. He still had his wife and family, he still had his health. He had put aside enough money over the years to live more than comfortably. He had invested wisely in west Texas lands, the money sufficient to support the family for two more generations.

It was time to retire.

CHAPTER 16

End of the Trail

AS HE APPROACHED THE HOUSE walking along Twelfth Street, Captain Rogers bundled his heavy coat around him a bit tighter, his tall white hat pulled down over his brow. The north wind was blustery that day, whistling down the hill as he reached the intersection and crossed to the front steps of his house. But that was not entirely the reason he kept his coat wrapped around his chest.

Two of his grandchildren met him as he reached the steps with cries of "Grandaddy!" calling the others from inside as well. Soon they had gathered around the gray headed gentleman. A tiny smile grew beneath the white mustache as the captain patted each of the little ones on their head. He stepped back from the wiggling entourage and his eyes widened. The children froze in anticipation; Grandaddy always brought some prize when they visited. The old Ranger reached inside the heavy coat and retrieved the tiny puppy from under his vest. The children squealed in delight and ran inside to tell their parents what a wonderful gift had just arrived.

Harriet looked from the front room window and smiled at her husband. He winked back at her, the puppy still squirming in his arms. He marched up the steps, his shoulders squared, and stepped inside. He handed the puppy to one of the grandkids, then stepped to the mantle in the living room. In a career-long custom, the captain unfastened his gun belt and placed the tools of his trade on the mantle shelf where they would remain until he left again for work. The children disappeared into the kitchen. It was a good day at the Rogers home.

Retirement seemed to fit John Rogers just fine. He and Hattie traveled on occasion, usually to San Antonio to see Charles and Lucile and, of course, the grandchildren—little Charles Mills, not so little now, the Captain's namesake John, Harriet, and young Blair. They welcomed Pleas on his infrequent furloughs from the army, and enjoyed his daughters Blaire and little Hattie. But mostly they stayed in Austin, enjoying the social life there, old friends, and their church. Rogers often gave the prayer now at church meetings and was in constant demand to teach the Men's Bible Class at First Presbyterian.[1]

The captain was less involved in politics but still gave his opinion on campaigns when asked. In 1926 Austin changed its form of city government from the commissioner system to the city manager system. P. W. McFadden became the first mayor under the new system which included four city councilmen and city manager Adam Johnson.

On the statewide scene Rogers had been pleased to vote for Pat Neff for governor in 1920 and again in his victorious reelection 1922. Neff, a fellow "dry" and big supporter of an expanded Texas Ranger force, had done well with many internal improvements for Texas but had caused a rift with Congress with his insistent reform demands. In 1924 Rogers faced a dilemma when Miriam "Ma" Ferguson ran against Klan-backed Felix Robertson, and he supported John Davis in his unsuccessful bid to unseat President Calvin Coolidge. Impressed by the young but energetic attorney general Dan Moody and his fight against Ma and Pa Ferguson's political chicanery, Rogers was pleased to cast a winning vote for Moody as governor in 1926.

Little did Rogers know that November day in 1926 what a difference that vote was going to make in his life.

They called it "Booger Town" at night. One of the wildest oil boom towns in Texas' history, Hutchinson County's community of Borger literally exploded onto the Llano Estacado prairie in the spring of 1926 when Ace Borger and John R. Miller promoted the two-hundred-and-forty-acre site along the Canadian River. As the "black gold" spouted into the Texas sky, forty-five thousand wide-eyed and trouble-prone men and women poured into the community from every direction. Brothels and saloons popped up like spring wildflowers; fights broke out over no more than a nod or a frown.[2]

The Panhandle and Santa Fe Railway came to town by the summer and Borger was officially incorporated with Miller as its first mayor. There was a post office and a school, a hotel and a jail scattered amidst the tents and lean-to's and shacks. By the end of 1926 there were even telephones and electricity in the community. But as Ranger William Warren Sterling personally observed, "Borger had no backlog of old timers to form a nucleus of good citizenship and law enforcement. It had gotten entirely out of control."[3]

What law enforcement existed in Booger Town was no more than Mayor Miller's henchman Two-Gun Dick Herwig and his sidekick and bootlegger Shine Popejoy, who meted out justice according to their own set of laws. With the proper "contribution," dope peddlers, madams, and card sharks could have their way in the town. Dixon Street became one of the most infamous sidewalks in the Southwest, strewn with drunken brawls, women of ill repute, and dead bodies.

The young governor of Texas Dan Moody would have none of it, however. Pressed by his good friend and political ally Speaker of the House Robert Lee Bobbitt, Governor Moody insisted that Borger be brought under control. When the local authorities could accomplish nothing, he decided to send in the Rangers.[4]

But the Rangers were in some disarray themselves in 1926, their powers to enforce the laws of Texas constricted since the Canales and Fall investigations. There was too much deadwood in the force, such as it had become anyway, and its once brazen reputation for staring down crime had become a legend now passed. At the behest of Speaker Bobbitt, Dan Moody looked into the problems of the state's law enforcement agencies. The first to be put under the reform knife was the highway department, followed by a general house cleaning of the Pa Ferguson political appointees spread across the administration. Then, in the spring of 1927, it was time to tune up the Texas Rangers. Once back in some semblance of order, Borger would be their first objective.

On April 30 Adjutant General Robert Lamar Robertson announced in Special Order #7 the sweeping changes that were to take place in the Ranger force. Nine Rangers, including several high-ranking officers, were to be "honorably discharged." Twelve officers were to be transferred within the force, a shake-up that was intended to bring fresh faces and energy to the unique organization. Frank Hamer, who had been serving as captain of Company D, was shifted to command the company at Ranger headquarters. William W. Sterling moved from captain of Company B to take Hamer's vacated position, while Tom Hickman became captain of Company B, and W. L. "Will" Wright was appointed captain of Company C and assigned to Del Rio.[5]

That left the command of Company A to be filled at its Marfa post. General Robertson made a special trip across Austin to 1200 San Antonio Street earlier in April to speak privately with the retired Ranger Captain John H. Rogers. The two spoke at length of the need for the Rangers to once more be seen as a viable and potent force for law enforcement in Texas. Who better to strengthen that fading reputation than one of the legendary "Four Captains" from the turn of the century? It was an invitation the now sixty-three-year-old Rogers could not resist.

John Rogers was reactivated as a Texas Ranger by Special Order #7, and assigned as captain of Company A in Marfa. The prospect of being moved to far west Texas and into the bleak mountains of Presidio County, however, must have given Rogers second thoughts. Or maybe Hattie had an opinion about such a move hundreds of miles away from grandchildren, nieces and nephews, and home. Whatever prompted the ensuing conversation between Rogers and Robertson, Special Order #8, dated May 14, made the following announcement: "Capt. J. H. Rogers, who by Special Order No. 7, dated April 30, 1927, was assigned to the command of Company A, Marfa, is hereby assigned to the command of Company C, Del Rio, in place of Capt. W. L. Wright, and Capt. Wright is hereby assigned to the command of Company A, Marfa." Seniority, and a lifelong reputation, apparently had its privileges.[6]

It certainly had its benefits nowadays. After all the years making no more than a pittance as a Ranger, Rogers must have been impressed by the wages of the 1920s. For although he had spent a life-time frugally saving and wisely investing and did not need the money, he would not have minded the eight hundred dollars per month salary package that included subsistence and camp expenses as well as an auto allowance that, in his case, went unspent. And in September, 1929, the state legislature thought enough of the Rangers' current work to nearly double the force's budget—Rogers made $1,122.50 every month after that plus the one-hundred-and-eighty dollar "subsistence."[7]

Re-activated Ranger Captain Rogers was spared the trip to Borger as well as the one to Marfa, although one of his privates, Y. A. Secrest, left for Borger immediately to do undercover work. Frank Hamer and Tom Hickman went next, followed soon thereafter by Captain Sterling. "'Judging from the time it took you to get here,' Hamer said to Sterling upon his arrival, 'you must have made the trip from Laredo on horseback and led your pack mule.'" Hamer and Hickman and Secrest soon departed leaving Sterling and men from Company D to restore order to Booger Town. They did. As Sterling tells it, "The gentlemen of the press asked me what tactics would be employed by the Rangers under my command. I replied that we were simply going to reverse the customary Borger procedure—where the criminals had been killing officers, we were going to kill off some of the crooks."[8]

John Rogers returned to the familiar confines of Del Rio and the Ranger post there around the first of June. Hattie stayed at their home in Austin and the captain commuted by train between home and office for the next three years, "re-upping" on May 15, 1929. In his reenlistment papers he is described as being sixty-five years, seven months old, five feet ten inches tall, with light blue eyes and "iron gray" hair.

Under his command were Sergeants W. W. Taylor and old *compadre* J. T. Laughlin, as well as Privates H. D. Glasscock, J. A. Miller, Y. A. Secrest, William Bangsley, and R. E. Poole. W. P. McConnell joined Company C later. Glasscock held "seniority" in the company having been there since 1919, and Miller since 1923. The rest joined up to be a part of the past meeting up with the future, the honor of serving under one of the great Rangers of their era.[9]

Company C served southwest Texas with distinction between 1927 and 1930, maintaining a presence along the always unruly borderlands, tracking smugglers and bootleggers, quieting riot-torn towns from Val Verde to Cameron counties, and arresting cattle rustlers and violent drunks. In July, 1927, Captain Rogers found himself in the west Texas hinterlands patrolling the oil boom community of McCamey. Situated five miles east of the Pecos River in Upton County, the boom town was surrounded by Rattlesnake Butte, Sugar Loaf Mountain, and the Bobcat Hills.

McCamey appeared on the west Texas landscape about the same time as Borger far to the north, and by the end of 1926 there were seven oil companies, including giants Shell and Humble, burrowing in and grabbing up land even as McCamey officially incorporated. Ten thousand people poured into McCamey the next year alone, and the typical lawlessness of that day erupted. Rogers traveled by train with several of his men from Del Rio to McCamey, a relatively short trip of only about ten hours, and went right to work. By sheer reputation the chaos began to subside almost immediately upon his arrival.

But as evidence that perhaps the years were catching up with the old Ranger, Rogers reported at the end of July that "things are quiet in McCamey but I could use some outside help." Speculation was that his old shoulder wound was now bothering him more often than not.[10]

Two months later Rogers made his way deep into the Rio Grande Valley to address trouble in San Juan, a thriving town located just a few miles east of McAllen. Although his report does not specify the trouble, the community was preparing to celebrate its tenth anniversary as an incorporated town and there may have been too much celebrating already going on.

In November, 1928, Company C spread itself thin across its area to observe the national and state elections; Rogers himself spent the first week of November in McAllen. Herbert Hoover was elected President of the United States, and Dan Moody was reelected as governor of Texas. On December 9 the captain was back at home long enough to write to an aunt: "I expect to spread Christianity with my wife and daughter in San Antonio. It's a great blessing to have this priviledge [*sic*] and to witness the grandchildren receive their things Christmas morning from Santa Claus."[11]

The duties of Company C were wide-ranging both geographically and in the usual variety of crimes investigated. Y. A. Secrest listed his work in 1929 in a later memoir: "I was detailed with Sergeant Taylor by Captain Rogers to catch three soldiers who had deserted the army at Marfa. After an extended automobile chase with them, they were finally captured.

"Sergeants Taylor, Laughlin and I with three other men went to Wink, Texas and made a raid on a gambling house. We caught seventy-three on Saturday night, and on the following Monday we caught two men running a still in Tulsa, Texas. Laughlin, Glasscock and I were sent to assist the sheriff of Medina County, near Lake Medina, and we caught one bootlegger with one hundred gallons of whiskey and wine, also two slot machines. I was detailed by the Captain to go with the constable at Rock Springs to aid Sheriff Young in capturing four bootleggers at Camp Wood. We seized car loads of whiskey in Rock Springs, in Bracketville, and in Sabinal.

"Captain Rogers, Henry Glasscock and I made numerous raids at Hondo, Castroville, Uvalde, and Del Rio. Another time, the South Pacific Railroad had quite a bit of stolen wire which could not be found. We worked three or four days and found the wire hidden in a deep canyon in the northwest part of Val Verde County about 100 miles from Del Rio."[12]

In September, 1929, Captain Rogers may have enjoyed the re-telling of some very old stories as he joined Captain Will Wright in El Paso to stop a prizefight. The old pugilism law was still on the books in Austin and a scheduled bout on September 27 garnered the attention of Governor Moody and Adjutant General Robertson. Rogers, Wright and several other Rangers arrived in El Paso a few days before the entertainment was to begin. The fight never took place; the Rangers departed.[13]

On October 19, 1930, John Rogers celebrated his sixty-seventh birthday at home in Austin. He had been feeling poorly for several weeks, weakened with occasional fever and what seemed to be severe stomach pains. Hattie and Lucile urged him to see his doctor, which he did. The diagnosis was unsure; a visit to Scott & White Hospital in Temple seemed in order. Rogers finally agreed. In Temple the tests were more clear: like his little brother years before, the captain's gall bladder was damaged and surgery would be required.

On the Sunday before he entered the hospital for the operation, Rogers went to church with his wife. There they prayed for the success of the surgery to come. Their pastor and the Men's Bible Class lifted him up in prayer.

The operation took place on the First of November. The captain's gall bladder was removed without any apparent difficulties. The doctors treating Rogers seemed very optimistic that after a period of recuperation he would be fine, better in fact, and able to carry on his duties.

On the night of November 10 the attending physician checked his patient once more and pronounced him well enough to be discharged the next morning and return to his Austin home. Rogers spent a fitful night at the hospital, ready for the next day and going home. When Hattie came into his room the next morning he was already out of bed, dressing himself.

He finished buttoning his shirt and pulled on his vest.

The aneurysm exploded in his brain as if a bullet had struck the Ranger. Even as Hattie reached for him, Rogers fell to the floor. Hattie bent down beside him, her cry having brought nurses rushing to her aid. It was already too late.

John Rogers was dead.

The obituary for John Harris Rogers, age sixty-seven, was published in more than fifteen Texas newspapers, and the word spread to towns as far away as Tuscon, Arizona and across the Rio Bravo into Mexico. The *Austin American* noted that Rogers "was Elder in First Southern Presbyterian Church. Former U. S. Marshal for the western district of Texas, and was Chief of Police during the administration of Mayor W. D. Yett. At the time of his death he was Captain of Company of Texas Rangers at Del Rio but maintained his home in Austin."[14]

Said the *Waco News-Tribune* obituary: "Taps have been sounded for Captain J. H. Rogers, for almost 45 years a gallant peace officer of the commonwealth and one of the bravest of the brave who never tarnished his oath of office, never turned his back upon a criminal fleeing from justice, never showed the white feather in the hour of conflict and in deportment and practice and custom and habit was a model for his kind. He had been wounded many times. Men said he bore a charmed life. He served with a whole host of the daring rough riders of Texas who battled for law observance with their sixshooters and made the resorts of smugglers and cattle thieves and robbers and gunmen places for the habitation for civilized men and women."[15]

Captain Rogers was buried in the Oakwood Cemetery in Austin in a plot next to his dear young son Lapsley. Members of Company C took care of all the funeral arrangements and served as pallbearers. John's son Pleas, stationed in the Philippines at the time, made it home by Christmas to be with the family. Years later the retired Army officer and veteran of two world wars would say, "I have seen many good men die, but my father was the best man I ever saw live."[16]

At the funeral service, Presbyterian pastor Reverend W. R. Minter spoke of Rogers as "a blessing," a "conscientious and devoted officer and servant of Texas," and a "constant worshiper and helper in the Lord." He waxed eloquent when he noted that "up in mountain-valleys and out on windswept plains are churches where people come to worship because, in part, of the loving gifts of John H. Rogers. A life such as this one is infinitely worthwhile. [And] we shall be unworthy of his friendship if we do not carry on for his Christ."[17]

Letters flooded in to Hattie from all over the country. Governor Moody wrote, "Captain Rogers was in every sense a Christian gentleman; he was a brave man and an officer who gave character and dignity to that field of service in which he had devoted so many years of his life." Pastor Bruce Roberts of First Baptist Church in Carrizo Springs noted that "all Texas has sustained a loss in the passing of Capt. Rogers. We could ill afford to lose one like him, for they are too few." Added Judge C. R. Sutton of Marfa, "The State has lost beyond question a valuable citizen and a useful servant."[18]

Four months later the *Sheriff's Association of Texas Magazine* eulogized the captain, quoting L. P. Sieker as naming Rogers "one who was as unafraid as any man who ever rode a horse on the trail of a desperado," and concluding the article: "When death called and his commission was returned it was clean and brilliant. He had never left a stain upon it."[19]

Perhaps most fitting and beautiful was the personal testimony of P. B. Hill, Ranger Chaplain who owed his office and his service to the captain, given at the service:

> "He was one of the bravest and best men I ever knew. In each of the three great departments of life—church, home and state—he was faithful and true. He was an earnest and sincere Christian with a genuine humility and purity of character that all men respected, and with a passion to win others to Jesus that led numbers to accept Christ as their Savior.
>
> "In his home he fulfilled in a faithful and beautiful manner the duties of husband and father—devoted and gentle, yet positive. In his home he honored the Lord before his family in worship, in word and in life.
>
> "He was known as one of the bravest men of the Texas Rangers and bore in his body bullet wounds from several battles with desperate outlaws. He was respected and feared by all who knew him. His fine integrity, devotion to duty and noble virtues, we who survive him will long endeavor to emulate.
>
> "He has fought his last fight."[20]

The Ranger's Prayer

O God, whose end is justice, Whose strength is all our stay,
Be near and bless my mission As I go forth today.
Let wisdom guide my actions, Let courage fill me heart
And help me, Lord, in every hour To do a Ranger's part.
Protect when danger threatens, Sustain when trails are rough;
Help me to keep my standard high And smile at each rebuff.
When night comes down upon me, I pray thee, Lord, be nigh,
Whether on lonely scout, or camped, Under the Texas sky.
Keep me, O God, in life And when my days shall end,
Forgive my sins and take me in, For Jesus' sake, Amen.

P. B. Hill, Ranger Chaplain

Abbreviations

AGP   Adjutant General of Texas, Papers of, 1882–1911. Texas State
             Archives, Austin.

MoR   Monthly Returns and Scout Reports of the Frontier Battalion,
             Texas Rangers, 1882–1901. Texas State Archives, Austin.

SR   Captain's Reports and Scout Reports of the Texas Ranger Force,
             1901–1911, 1927–1930. Texas State Archives, Austin.

Endnotes

INTRODUCTION

1. Statement by John H. Rogers, U. S. Marshal, Western District of Texas, April 3, 1913, in possession of Rogers Family, Bulverde, Texas, and this author.

2. Walter P. Webb, *The Texas Rangers: A Century of Frontier Defense*, 460.

3. "A Man Unafraid—Capt. J. H. Rogers," from the *Del Rio Presbyterian*, quoted in C. Rogers McLane, *The Rogers Family Genealogy*, 31.

4. T. R. Fehrenbach, *Lone Star: A History of Texas and the Texans*, 475.

5. Fehrenbach, 473. See Bob Scott's biography of Leander McNelly (Austin: Eakin Press, 1998).

6. *Bi-annual Report of the Adjutant General of Texas, 1891-1892*, 8.

7. "Texas Rangers" and other biographical articles, *New Handbook of Texas*.

8. A. J. Sowell, *Early Settlers and Indian Fighters of Texas*, 134.

9. McLane, *The Rogers Family Genealogy*, 33.

10. *Waco News-Tribune*, November 14, 1930, and reprinted by the *Dallas News* in December, 1930, as an "Editorial of the Month." McLane, 33.

CHAPTER ONE

1. "Hardeman County, Tennessee, Vital Records," in C. Rogers McLane, *The Rogers Family Genealogy*, 4-7.

2. Hardeman County, Tennessee, Marriage Records, Book I, 72, March 18, 1834; also, United States Census 1840, 1850 for Mississippi and Tennessee.

3. Robert Miller, *The Life of Robert Hall*, 36-38.

4. Land Contract of Isaac Rogers, Guadalupe County, Texas, Deed Records, Vol. G:114 (1856), Guadalupe County Courthouse, Seguin. Today the homestead property is located down a sloping valley in eastern Guadalupe County, just south and west of Red Rock Road and the Old Seguin-Luling Road.

5. 1860 Census of the United States, Guadalupe County, Texas, 645, 678.

6. Probate Cases of Guadalupe County, Texas, 539; also, *Guadalupe Valley Trails*, 4:2 (1998). Martin Rogers purchased most of the auction items.

7. Arward Max Moellering, "History of Guadalupe County" (Masters Thesis, University of Texas, 1938), 74-79.

8. Willie Mae Weinert, *An Authentic History of Guadalupe County* (1951), 27. The Harrises, Bentons, and others from Guadalupe County are mentioned in some detail throughout this county history.

9. Carl L. Duaine, *The Dead Men Wore Boots: An Account of the 32nd Texas Volunteer Cavalry* (1966), 163-168.

10. Josephine Etlinger, *Sweetest You Can Find: Life in East Guadalupe County, 1851-1951*, 270.

11. *Official Records of the Union and Confederate Armies*, Part I, Vol. 6 (Addendum), 378-390; also, L. E. Daniell, *Texas: the Country and Its Men* (1901), 483 (from a personal interview with John H. Rogers in 1899.)

12. Story taken from author's interview with John, Dub, Mills, and Charlie Reeves, descendants of John H. Rogers, July, 2001.

13. A. J. Sowell, *Incidents Connected with the History of Guadalupe County* (1887), 56-59.

14. "The Fourth Texas Confederate Infantry Regiment," www.cba.uh.edu/~parks/tex.

15. McLane, 29. Part of the nickname's derivation came from the fact that when he joined the Rangers he was John's kid brother and barely sixteen years old, one of the youngest Rangers to serve in the Frontier Battalion at that time.

16. A. J. Sowell, *Rangers and Pioneers of Texas* (1884), 233.

17. Probate Records, Guadalupe County (Texas), Vol. C, 506; Vol. E, 569-573.

18. Moellering, 77.

19. *Guadalupe Valley Trails*, 7:3 (1991): 23-26. William George Kingsbury was born in New York and moved to Texas during the Mexican War. He ran a dental clinic in San Antonio until 1869 when he moved to Boerne. As an immigration agent for the railroads, Kingsbury lived for a time in London, England. He was highly respected as a Texas scholar and writer. John Henry Brown, *Indian Wars and Texas Pioneers* (Austin: L. E. Daniell, 1896), 552.

20. 1880 Census of the United States, Guadalupe County (Texas), 230B.

CHAPTER TWO

1. Vertical Files, John H. Rogers, Center for American History, Austin; Van Denmark, "Religion and Bullets," *Texas Monthly* (March 1929), 349-351. The family believes, and Rogers himself mentioned this later in life, that his marriage to Hattie Burwell was the real "spark" for his faith. The seeds had been planted in his youth.

2. Omer W. Cline, "History of Mitchell County to 1900," (Masters Thesis, East Texas Teachers College, 1948), 34-51f; S. G. Reed, *History of the Texas Railroads*, 154-155, 180-181; Wayne Gard, "The Mooar Brothers, Buffalo

Hunters," *Southwestern Historical Quarterly* 63:1 (1959), 31-45; W. C. Holden, "Law and Lawlessness on the Texas Frontier, 1875-1890," *Southwestern Historical Quarterly* 44:2 (1940), 199-200; Don Watson and Steve Brown, *From Ox Teams to Eagles,* 28; Giles Edward Bradford, Jr., "History of Mitchell County, Texas" (Masters Thesis, University of Texas 1937), 56-99.

3. Bradford, 154. The shootout that mortally wounded Sam Bass in Round Rock, Texas, was a flurry of gunfire from several angles by numerous guns as Bass fled through the town streets and alleys. More than one person ultimately claimed credit for his death. Also, Ranger Ira Aten's father, a local minister, is said to be the one who administered last prayers over the dying Bass.

4. J. Evetts Haley, *Jeff Milton: A Good Man with a Gun,* 45-50; Frederick Wilkins, *The Law Comes to Texas,* 224-227.

5. Adjutant General Official Papers & Records (hereafter *AGP*), Box 401-62:1.

6. Texas Rangers Official Records and Monthly Returns of the Frontier Battalion (hereafter *MoR*) 1883; also, Family Papers of John Harris Rogers, in possession of John M. Reeves, Bulverde, Texas.

7. John Leffler, "Cotulla," *New Handbook of Texas.*

8. *AGP,* February 28, 1882.

9. H. W. King, "Texas Rangers Service and History," in Wooten, *History of Texas,* 361.

10. General Order #13 (January 7, 1884) in *AGP.* The family enjoys telling the story of Rogers' "gimlet eyes." They also note his stern warning to any Ranger private caught "slouched in the saddle."

11. *MoR,* Box 401-70:2 (1884-1885).

12. *MoR,* February and March, 1886.

13. Florence Fenley, *Oldtimers: Frontier Days in Uvalde, Texas,* 23-27; also, *A Proud Heritage: A History of Uvalde County, Texas,* 11-19.

14. *MoR* Annual Report, 1885.

CHAPTER THREE

1. Vertical Files, John Harris Rogers, Center for American History, Austin.

2. *MoR* December 1-20, 1885.

3. *AGP* April 30, 1886.

4. W. W. Sterling, *Trails and Trials of a Texas Ranger,* 308.

5. "Harrold," *New Handbook of Texas.*

6. Scott to Sieker, July 31, 1886, Frontier Battalion Records, Correspondence Files, Texas State Archives, Austin.

7. Sterling, 309. Combs, *Gunsmoke in the Redlands,* 111-118, tells the story from the version presented him by Elmer Harper. It is not unsympathetic to

the Conners' plight, their being accused perhaps falsely of the murders and then hunted down like the "animals" they may have become in order to survive.

8. Daniell, 484, Combs, 115.

9. Francis Abernethy, "Scrappin' Valley," *New Handbook of Texas*.

10. Scott to Sieker, July 31, 1886, in the Files of the Frontier Battalion (Correspondence); also, *AGP* August, 1886.

11. *MoR*, September 1886.

12. *MoR*, July and September 1887. This is a strange and mysterious side story of Brooks' activities related to the murder of which he was accused, made all the more peculiar that it certainly seems to have happened in the line of duty. Whatever "politics" may have been involved, Brooks' exoneration spared him the ignominy and put him back on the trail where he belonged.

13. "Brownwood," *New Handbook of Texas*.

14. Walter Prescott Webb, *History of the Texas Rangers*, 426.

15. T. R. Havins, *Something About Brown: A History of Brown County*, 37.

16. Havins, 38.

17. Henry McCallum, "The Wire That Fenced the West," *Southwestern Historical Quarterly* 61:2 (1957), 207-219.

18. Havins, 39. Brown County Court Records, September, 1886.

19. Webb, 428-437; Wilkins, 268-269; Havins, 39; Aten, *Six and One-Half Years in the Ranger Service,*17-20.

20. Roy D. Holt, "Introduction of Barbed Wire into Texas and the Fence Cutting War," *West Texas Historical Association Yearbook* VI (1930), 65-79.

21. Wayne Gard, "Brown County Six Shooter Days," *Dallas News,* July 9, 1956.

22. *MoR*, January 1887.

CHAPTER FOUR

1. Joe F. Combs, *Gunsmoke in the Redlands,* 111. Milton Anthony's name is conjecture, based on other local sources that include him and Redden Alford.

2. Scott to Sieker, July 31, 1887; *MoR*, March 31, 1887.

3. The unmarked gravesites are ten miles south of Hemphill and one-half mile east of the tiny community of Six Mile Creek, Texas. They sit behind the remains of a home that Combs believes once belonged to the Conner family. Combs, 112. Uncle Willis Conner is also buried there.

4. Daniell, 484-488; Sterling, 309-313; Combs, 111-113; *MoR* March 1887; W. S. Adair, "Rangers 40 years Ago Had No Easy Life," *Frontier Times* 4 (1927), 41-43.

5. *AGP,* April, 1887; Combs, 112. The Conners had a superior position on Lick Branch. More of the posse present may have only meant more casualties.

6. Daniell, 488; Sterling, 381.

7. Report of Dr. Frank Tucker to the Adjutant General, April, 1887. Mike Cox, *Texas Ranger Tales II,* 137.

8. Smith to Sieker, May 19, 1887, John H. Rogers Vertical Files, Texas Ranger Archives, Waco. Both Tucker and Smith claim responsibility for the care of the wounded Rangers, perhaps each vying for whatever compensation might have been available.

9. Combs, 112; Sterling, 372.

10. *MoR* June 1887. Curren "Kid" Rogers Vertical Files, Texas Rangers Museum and Archives, Waco.

11. Combs, 114-115; Adair, 42. There is a sign on the highway that will direct a visitor to the otherwise unmarked cemetery. Down the steep banks and less than a mile from there through the thicket is the battle site itself, located on Lick Branch.

12. *San Antonio Daily Express,* June 19, September 23-27, 1887; *Fort Worth Daily Gazette,* June 19, 23, 24, 1887.

13. *MoR* July 1887. The 1900 Fugitive List still had Barber's name with a detailed physical description including: "occupation, horse thief; foot No. 5 or 6 boot; always well dressed; has had one hand torn up in a gin and fingers are drawn up; has been crippled in hip, which makes one leg shortest, and gives scarcely perceptible limp in walking. Indicted 1884."

14. Sterling, 313. Leaving a Ranger in charge with officers dispersed was not an altogether rare occurrence; most of the time a sergeant would have been available.

15. *MoR* August 1887. Also, "Ballinger, Texas," *New Handbook of Texas.*

16. *San Saba News,* October 2, 1886.

17. *MoR* October 31, 1887.

18. Report of the Adjutant General, 1886-1887, Official End of the Year Report, 1887, *AGP.*

19. *MoR* March 1888. Cf. Also, information on Tupper Harris and the Harris family in McLane, *The Rogers Family Genealogy.*

CHAPTER FIVE

1. Fort Smith *Elevator,* December 13, 1889; *MoR* March and April, 1888.

2. *MoR* May 1888. Brooks and Rogers would now serve as officers in the Frontier Battalion and the Ranger Force for the next eighteen years.

3. *MoR* May and July, 1888. The mysterious robber was never identified or captured. Diarist George Wedemeyer gave his Fort Concho assessment in the summer of 1886, Mike Cox, *Texas Ranger Tales II,* 117.

4. *MoR* July, August and September 1888.

5. Arnoldo De Leon, *They Call Them Greasers: Anglo Attitudes Toward Mexicans in Texas, 1821-1900;* Alicia Garza, "Rio Grande City Riot of 1888," *New Handbook of Texas.*

6. *MoR* October, November, and December 1888; Dick Heller, Jr., "Salineno," *New Handbook of Texas.*

7. *MoR* February through August 1889.

8. *MoR* September through December 1889. Tupper Harris was tall and lean, and sported a somewhat delicate black mustache during his Ranger career; he looked more the sporting gentleman than the tough law officer he was.

9. "Cotulla," *New Handbook of Texas.*

10. *Report of the Adjutant General,* 1889-1890, 25-26. The story of the "special" or later "Loyalty" Rangers is one unto itself. In the beginning it had some merit, a kind of elevated citizens' posse that became a support system for the Frontier Battalion. But over the years it became so heavily politicized that it soured. The appointment of hardened gunslingers to this post did not help its reputation. Robinson, *The Men Who Wear the Star,* 274-280.

11. *MoR* March through May 1890.

12. *MoR* June through September 1890.

13. Vertical Files, John H. Rogers, Center for American History, Austin.

14. *MoR* January and February 1891. The four captains served alongside one another for the next twelve years.

15. *MoR* January through May 1891.

16. Burwell Family History, Vertical Files, John H. Rogers, Center for American History, Austin; also, McLane, *The Rogers Family Genealogy.*

17. Daniell, 488-489.

18. *Bi-annual Report of the Adjutant General, 1891-1892,* 10; Cox, 140.

19. McNeel to Mabry, December 18, 1891, Frontier Battalion (Correspondence).

20. *Bi-annual Report of the Adjutant General, 1891-1892,* 11.

21. *MoR* April and October, 1891.

22. Richard Harding Davis, *The West from a Car-Window;* mentioned in Sterling, 316; Cox, 140.

23. *MoR* March 1892.

24. *Texas Volunteer Magazine* (June 15, 1892), 6-7.

25. *MoR* December 1892, January through March 1893.

26. *MoR* January, February 1893. Other accounts of this remarkable event consider the highly political agenda that Captain McNeel carried with him as a detriment to his ability to perform his duties. This, as well as the fact that perhaps his political perspective differed widely from his superiors, would have cost him the job.

CHAPTER SIX

1. *MoR* February through August 1893. There's something of an apologetic tone in the report in Rogers' reference to having to purchase supplies from the local merchants, as if this was an embarrassment to the Frontier Battalion.

2. *MoR* May, July, November 1893.

3. Wilkins, p. 314. During Rogers' service in the Frontier Battalion and the Ranger Force, there were a dozen Rangers lost in the line of duty, only one, Tom Goff, was serving under Rogers at the time of death.

4. Daniell, 489. Cf. also, McLane's *The Rogers Family Genealogy,* for more information on the captain's family.

5. *MoR* December 1894.

6. *MoR* 1895. In McLane see more information about the Chesshers, Kid and Bettie's children, and the death of John Harris.

7. *El Paso Daily Herald,* October 21, 1895, January 7, 1896. The most complete study of the El Paso prizefight has been done by Leo Miletich, *Dan Stuart's Fistic Carnival* (1994).

8. *New Orleans Picayune,* December 27, 1891.

9. *Dallas Morning News,* September 9, 1895; Miletich, 42.

10. *Texas Christian Advocate,* October 19, 1892. The ministers' union in El Paso was manifestly involved over the issue from the beginning. In fact, ministers from New Mexico also became involved.

11. *Dallas Morning News,* December 12, 1895.

12. *Austin Daily Statesman,* November 18 and 24, 1895; Report from the Adjutant General's Office, February 27, 1896, in *Bi-annual Report of the Adjutant General, 1895-1896,* 11-12. *Dallas News,* September, 18, 20, 22, 26, 1895. The revised penal code was passed by the House on April 16, 1895 and became law without the governor's signature. From July 13 to October 7 the controversy over the revised code battled its way through the court of Judge J. M. Hurt, Criminal Appeals. Although a test case failed to uphold the revisions, Judge Hurt eventually ruled that the revised statute was to be incorporated. This did not settle the question, and Governor Culbertson threatened to send troops to stop the fight regardless of the law. Elmer Million, "The Texas Prize Fight Statute," 156-157.

13. *El Paso Daily Herald,* October 2, 1895.

14. *El Paso Daily Herald,* December 19, 1895.

15. "An Appeal to the Citizens of El Paso," published and circulated as a flier by the El Paso Ministers' Union, and paid for by the Methodist Church. The women's appeal may have an even broader impact because of the strength of the Methodist Women's Temperance Society behind it.

16. Robinson, *The Men Who Wear the Star,* 258.

17. Miletich, 145. This was a bold statement, but Stuart was never shy, especially in public. His demeanor alone carried the event for weeks.

18. Official Report of Captain John H. Rogers, *AGP* February 28, 1896.

19. *El Paso Daily Herald,* February 12, 1896.

20. Miletich, 158. In fact Stuart had issued a standing invitation to pay for any law officer who wished to board the trains to follow his front men. The Rangers paid their own way, however, not falling prey to the promoter's gimmick.

21. *MoR* February 1896. Other Monthly Records show that crime was confronted on several occasions during this event.

22. Albert Bigelow Paine, *Captain Bill McDonald,* 196-198. Sonnichsen, *Roy Bean, Law West of the Pecos,* 180-185.

23. Webb, 446; Robinson, 261; interview by author with Rogers' descendants, July, 2001.

24. *Chicago Tribune,* February 22, 1896; *El Paso Daily Herald,* February 22, 1896.

25. *Dallas Morning News,* February 22, 1896.

26. *AGP* Official Report Rogers to Mabry, February 28, 1896.

27. *MoR* April 1896, story from the Rogers' descendants.

28. *MoR* 1896-1897. The information that follows comes from the *Bi-annual Report of the Adjutant General, 1897-1898.* There were three men of the DuBose family who served with Captain Rogers: C. B. (Charlie) for six months in 1896, Edwin M. who served between 1899 and 1902, and H. G. (Harry) from 1897 to 1900, the latter two as officers. Rogers wrote this about Harry in an 1899 report: "an all around good officer of whom I am proud." *Records of Service of the Adjutant General.* The DuBose family became good friends with the Rogers kin over the years. Interview with Curren Rogers McLane, June, 2002.

CHAPTER SEVEN

1. Culberson to U. S. Senator Horace Chilton, May 8, 1898, in *AGP.*

2. Culberson to Rogers, May 13, 1898, in *AGP.*

3. *MoR* April, May and June, 1898.

4. *MoR* June 1898. Office of the Secretary of the Treasury Department to C. L. Rogers, September 1, 1898. The title was Special Treasury Employee, "to assist in the prevention and detection of frauds upon the Customs Revenue, with compensation at the rate of $100 per month."

5. Interview with Rogers' descendants, July 2001; *MoR* July 31, 1898.

6. *MoR* July 1898.

7. *MoR* July through October 1898. Frank McMahon hailed out of the El Paso area and, according to one story, had once been hired by outlaw-turned-

attorney John Wesley Hardin to "knock off" the husband of a woman Hardin was eyeing at the time. If true, it is certainly unlikely Captain Rogers was aware of it when he signed McMahon on.

8. Culberson to Rogers, November 26, 1898, in *AGP.*

9. This pocket New Testament is in the possession of Kid's grandson, Rev. Curren Rogers McLane, Fort Worth.

10. *Bi-annual Report of the Adjutant General, 1897-1898; MoR* January, February and March 1899.

11. Official Report of Captain John H. Rogers, *AGP;* Report of Dr. W. T. Blunt to the Adjutant General, April 1899, *AGP.*

12. Report of Captain Rogers to Adjutant General Mabry, *AGP, 1897-1898.*

13. Rogers got off a shot at Herrera, wounding him but not mortally. Even recent accounts of this fight have Rogers and Herrera squared off in a street duel (Utley, 270), which is not so. See Rogers' own report, and his interview with Daniell, 490-492. The family lauds Creed Taylor with saving the captain's life, and insists that it was not Herrera who fired the deadly shot but an unknown shooter from the rooftop. Author's interview with John Leslie Reeves, July, 2001.

14. Webb, 450-451; McLane, *Rogers Family Genealogy*, 22-24. According to the family account, Augie Old walked up to the wounded Herrera and fired two shots point blank to his head.

15. Interview with Rogers' family descendants, July, 2001. Sergeant H. G. DuBose to General Thomas Scurry, March 28, 1899, *AGP.*

16. Daniell, 493. Rogers, as most Rangers in those days, was not pleased with the small .351 caliber of the rifle and always kept his Model 97 .44 caliber Winchester close at hand. The Rogers family still enjoys the Captain's tale of a Ranger gunfight involving mostly smaller caliber guns, the shootout more like a fireworks display than doing any harm. That bent stock gun now resides in a special display case featuring artifacts of Captain Rogers's career in the Pioneer Hall Museum in San Antonio.

17. Sterling, *Trails and Trials of a Texas Ranger*, 376-377; Sonnichsen, *I'll Die Before I Run*, 299-315.

CHAPTER EIGHT

1. *MoR* August, September, October, and November, 1899. The report does not say specifically that the medicine bill from a Dr. Williams was only Rogers'.

2. *MoR* November 1899 through January 1900. It was Sgt. DuBose's first trip back to Langtry since the prizefight episode.

3. *AGP* Official Report of Captain John H. Rogers, January 10, 1900.

4. *MoR* May and June 1900.

5. General Order No. 24, *AGP* 1900. Augie Old is often listed with Rogers and Thalis T. Cook as the "Christian Rangers;" not so Augie's brother Will.

6. *MoR* June through September 1900.

7. *AGP* Official Report of Captain John H. Rogers, October 1900; Sterling, 409-411: "It closed the stormy career of an outlaw and firmly established the reputation of Will Wright as a man among men." Wright was called to the scene from his home where his family anxiously awaited word after hearing gunshots down the street. "Wright's trial by fire proved to the hard cases around Cotulla that he was more than a match for any of them, and he had no further trouble there."

8. *MoR* November and December 1900. "Marathon," *New Handbook of Texas.*

9. *MoR* January through May 1901. Ed DuBose followed his younger brother Harry as Rogers' sergeant. He later joined Hughes' Company D on September 3, 1904.

10. "El Corrido de Gregorio Cortez," several sources, including Americo Paredes, *"With His Pistol in His Hand," A Border Ballad and Its Hero,* 171-172. Also Daniell, 493-494.

11. Maurice Kildare, "The Rangers Got Their Man," *The New Mexico Lawman,* 6-7; Sterling, 497-500.

12. Julian Samora et al, *Gunpowder Justice,* 60.

13. Samora, 61; Daniell, 494; Kildare, 7-13; Sterling, 501-507.

14. Sterling, 507-511; Samora, 60; Kildare, 13-14.

15. *AGP* Official Report of Captain John H. Rogers, July 1901. The family tells how upset the captain was years later when he spotted a just pardoned (by Governor Colquitt) and released Cortez walking down the city street. Interview with Rogers' family descendants, July 2001. Bill Merriman's name is sometimes noted as Merren, as in a letter from Gov. Joseph Sayers to Rogers, August 17, 1901. But both Kildare and Sterling use Merriman, a name also found in a Laredo directory at about that time.

16. Act of the Twenty-seventh Texas Legislature, March 29, 1901, to be instituted within ninety days time; the law printed in full as General Orders No. 62, *Bi-annual Report of the Adjutant General, 1901-1902,* 126-129.

CHAPTER NINE

1. McLane, *Rogers Family Genealogy;* Interview with Rogers Family descendants, July 2001. *MoR* January through August 1902.

2. Morphis, *History of Texas,* 451. This quote is attributed to an officer named McCown at the outset of an assault against Monterrey during the Mexican War. The more entertaining version includes this: "We would mightily like for you to be on our side and help us; but if you can't do it, for

Christ's sake don't go over to the Mexicans, but just lie low and keep dark, and you will see one of the damnedest fights you ever saw in all your born days." Paraphrases of such a prayer would have been common.

3. Sterling, *Trails and Trials of a Texas Ranger,* 369-370. The top hat story probably took place in Laredo, not Cotulla, as an elderly DuBose remembered it to Sterling years later. In 1903 poet and short story artist O. Henry (Will Porter), writing out of Austin and after spending some time on a local ranch, penned a tale he called "The Marquis and Miss Sally." In the cowboy story a camp is disrupted with the arrival of a top-hatted judge, whose chapeau is soon the target of several of the cowpokes' pistols. Coincidentally, Will Porter sang bass in the Presbyterian church choir where Rogers attended.

4. Scout Reports of the Ranger Force (hereafter *SR*), November 1902. The Scout Reports, though not as organized or detailed, replaced the Monthly Returns of the previous two decades as part of the general reorganization of the Texas Rangers from the now-defunct Frontier Battalion.

5. *SR* December 1902 through May 1903.

6. Marilyn Rhinehart, "The Thurber Coal Miners, 1888-1903," *Southwestern Historical Quarterly,* 532-539. Reported by Captain Rogers in the *Bi-annual Report of the Adjutant General, 1903-1904,* 161.

7. *SR* October 1903 through February 1904.

8. James Fenton, "Tom Ross: Ranger Nemesis," *National Association for Outlaws and Lawmen Quarterly* 1979, 4. Captain McDonald would later dismiss a drunk and disorderly Sullivan from the Ranger Force.

9. John H. Rogers, Vertical Files, Center for American History, Austin.

10. Fenton, 19-20. Also mentioned by Rogers in his presentation for the *Bi-annual Report of the Adjutant General, 1903-1904,* 161-162.

11. Interview with Rogers' family descendants, July 2001.

12. *AGP* Official Report of Captain John H. Rogers, January 1906.

13. *SR* November 30,1905.

14. Daniell, 495-496. Rogers to Lanham, October 7, 1905; Lanham to Rogers, October 19, 1905. *Records of the Governor of Texas* (Correspondence), October 1905.

15. *AGP* Official Report of Captain John H. Rogers, January 1906.

CHAPTER TEN

1. Jenkins and Frost, *I'm Frank Hamer,* 20-21.

2. McLane, *Rogers Family Genealogy,* 40.

3. *AGP* Official Report of Captain John H. Rogers, October 1906.

4. Sterling, 332. "John Abijah Brooks," *New Handbook of Texas.* Brooks served thirty-eight years as a district judge, longer than his service as a Ranger.

5. *History of Shelby County, Texas* (1988), 27.

6. Vertical Files, John Harris Rogers, Center for American History, Austin. Jenkins and Frost, *I'm Frank Hamer,* 29-30.

7. Official Report, Rules and Regulations for Company C, Ranger Force, Captain Rogers, December 1906.

8. Albert Bigelow Paine, *Captain Bill McDonald, Texas Ranger,* see this source for the glorified account as Colonel Edward House wanted it written; Harold Weiss Jr., "Yours to Command: Captain William J. 'Bill' McDonald and the Panhandle Rangers of Texas" and "William Jess McDonald," *New Handbook of Texas,* see these sources for a more factual account of McDonald's life.

9. *AGP* Monthly Reports, January through June 1907.

10. *AGP* Monthly Reports, July and August 1907.

11. Vertical Files, History of the Austin Dam & Town Lake, Austin History Center.

12. *Austin Daily Statesman,* August 28, 1907; interview with Rogers' family descendants, July 2001. First Southern Presbyterian is today Central Presbyterian Church, still located on East Eighth Street in Austin.

13. McLane, *Rogers Family Genealogy,* 33.

14. Author's interview with the Reeves family, July, 2001; *SR* October 1907.

CHAPTER ELEVEN

1. Judge James Perkins to Rogers, September 1, 1908, Family Papers in possession of John Reeves, Bulverde, Texas.

2. Official Report, Captain Rogers, May 1908.

3. *SR* June 30, 1908; Jenkins and Frost, *I'm Frank Hamer,* 31.

4. Official Report, Captain Rogers, July through September 1908.

5. William McLeod, *Story of the First Southern Presbyterian Church of Austin,* 101.

6. Daniell, 497; Official Reports, Captain Rogers, January 1909.

7. Official Reports, Captain Rogers, May, September 1909.

8. C. L. Sonnichsen, *Pass of the North,* 387: "Diaz was cheered and viewed with patriotic interest when he came to the border for his historic meeting with President Taft on October 16, 1909—an affair of great pomp and circumstance on both sides of the boundary. But only a year later the whole northern country was in the process of rising against him."

9. Official Reports, Captain Rogers, December 1909.

10. Program for the Dedication of the New Austin Dam, Spring 1910, Vertical Files, Austin History Center.

11. Official Reports, Captain Rogers, April and May, 1910.

12. *SR* July 31, 1910. Rogers did not participate in the chase itself. During his entire life the captain never drove an automobile and rarely even sat in a passenger's seat.

13. Official Reports, Captain Rogers, July through November 1910.

14. Rogers to Adjutant General J. O. Newton, December 3, 1910, Vertical Files, Center for American History, Austin.

15. Frederick S. Calhoun, *The Lawmen: United States Marshals and their Deputies, 1789-1989*, 215 ff; W. H. Timmons, *El Paso: A Borderlands History*, 209ff.

16. Calhoun, 230; Official Reports, Captain Rogers, 1910.

17. Report of the U. S. Marshal's office to the Attorney General, December 1, 1911, in Calhoun, 233.

18. Interview with Rogers family descendants, July 2001.

19. Official Report, Captain Rogers, January 1911. Information on the New Mexico "white cappers" can be found in Ball, *History of the U. S. Marshals in New Mexico and Arizona, 1846-1912,* 150.

20. Records of the U. S. Marshal Service, Fort Worth, Texas, Vertical Files, John H. Rogers.

21. "Texas Presbyterian College for Girls," *New Handbook of Texas;* Daniell, 494. Lucile graduated in May, 1913, and then attended The University of Texas in Austin.

CHAPTER TWELVE

1. Office of the U. S. Attorney General, February 21, 1911.

2. Sonnichsen, *Pass of the North*, 390.

3. Frederick Calhoun, *The Lawmen*, 212-216.

4. Timmons, *El Paso, A Borderlands History*, 212-213.

5. Calhoun, 219.

6. U. S. Marshal Calvin Brewster to Attorney General Newton, March 1, 1912; U. S. Marshal Eugene Nolte to Attorney General Newton, March 17, 1912.

7. *El Paso Herald,* July 13, July 17, November 17, 1911, Vertical Newspaper Files, Center for American History, Austin.

8. *El Paso Herald,* April 10, 1912.

9. Records of the U. S. Marshal Service, October, 1912. National Archives and Records Administration, Fort Worth, Texas.

10. Sonnichsen, *Pass of the North*, 370-374.

11. Ibid, 375. "Exploits like that," Sonnichsen continues, "convinced the voters that it would be unwise to change mayors in mid-stream."

12. Sonnichsen, 287-290. "There were five important madams in El Paso between 1881 and 1915—all of them shrewd and capable businesswomen of considerable force and charm: Alice Abbott, Etta Clark, Gypsy Davenport, May Palmer, and Tillie Howard were their professional names."

13. Sonnichsen, 363,364, 374-375. Slater in the *El Paso Herald,* January 10, 1912.

14. *El Paso Herald,* July 17, 1911.

15. Calhoun, 222. Politically astute, Rogers certainly would not have been surprised by the loss of his job, and would likely have known weeks ahead and begun making preparations to move on.

16. Edward M. House to Z. T. Fulmore, November 12, 1912; John Nance Garner to Rogers, February 7, 1913. Rogers Family Papers in possession of Charlie Reeves, San Antonio. Colonel House was a governor- and president-maker with Woodrow Wilson's full attention. Zachary Taylor Fulmore was a Civil War vet, president-elect of the Texas State Historical Association, and a friend of Rogers whose families sat in church together. Garner had twenty more years still in Congress and two stints as Vice-President awaiting him.

17. Petition for support of John H. Rogers' nomination, Rogers Family Papers in the possession of John Reeves, Bulverde, Texas, and the author.

18. John Hughes to President-elect Woodrow Wilson, January 5, 1913. Paper of John Reeves, Bulverde, Texas.

19. Frank Hamer to President-elect Woodrow Wilson, January 10, 1913. Papers of John Reeves, Bulverde, Texas.

20. Petition in the Rogers Family Papers; also, Daniell, 498.

21. *State Topics,* April 12, 1913, 10.

CHAPTER THIRTEEN

1. Letter of John H. Rogers, April 3, 1913, Vertical Files, Center for American History, Austin; also in possession of John Reeves, Bulverde, Texas.

2. Files of The Western District of Texas, Records of the U. S. Marshal Service, Fort Worth.

3. McLane, *The Rogers Family Genealogy,* 33. Reverend Minter followed the long-standing and highly esteemed pastorate of Dr. William McLeod. During this same period John R. Hughes became the last of the "Four Captains" to retire from the force. A story is told of him and automobiles as well—that a Model T bought as a wedding present became instead a reminder of a lost love when his fiancée died. Hughes kept the car in pieces in a garage, once a year reassembling it only to drive to her grave in Rockport. Martin, *Border Boss,* 75-76; recounted in *Corpus Christi Caller Times,* January 2, 2002.

4. Calhoun, *The Lawmen,* 237.

5. Files of the U. S. Marshal Service, 1913-1914, Western District, Fort Worth Archives.

6. *US v. Brady,* Case No. 174 (1913).

7. Files of the U. S. Marshal Service, Western District of Texas, 1913-1914. Postal fraud and theft remained high on the list of crimes for the marshals to investigate and prosecute. Rogers' experience here would serve him well as an investigator for American Railway Express.

8. *US v. Floyd Davis*, May 18, 1913 (San Antonio Docket), U. S. Marshal Records.

9. *US v. Dave Blumenfield*, May 6, 1915 (San Antonio Docket), U. S. Marshal Records.

10. Jenkins and Frost, *I'm Frank Hamer,* 66.

11. Harrison Act, December 17, 1914, Records of the U. S. Congress.

12. Records of Special Agent Charles B. Braun, Bureau of Investigation, September 23, 1915, U. S. Marshal Records, Fort Worth.

13. *US v. M. K. Ross et ux,* September 3, 1915 (San Antonio Docket), U. S. Marshal Records.

14. *US v. Herman and Otto Schempf,* May 29, 1915 (San Antonio), U. S. Marshal Records.

15. Warren to Gregory, Records of the U. S. Attorney General (Official Correspondence), in Calhoun, 236.

16. *US v. C. T. Schaine et ux,* June 1, 1917 (Austin Docket), U. S. Marshal Records.

17. Charles Braun Papers, April 4-12, 1917.

18. Sheriff Fred Long to Marshal John Rogers, April 7, 1917, Braun Papers.

19. Charles Braun to John Rogers, June 2, 1917, Braun Papers.

20. Rogers to R. L. Barnes, August 10, 1917; Braun to Barnes, August 17, 1917, Braun Papers.

21. *US v. Willie Rolff,* July 19, 1918 (Austin Docket), U. S. Marshal Records.

22. *US v. Irene Miller,* July 2, 1918 (Austin Docket), U. S. Marshal Records.

CHAPTER FOURTEEN

1. Testimony of J. B. Scarborough, 279, and Virginia Yaeger, 323, *Proceedings of the Joint Committee of the Senate and of the House in the Investigation of the Texas State Ranger Force,* January 31-February 14, 1919, Austin.

2. Frank Cushman Pierce, *A History of the Lower Rio Grande Valley,* 114.

3. Evidence by the Prosecution, January 31-February 2, 1919, *Proceedings.*

4. "Jose T. Canales," *New Handbook of Texas;* Scarborough, 279, *Proceedings.*

5. Interrogation by Knight, February 12, 1919, 1233, *Proceedings.* The interrogation took place on Wednesday, February 12, and began at 10:00 A.M. Knight was a partner in the Dallas law firm Thompson, Knight, Baker, & Harris. He was fifty-four years old, and had just left a three-year position as president of the Texas State Fair.

6. Testimony of Captain J. H. Rogers, February 12, 1919, 1233-1250, *Proceedings.*

CHAPTER FIFTEEN

1. Eighteenth Amendment to the United States Constitution; Volstead Act of Congress, October 28, 1919.

2. Calhoun, 241.

3. James C. White, Special Agent, testimony in *US v. Tom Hamby & Leon Koch,* June 8, 1921, San Antonio.

4. *US v. Ted Tobin,* June 24, 1920; *US v. J. W. Roach & S. H. Ramsey,* June 28, 1920 (Rogers as arresting officer), Records of the U. S. Marshal Service, Western District of Texas, Austin Docket.

5. *US v. Rose Weathers & Robert Gilmore,* May 23, 1921 (Rogers as arresting officer), U. S. Marshall Service.

6. John Rogers to Tom Roe, October 8, 1917, Rogers Family Papers, in possession of John Reeves, Bulverde, Texas.

7. Pamphlet in the Family Papers, Bulverde, Texas.

8. *Austin Statesman,* May 2, 1921, Austin History Center.

9. Rogers to Cureton, February 13, 1922. Letter in Rogers Family Papers, John Reeves, Bulverde, Texas; Cox, 146; Interview with Rogers family descendants, July, 2001.

10. Rogers to Culberson, January 5, 1922. Rogers to Culberson, June 22, 1922. Papers of the Governor of Texas (Personal Correspondence); Rogers Family Papers, John Reeves, Bulverde, Texas.

11. Earle Mayfield to Rogers, November 17, 1922, Rogers Family Papers.

12. Rogers to W. P. Hawkins, June 22, 1922; J. W. Galbreath to Rogers, November 19, 1922; Rogers to T. N. Campbell, September 23, 1922; Thomas Greenwood to Rogers, October 17, 1922. Rogers Family Papers, Bulverde.

13. Rogers to J. B. McCarl, Comptroller General of the United States, October 17, 1922. Rogers Family Papers.

14. Rogers to Gillette, February 25, 1922, Rogers Family Papers.

15. *Austin Statesman,* May 1, 1923, Austin History Center.

16. *Austin American,* May 3, 1923.

17. Records of the Police Chief, City of Austin, March 23, 1924.

18. Police Blotter, Austin Police Department, March 20, March 23, April 23, 1924. Austin History Center.

19. *Austin American,* April 21, 1924.

20. *Austin American,* April 22, 1924.

21. *Austin American* and *Austin Statesman,* May 1-3, 1924. Interview with Rogers family descendants, July, 2001.

CHAPTER SIXTEEN

1. Interview with Rogers family descendants, July, 2001.

2. "Borger," *New Handbook of Texas.*

3. Sterling, 97. "Borger presented a new and unprecedented problem in the maintenance of decency and order unlike other oil fields heretofore found in Texas."

4. Sterling, 99-107. The promoter of Borger "even brought his own doctors and undertakers, the latter being paid $100 for interring paupers." But, says Sterling, "At this critical time, Texas had a chief executive [Dan Moody] whose record showed he would not permit such conditions to flourish under his administration."

5. Special Order No. 7, April 30, 1927, Records of the Texas Rangers, Ranger Museum and Archives, Waco.

6. Special Order No. 8, May 14, 1927, Records of the Texas Rangers, Waco.

7. Paymaster Records, Texas Rangers, Company C, 1927-1928, Waco.

8. Sterling, 100. "This statement had a good psychological effect," remembers Sterling, "and we did not have to shoot anybody. The exodus of crooks and parasites, which had started with the arrival of the first Rangers, was given added impetus by this announcement."

9. Vertical Files, John H. Rogers, Waco Texas Rangers Hall of Fame and Museum, Waco.

10. "McCamey," *New Handbook of Texas;* Papers of Governor Dan Moody, July, 1927, Texas State Archives, Austin; "Combined Recollections of Lucile and Pleas (Rogers)," John Harris Rogers Vertical Files, Texas Rangers Hall of Fame and Museum, Waco.

11. Rogers to Aunt Lollie (probably his sister Leonora), December 9, 1928, John H. Rogers Vertical Files, Center for American History, Austin.

12. "Reminiscences of a Texas Ranger," Y. A. Secrest, Vertical Files, Texas State Archives, Austin.

13. *Report of the Adjutant General,* September, 1929.

14. *Austin American,* November 12, 1930.

15. *Waco News-Tribune,* November 13, 1930.

16. "Combined Recollections of Lucile and Pleas," Vertical Files, John Harris Rogers, Texas Rangers Hall of Fame and Museum, Waco.

17. Eulogy for John H. Rogers by Rev. W. R. Minter, Pioneer Hall Museum in San Antonio.

18. Rogers Family Papers, Bulverde, Texas.

19. "Many Brilliant Exploits Manifest Courage of Captain Rogers," *Sheriff's Association of Texas Magazine,* Volume 1 No. 2, March 1911, 11.

20. Eulogy of P. B. Hill, Texas Ranger Chaplain, Pioneer Hall Museum in San Antonio. The captain's beloved Hattie passed away on July 5, 1948, in San Antonio. Their son Pleas died in 1974 and their daughter Lucile was ninety-three when she passed away in 1987.

Bibliography

UNPUBLISHED PRIMARY SOURCES

The preponderance of the information for this biography came from primary sources related directly to the Texas Rangers collections, from the Frontier Battalion and Ranger Force papers, and including records from the adjutant general, the governors, and other archival files. Specifically these collections include:

Adjutant General Papers, Letter Press Books & Correspondence, Texas State Archives, Austin.

Adjutant General of Texas, Papers of, 1882-1911. Texas State Archives, Austin.

Adjutant General of Texas, Official Bi-annual Reports of the Office of, 1895-1906. Texas State Archives, Austin.

Austin, City of, Police Records, 1923-1924, Austin History Center.

Census Records of the United States and Texas, 1850, 1860, 1870 and 1880.

Governor of Texas, Papers of, 1884-1911, 1927-1930, Texas State Archives, Austin.

Governors of Texas Records, Letter Press Books & Correspondence, Texas State Archives, Austin.

Guadalupe County, Texas, Deed, Marriage, Census, Tax Rolls, and Probate Records of, Guadalupe County—Seguin Public Library Archives.

Government Documents, "Proceedings of the Joint Committee of the Senate and the House in the Investigation of the Texas State Ranger Force" [The Canales Investigation], January 3-February 14, 1919. Texas State Archives, Austin.

Government Documents, "Proceedings of the U. S. Senate Subcommittee on Mexican Relations in the Investigation of Mexican Affairs" [The Fall Hearings], September 19, 1919-April 20, 1920. Texas State Archives, Austin.

McLane, C. Rogers, The Rogers Family Genealogy, Vertical Files, Rangers Archives, Texas Ranger Hall of Fame & Museum, Waco.

Newspaper articles from various newspapers in Austin, San Antonio, El Paso, Waco, Fort Worth, and Dallas.

Newspaper files, Austin History Center, Austin City Library System.

Reeves, John, Mills, and Charlie, descendants of Lucile Rogers Reeves, author's personal interview with, at Bulverde and San Antonio, Texas, July, 2001.

Rogers, Curren "Kid", Vertical Files, Texas Ranger Archives, Waco.

Rogers, John H., Papers, Center for American History, University of Texas, Austin.

Rogers, John H., Papers of, Vertical Files, Texas Rangers Hall of Fame and Museum, Waco.

Rogers, John H., Papers of, Vertical Files, Texas State Archives, Austin.

Rogers, John H., Articles and Papers from display case, Pioneer Hall Museum of San Antonio.

Texas Rangers, Monthly Returns and Scout Reports of the Frontier Battalion of, 1882-1901. Texas State Archives, Austin.

Texas Ranger Force, Captain's Reports and Scout Reports of, 1901-1911, 1927-1930. Texas State Archives, Austin.

U. S. Marshal Service, Archival records of, Western District of Texas, 1911-1921, National Archives and Records Administration, Fort Worth, Texas.

PUBLISHED PRIMARY SOURCES

Aten, Ira. *Six and One-Half Years in the Ranger Service: The Memoirs of Sergeant Ira Aten, Company D, Texas Rangers.* Bandera, Texas: Frontier Times, 1945.

Daniell, L. E. *Texas: The Country and Its Men.* Austin: 1916.

Sowell, A. J. *Early Settlers and Indian Fighters of Southwest Texas.* 2 vols. Austin: Ben Jones, 1900.

_____. *Rangers and Pioneers of Texas.* San Antonio: Shepard Brothers, 1884.

Sterling, William Warren. *Trails and Trials of a Texas Ranger.* Norman: University of Oklahoma Press, 1959.

Sullivan, W. John L. *Twelve Years in the Saddle for Law and Order on the Frontiers of Texas.* Von Boeckmann-Jones, 1909.

SECONDARY SOURCES

Adair, W. S. "Rangers 40 Years Ago Had No Easy Life." *Frontier Times* 4 (1927): 41-43.

Ball, Larry. *United States Marshals of New Mexico and Arizona Territories, 1846-1912.* Albuquerque: University of New Mexico Press, 1999.

Baugh, Virgil E. *A Pair of Texas Rangers: Bill McDonald and John Hughes.* Washington, D.C.: Potomac Westerners Corral, 1970.

Bradford, Edward Jr. "History of Mitchell County, Texas." Masters Thesis, University of Texas, 1937.

Brookshire, William Riley. *War Along the Bayous: The 1864 Red River Campaign in Louisiana*. Washington, D. C.: Brasseys, 1998.

Burton, Art. *Black, Red, and Deadly: Black and Indian Gunfighters of the Indian Territories*. Austin: Eakin Press, 1991.

Calhoun, Frederick C. *The Lawmen: United States Marshals and their Deputies, 1789-1989*. Washington, 1989.

City Directories of Austin, Texas. 1905-1916, 1926-1931. Austin History Center.

Cline, Omer W. "History of Mitchell County to 1900." Masters Thesis, East Texas Teachers College, 1948.

Combs, Joe F. *Gunsmoke in the Redlands*. San Antonio: Naylor Company, 1968.

Conger, Roger N. et al. *Rangers of Texas*. Waco: Texian Press, 1969.

Cox, Mike. *Silver Stars and Sixguns: The Texas Rangers*. Austin: Department of Public Safety, 1987.

_____. *Texas Ranger Tales: Stories That Need Telling*. Plano: Republic of Texas Press, 1997.

_____. *Texas Ranger Tales II*. Plano: Republic of Texas Press, 1999.

Davis, John L. *The Texas Rangers: Images and Incidents*. San Antonio: Institute of Texan Cultures, 1991.

_____. *The Texas Rangers: Their First 150 Years*. San Antonio: Institute of Texan Cultures, 1975.

Davis, Richard Harding. *The West From a Car-Window*. New York: Harper, 1892.

Day, James M. "El Paso's Texas Rangers." *Password* 24 (Winter 1979): 153-172.

DeArment, Robert. "That Masterson McDonald Standoff." *True West* 45 (January 1998): 12-15.

De Leon, Arnoldo. *They Call Them Greasers: Anglo Attitudes Toward Mexicans in Texas, 1821-1900*. Austin: University of Texas Press, 1983.

Denmark, Van. "Religion and Bullets." *Texas Monthly* (March 1929): 349-351.

Duaine, Carl L. *The Dead Men Wore Boots: An Account of the Thirty-Second Texas Volunteer Cavalry, CSA, 1862-1865*. Austin: San Felipe Press, 1966.

Etlinger, Josephine. *Sweetest You Can Find: Life in East Guadalupe County, 1851-1951*. San Antonio: Watercress Press, 1987.

Fehrenbach, T. R. *Lone Star, a History of Texas and the Texans*. New York: MacMillan, 1968.

Fenton, James I. "Tom Ross: Outlaw and Stockman." Masters Thesis, University of Texas at El Paso, 1979.

_____. "Tom Ross: Ranger Nemesis." *Quarterly of the National Association for Outlaw and Lawman History* 14 (1990): 4-21.

Fitzsimon, L. J. *Seguin, Texas*. Seguin Centennial Commission, 1938.

Gard, Wayne. "The Fence-Cutters." *Southwestern Historical Quarterly* 51 (July 1947): 1-15.

_____. "The Mooar Brothers, Buffalo Hunters." *Southwestern Historical Quarterly* 63 (1959): 31-45.

Haley, J. Evetts. *Jeff Milton: A Good Man with a Gun.* Norman: University of Oklahoma Press, 1948.

Hardin, Stephen. *The Texas Rangers.* London: Osprey Press, 1991.

Havins, T. R. *Something About Brown: A History of Brown County.* Brownwood: Banner Press, 1958.

Hewett, Janet B. ed. *Texas Confederate Soldiers.* 2 vols. Wilmington: Broadfoot Press, 1997.

Holden, W. C. "Law and Lawlessness on the Texas Frontier, 1875-1890." *Southwestern Historical Quarterly* 44 (1940): 199-200.

Holt, Roy D. "The Introduction of Barbed Wire into Texas and the Fence Cutting War." *West Texas Historical Association Yearbook* 6 (1930): 72-88.

Jenkins, John H. and H. Gordon Frost. *I'm Frank Hamer: The Life of a Texas Peace Officer.* Austin: Pemberton Press, 1968.

Johnson, Ben. "The Plan de San Diego Uprising and the Making of the Modern Texas-Mexico Borderlands." Presented at Western Historical Association Conference, San Antonio, October 11-14, 2000.

Kildare, Maurice. "The Rangers Got Their Man; Gregorio Cortez." *The New Mexico Lawman* 4 (1978): 6-15.

Kilgore, Dan. E. *A Ranger Legacy: 150 Years of Service in Texas.* Austin: Madrona Printing Company, 1973.

King, W. H. "The Texas Ranger Service and History of the Rangers, with Observations on their Value as a Police Protection." In *A Comprehensive History of Texas, 1685 to 1897,* edited by Dudley G. Wooten, 2 vols. Dallas: Scharff Company, 1898: 329-367.

Knowles, Thomas W. *They Rode for the Lone Star: The Saga of the Texas Rangers.* Dallas: Taylor Publishing, 1998.

Malsch, Brownson. *Lone Wolf Gonzaullas, Texas Ranger.* Austin: Shoal Creek Publishers, 1980. Reprint, Norman: University of Oklahoma Press, 1998.

Maltby, William J. *Captain Jeff; or, Frontier Life in Texas with the Texas Rangers.* Colorado City, Texas: Whipkey, 1906.

"Many Brilliant Exploits Manifest Courage of Captain Rogers." *Sheriff's Association of Texas Magazine* 1 (March, 1931): 1-2.

Martin, Jack. *Border Boss: Captain John R. Hughes, Texas Ranger.* San Antonio: Naylor, 1942.

Mason-Manheim, Madeline. *Riding for Texas: The True Adventures of Captain Bill McDonald of the Texas Rangers, as Told by Colonel Edward M. House to Tyler Mason.* New York: Reynal & Hitchcock, 1936.

Mason, Herbert Molloy, Jr. *The Texas Rangers.* New York: Meredith Press, 1967.

McCallum, Henry D. "Barbed Wire in Texas." *Southwestern Historical Quarterly* 61 (October 1957): 207-219.

_____ and Frances T. McCallum. *The Wire That Fenced the West.* Norman: University of Oklahoma Press, 1965.

McLeod, William. *The Story of First Southern Presbyterian Church, Austin.* Austin: Presbyterian Synod, 1939.

Mertz, Richard J. "'No One Can Arrest Me': The Story of Gregorio Cortez." *Journal of South Texas* 1 (1974): 1-17.

Miletich, Leo. *Dan Stuart's Fistic Carnival.* College Station: Texas A & M Press, 1994.

Miller, Robert. *The Life of Robert Hall.* Austin: State House Press, 1992.

Million, Elmer M. "History of the Texas Prize Fight Statute." *Texas Law Review* 17 (February 1939): 152-159.

Moellering, Arward Max. "History of Guadalupe County, Texas." Masters Thesis, University of Texas, 1938.

Montejano, David. *Anglos and Mexicans in the Making of Texas, 1836-1986.* Austin: University of Texas Press, 1987.

Morphis, J. M. *History of Texas.* New York: United States Publishing, 1875.

Niemeyer, Vic. "Frustrated Invasion: The Revolutionary Attempt of General Bernardo Reyes from San Antonio in 1911." *Southwestern Historical Quarterly* 67 (1963): 213-225.

Paine, Albert Bigelow. *Captain Bill McDonald, Texas Ranger: A Story of Frontier Reform.* New York: Little & Ives, 1909.

Paredes, Americo. *"With His Pistol in His Hand:" A Border Ballad and Its Hero.* Austin: University of Texas Press, 1958.

Pierce, Frank Cushman. *A Brief History of the Lower Rio Grande Valley.* Menasha, Wisconsin: n.p., 1917.

Preece, Harold. *Lone Star Man: Ira Aten, Last of the Old Texas Rangers.* New York: Hastings Publishing, 1960.

Procter, Ben. *Just One Riot; Episodes of Texas Rangers in the 20th Century.* Austin: Eakin Press, 1991.

Reed, S. G. *A History of the Texas Railroads and of transportation conditions under Spain and Mexico and the republic and state.* Houston: St. Clair Printing, 1941.

Rhinehart, Marilyn. *A Way of Work and a Way of Life: Coal Mining in Thurber, Texas, 1888-1926.* College Station: Texas A & M University Press, 1992.

_____. "Thurber Coal Miners." *Southwestern Historical Quarterly* 92 (1989): 509-542.

Ribb, Richard. "Patrician as Redeemer: José Tomás Canales and the Salvation of South Texas, 1910-1919." *Journal of South Texas* 14 (Fall 2001): 189-203.

Rickard, John A. "The Ranching Industry of the South Texas Plains." Masters Thesis, University of Texas, 1937.

Roberts, Daniel W. *Rangers and Sovereignty.* San Antonio: Wood Printing, 1914.

Robinson, Charles M. III. *The Men Who Wear the Star: The Story of the Texas Rangers.* New York: Random House, 2000.

Ruhlen, George. "Fort Hancock: Last of the Frontier Forts." *Southwestern Historical Quarterly* 66 (January 1959): 487-492.

Samora, Julian, Joe Bernal, and Albert Pena. *Gunpowder Justice: A Reassessment of the Texas Rangers.* Notre Dame: University of Notre Dame Press, 1979.

Sandos, James A. *Rebellion in the Borderlands: Anarchism and the Plan of San Diego, 1904-1923.* Norman: University of Oklahoma Press, 1992.

Shelby County Historical Commission. *History of Shelby County, Texas.* Center, Texas: Curtis Printing, 1988.

Sonnichsen, C. L. *I'll Die Before I Run: The Story of the Great Feuds of Texas.* New York: Devon Adair, 1962.

_____. *Pass of the North: Four Centuries on the Rio Grande.* El Paso: Texas Western Press, 1968.

_____. *Roy Bean, Law West of the Pecos.* New York: Devon Adair, 1958.

Sowell, A. J. *Incidents Connected with the History in Guadalupe County, Texas.* Austin, 1887.

Spellman, Paul N. "Dark Days of the Texas Rangers, 1915-1918." *Journal of South Texas Studies* 12 (Spring 2001): 79-97.

Stambaugh, J. Lee and Lillian J. *The Lower Rio Grande Valley of Texas.* San Antonio: Naylor Company, 1954.

Stephens, Robert W. *Texas Ranger Sketches.* Dallas: n.p., 1972.

Tenayuca, Emma and Homer Brooks. "The Mexican Question in the Southwest." *Political Affairs* (March 1939): 257-268.

Texas State Historical Association. *The New Handbook of Texas.* 6 vols. Austin: TSHA, 1995.

Timmons, W. H. *El Paso, A Borderlands History.* El Paso: University of Texas at El Paso, 1990.

Utley, Robert M. *Lone Star Justice: The First Century of the Texas Rangers.* New York: Oxford Press, 2002.

"Two New U. S. Marshals." *State Topics.* Houston, April 12, 1913.

Watson, Don and Steve Brown. *From Ox Teams to Eagles; A Company History of the Texas & Pacific Railway.* n.d.

Webb, Walter Prescott. *The Texas Rangers: A Century of Frontier Defense.* Austin: University of Texas Press, 1935.

Weinert, Willie Mae. *An Authentic History of Guadalupe County, Texas.* Seguin, 1951.

Weiss, Harold J. Jr. "Yours to Command: Captain William J. 'Bill' McDonald and the Panhandle Rangers of Texas." PhD dissertation, Indiana University, 1982.

_____. "The Texas Rangers Revisited: Old Themes and New Viewpoints." *Southwestern Historical Quarterly* 97 (April 1994): 621-640.

"When Rogers Courted Death." *Frontier Times* 4 (December, 1926): 8.

Wilkins, Frederick. *The Law Comes to Texas: The Texas Rangers, 1870-1901.* Austin: State House Press, 1999.

_____. *The Legend Begins; The Texas Rangers, 1823-1845.* Austin: State House Press, 1996.

Index

A

B

Y